BILINGUAL EDUCATION AND BILINGUALISM 5
Series Editor: Colin Baker

A Parents' and Teachers' Guide to Bilingualism

Colin Baker

MULTILINGUAL MATTERS LTD
Clevedon • Philadelphia • Adelaide

Library of Congress Cataloging in Publication Data

Baker, Colin, 1949-
A Parents' and Teachers' Guide to Bilingualism/Colin Baker.
(Bilingual Education and Bilingualism: 5)
Includes bibliographical references and index.
1. Bilingualism in children–Handbooks, manuals, etc. I. Title. II Series.
P115.2.B35 1995
649'.157–dc20 94-49737

British Library Cataloguing in Publication Data

A CIP catalogue record for this book is available from the British Library.

ISBN 1-85359-265-X (hbk)
ISBN 1-85359-264-1 (pbk)

Multilingual Matters Ltd

UK: Frankfurt Lodge, Clevedon Hall, Victoria Road, Clevedon, Avon BS21 7SJ.
USA: 1900 Frost Road, Suite 101, Bristol, PA 19007, USA.
Australia: P.O. Box 6025, 83 Gilles Street, Adelaide, SA 5000, Australia.

Cover design by Bob Jones Associates.
Printed and bound in Great Britain by WBC Ltd, Bridgend.

Contents

Section B: Language Development Questions

Section C: Questions About Problems

Section D: Reading and Writing Questions

Section E: Education Questions

Basic Education Questions

Types of Bilingual Education

Section F. Concluding Questions

Acknowledgements

The idea for this book was not mine. It came as a 'one liner' during a telephone conversation. 'Have you thought of writing a book to help parents?'. No, I hadn't. I didn't really give the matter more thought. There were other projects ongoing, other commissions requiring writing time.

One event changed all. An operation was required with a few weeks convalescence at home. I decided that recovery would be enjoyable if something was accomplished. The parent book could be written. A highly skilled surgeon, Mike Jamison, ensured those weeks were totally trouble free.

Before the hospital operation, the structure of the book was planned. The questions were provisionally agreed with the guardian angel of the project, Marjukka Grover. She grafted more questions onto the initial skeleton. After the first draft was completed, Marjukka nursed the project through its successive stages. When a publisher like Marjukka Grover is so enthusiastic about the potential impact of the book on parents and teachers, the author is given extra enthusiasm. No author could have been more kindly treated or more sagaciously advised. Marjukka spent considerable time advising me on the draft, and made many comments that added much to the width of the book. A thousand thanks to my favorite Finn.

Marjukka Groverin innostus kaksikielisyyteen, ja tuottamaan kaksikielisyyttä edistäviä jäsenkirjeitä, aikakauslehtiä ja kirjoja, on ollut tärkeä kansainvälinen kontribuutio. Tämä panos on tehnyt mahdolliseksi tutkijoille, opettajille ja erilaisille asiantuntijoille, ja mikä tärkeintä vanhemmille, ymmärtää täydellisemmin ja herkemmin kaksikielisiä ihmisiä ja monikielisiä yhteisöjä.

Hänen henkilökohtainen esimerkkinsä suomea ja englantia puhuvien poikien onnistuneena kasvattajana, on osoituksena syvästä ja voimakkaasta sitoutumisesta kaksikielisyyteen.

Marjukan kannanotto kaksikielisyyteen oli tärkeä aloitettaessa Multilingual Matters ja MLM julkaisujen puhjettessa kukkaan. Tämä kirja saa myöskin kiittää paljon olemassaolostaan hänen innostustaan, kannatustaan ja tukeaan.

Sinulle, Marjukka, ja Sinun elämäntehtävällesi tämä kirja on omistettu.

Anne Sanderson kindly typed the first draft. With impeccable accuracy, incredible patience and infinite care, she produced a fast turn-round that impelled me to continue at full speed. Thanks also to her husband, Barry, who for over 20 years has been the University's computing backbone and has always responded helpfully to my computing requests.

The draft manuscript was shown to a variety of people. There were anonymous Readers appointed by the publishers who gave searching, valuable and constructive advice. I am most grateful to these people for their sound recommendations and careful examination of the draft text. One of the academic reviewers appointed by the publishers kindly contributed her unique combination of personal, family multilingualism with academic expertise in bilingualism. That contribution from Charlotte Hoffmann gave much help, thoughtful guidance and needed reassurance.

Dr Jean Lyon, a highly experienced clinical psychologist, kindly provided judicious and astute advice. She is an expert on bilingualism in families, and is sensitive and seasoned in problems met by bilingual families. I'm grateful for that dimension of understanding sensitively taught to me. Geraint Wyn Jones has shared with me his perceptions about bilingualism across many years. A colleague in the School of Education, he asks all the right, awkward questions, and provides a fresh, original and highly experienced viewpoint. We've discussed bilingualism in Bangor and the Bronx, in scholarly chambers in Gwynedd and on street corners in Harlem. I'm much the richer.

Dr Sylvia Prys Jones dropped out of heaven into the Bangor's School of Education. She came at a crucial time in the School's development — when the chance to expand our contribution to bilingualism and bilingual education became possible. Appointed as a Postdoctoral Fellow, with an outstanding and distinguished student career in Oxford and Wales, she provides an fresh intellectual dimension combined with a knowledge of more languages than seem possible: English, Welsh, Breton, French, Irish, Hebrew and Spanish. While working with me on an Encyclopedia Project, Dr Sylvia Prys Jones kindly agreed to read the draft of this book. Herself a mother with three bilingual children, she at once spotted the virtues and vices of the written style adopted. The less effective and more vague passages were immediately and accurately detected. (My feeble excuse was that these were written while the anesthetic was still present in the system). Many highly original points were made — including locating issues that academics ignore because the issues are uncomfortable. My sincere and grateful thanks.

Only half this book would have been written if I hadn't met Professor Ofelia García of City College New York. For a previous book (*'Foundations of Bilingual Education and Bilingualism'*), she was wisely appointed as Academic Advisor. In our discussions in New York, Professor García has added considerable depth and width to my British and European perspective. She taught me much about the plight of language US minorities. When Professor García reads my drafts, it is like having an academic psychoanalysis. She detects exactly where I'm coming from, what are the prejudices I've failed to conceal, and what is embedded in the heart as well as the mind. My enormous appreciation goes to Ofelia for her continued support, help, encouragement, unselfish giving of time and her wisdom. She provides such sensible, 'street-wise', perceptive and thoughtful advice. It is an enormous privilege to work across the Atlantic with such an outstanding, 'top-rate' international scholar.

I wish to express my gratitude to my Head of Department, Professor Iolo Wyn Williams, for his undoubted part in my managing to write five books in a decade. While he is quick to understand all matters educational and political, I've failed to get him to understand that his style of leadership has been absolutely crucial. He has always given me the freedom to choose in which direction and on what projects I spend my time. When I've needed support, he has always given it. When I've needed equipment or funds, he has always responded in a positive way. When I need advice, this has always been given with sensibility and consideration. Few come to the School of Education without picking up very quickly the friendly, happy, cooperative atmosphere that exists. To work in such a Department has been a pleasure and has been much treasured.

This book would never have been written if I didn't live in a bilingual nuclear and extended family. In the home, my wife Anwen, teenagers Sara and Rhodri, and footballer Arwel, provide the experience, the stimulus for thinking, and a range of hilarious incidents that form one basis for this book. All four are fully bilingual. They respond to my unending questions about their experience of bilingualism and bilingual education with honesty, openness and humor. They lovingly provide a homely, 'feet on the ground' dimension that balances the academic study of bilingualism. As time has advanced, each has understood better the reasons for mealtime interrogations about personal bilingualism. I'm grateful for the unending replies, and for the teasing and wit that keeps me 'down to earth'. The extended family are bilinguals — most speaking Welsh and English, but also French and German. Their variety of bilingual use and attitude is a glorious learning experience. I especially want to mention 'Taid' (my children's Welsh grandfather). His deep love of language, constant inspection of language and willingness to translate important texts for me, despite severe disablement, will never be forgotten. *Heddwch fyddo o fewn dy ragfur: a ffyniant yn dy balasau.*

Ken Hall of Multilingual Matters advised on presentation and production. It is a great encouragement for an author to have someone of his expertise and experience to advise. Methodical, dependable and serene, Ken has safely guided me through four books. To all who read the drafts, and gave me help and support, I am most grateful. However, the responsibility for anything in this book that is not as fair or just as it should be is totally mine.

Finally, my thanks to Mike Grover for the telephone call. The operation of this book would never have occurred without that invitation. When a physician's care was needed, he gave it on time, without postponements. The post operative support was perfect.

Introduction

The different situations addressed in the book

The style of the book is to pose those **questions** that parents, teachers and others most often ask about raising bilingual children. Straightforward **answers** follow, written in direct, plain language. The book deals with family questions, educational questions, language issues and particularly focuses on problems that arise. Such questions reflect **central issues** that people regularly meet in deciding about bilingualism in the home. Important questions about advantages and disadvantages, schemes and strategies of language development are posed. The answers to the questions will raise awareness of what **challenges** may be faced as bilingual family life develops and what decisions may have to be made.

The book is partly for parents and teachers who are bilinguals themselves. It is also written for monolingual parents and teachers (and other professionals such as doctors, speech therapists, practicing psychologists and counselors) who want to know more. The book is for those who are searching for answers to their questions. It is also written for those who are just starting to think about the important questions. The book is written for those with some intuitive understanding of bilingual situations. It is also written for those who are starting from the very beginning.

The language of bilingualism

The book is about **bilingual children, bilingual parents and bilingual education**. Unfortunately, much fog surrounds these words. There is no agreed, common definition or understanding of these terms. Bilingualism is a simple term that hides a complex phenomenon. Does the term 'bilingual' cover those who are able to speak a language but don't? Those who understand what others say in one of their languages but rarely or never use that language? Does the term 'bilingual' cover those who are proficient in one language but are only just beginning to learn a second language? Does the term 'bilingual' cover those who can speak a language without literacy, or only those who speak, read and write in both languages?

Such questions highlight that there is not just one dimension of language. We can examine people's proficiency in two languages in their **listening (understanding), speaking, reading and writing** skills. Across these four basic dimensions of language will be many shades of gray. In between those who are fluent in two languages and those who are learning a second language there are many variations. Where second language learning stops and bilingualism exists is endlessly debated. Any cut-off point will be arbitrary and contentious. There are some people who do become approximately equally fluent in both their languages (sometimes called balanced bilinguals). These tend to be the few rather than the many. Most people are more competent in one language than another. Bilinguals often find it easier to use one of their languages in one set of circumstances, another language in a different set of circumstances. Languages often have different uses in different places, with different people.

Calling someone a **bilingual** is therefore an **umbrella term**. Underneath the umbrella rest many different skill levels in two languages. Being bilingual is not just about proficiency in two languages. There is a **difference** between **ability and use** of language. Someone may be quite competent in two languages, yet rarely or never use one of those languages. Such a person has bilingual ability but does not act or behave bilingually. A different case is a person who regularly uses both their languages, even though one language is still developing. Such a person may be hesitant in speaking, finding it difficult to speak with correct grammar or unable to use a wide vocabulary. In practice, that person may be bilingual, although ability in one language is lacking (but improving steadily). Such a distinction between ability in a language and use of a language again shows why the simple label 'bilingual' hides a complex variety beneath its simplicity.

Types of family bilingualism

Bilingual families and parents raising bilingual children are constantly referred to in this book. However, the language abilities of mother and father, the availability of language practice with the extended family, the nature of the local language community or region creates a **wide variety of bilingual families**.

Bilingual families include many **different combinations** of answers to the following questions:

(1) What language(s) does the mother speak to the child?
(2) What language(s) does the father speak to the child?
(3) What language(s) do brothers/sisters speak to each other?

(4) What language(s) do the extended family (grandparents, aunts uncles etc.) speak to the child?
(5) Are the language(s) of the home?
 (a) majority languages
 (b) a majority and a minority language
 (c) minority languages/dialect
 (d) one minority language
(6) Is a different language to the home being acquired outside the home (e.g. in the street, in school)?
(7) Are the language(s) of the home spoken in the local community/region? and/or...
(8) Are the language(s) of the home spoken in a different region/abroad?
(9) Is the family geographically stable or mobile with changing language needs?

A variety of **language strategies** are thus used by parents to produce bilingual children. The **main strategies** are as follows (with other alternatives possible, e.g. changing patterns over time):

Strategy 1: Each parent speaks a different language to the child. This is often called the 'one person–one language' strategy.

Strategy 2: The parents speak one language to the child who acquires a second language outside the home. This often occurs in language minority situations.

Strategy 3: Both parents speak both languages to the child.

This book attempts to cover a wide variety of **bilingual family** situations (including other situations not listed above). Some answers to questions cover all types of situation. There is a generalization irrespective of the type of bilingual family. There are other questions specifically posed for specific circumstances. For example, there are **minority language parents** living in a region where the minority language has a long and valued past. Such indigenous minority languages are often surrounded and threatened by a majority language such as English, French, German, Spanish, Arabic or Italian. The attitudes and motivations with regard to language and culture of such families will differ widely. This book covers the issues raised by parents in such contexts.

The book is also equally written for parents in **mixed language marriages** (and inter-cultural marriages). Mixed language marriages are on an increase as international borders open and communications between countries become easier. For example, if the mother speaks French, German or Swedish as her first language and is married to a monolingual English-speaking father, there are many answers in this book for such a mixed language situation. If both parents have a **different language from the majority language of the host country**, this book also applies. Advice covers those families with **two internationally prestigious languages** such as French and English, and when there is a **combination of a majority and a minority language**.

Other families travel to neighboring or distant countries for employment, advancement or because of the **international nature of their employment** (e.g. those working for the European Union, the Council of Europe, the United Nations and transnational companies). Such mobile, 'international' families are on the increase. There is guidance in this book for such situations.

Another situation covered in this book is that faced by **refugees, guest workers, migrants and recent or established immigrants** into a country. (The term **in-migrants** is used hereafter as a more neutral term to encompass immigrants, migrants, guest workers and refugees.) For example, there are various language minority groups residing in Germany, the different Asian, Turkish and Greek language groups in England, and many in-migrants in the Scandinavian countries. In such cases, the home language (heritage language) is a minority language and the 'new' or 'host' country operates in a majority language. One example is the Punjabi, Bengali, Hindi and Gujerati speakers in Canada, England and the United States who are surrounded by mass media and education in the dominant English language. This book also provides advice for such situations.

Different bilingual situations

These different bilingual situations lead to an important distinction. There is a dimension ranging from **additive bilingualism** to **subtractive bilingualism**. When children use a majority language and have the possibility of becoming bilingual in another majority or a minority language, this is usually regarded as an **additive** bilingual situation. The first language, a prestigious majority language, is not under threat. It won't be replaced by the second language, be it a majority or a minority second language. Through the home and/or the school, a child adds a new language and culture without loss.

A different situation is where a **minority language child** is expected to learn a second majority language in the home or more often at school. The idea is that the second (majority) language should become dominant, even replace the minority language. This is termed **subtractive bilingualism**. For example, Asian families in England often find that the school depreciates the home language and only promotes the dominant language of school and society — English. In the United States, children who acquire Spanish at home as their first language attend schools that often insist on the English language becoming dominant in their lives.

Politicians, administrators, educationists often seek to replace the minority language with the majority language. Their arguments for majority language supremacy range around: finding employment, equality of opportunity, the importance of a common denominator language such as English in integrating society, the melting pot idea that inmigrants should become part of the majority by losing their minority language and becoming, for example, English-speaking. The drive is to assimilate language minorities into mainstream life. Differences are to be replaced by similarities. Language variety is to be replaced by language uniformity. This can result in **subtractive** bilingual situations. The attempt is often to replace the home language by the majority language. The learning of a second language may be at the expense of the first language, unless parents take care. The term 'bilingual children' is sometimes a euphemism for children whose home language is being replaced by the majority language of the region.

This book deals with both types of situation — the **additive** bilingual situation **and** the **subtractive**. It provides advice for both majority language and minority language parents, whether they are in their home country or have traveled to a host country. The book addresses parents living in a community that supports their home language or depreciates it. There is information for those in a region that has a large or small number (or no speakers) of the languages of the home.

The content of the book

The intention of this book is to provide a **readable introduction** that is of practical value to parents. No attempt is made to provide an introduction to the terminology academics use to discuss bilingualism. Technical jargon and academic theories have been translated into everyday language wherever possible. Readers wishing to progress to books with a more academic bias are invited to study a list given at the end of this book.

Since **education** affects the bilingual development of the child, a separate section discusses the role of the school in fostering and sometimes hindering bilingual development. Different and varied circumstances are covered by such questions. The book covers a variety of school and classroom contexts: where the language of schooling is different from the language of the home, where parents have a choice of maintaining their minority language in the school, where the only available schools are majority language schools that foster monolingualism, where parents frequently move from country to country as part of their employment, and where children move from one school to another. No technical discussion is given about the variety of bilingual education that exists worldwide. The author's book *Foundations of Bilingual Education and Bilingualism* (1993) provides such an introduction.

At the end of this book, a **glossary** is given. This provides a quick and easy understanding of key terms used in this book. For example, the term in-migrant is used instead of immigrant. The reason will be clear from the glossary ('in-migrant' is more inclusive and has less negative connotations in English). The glossary also includes some oft employed technical terms, deliberately not used in this book but which are common in other writings on bilingualism. For example, United States parents will encounter specific US terms used to describe bilingual children and bilingual education. Where these are not explained in a particular question, their meaning is given in the glossary.

Some **readers** will read through the book question by question. For those, the book has been arranged in an order that seems logical and developmental. Foundations laid early in the book will increase understanding of later issues. However, many readers will dip into the book. Some questions will be read, others returned to at a later date, yet others regarded as not important. The book has, from the beginning, been designed with such readers in mind. Each question and answer can be read in isolation. Each answer attempts to give sufficient important information to help the inquirer. This means that there is a little duplication of content to achieve the self-sufficiency of each answer.

Answers will lead to other questions, other answers. Hence, there is some cross-referencing in the book. Also an **index** at the back of the book will help readers to find other related topics to build on answers. The use of emboldening certain words is used to enable readers to quickly scan the text for important and relevant topics. Such highlighting will make it quicker to find the information needed.

Wherever possible, answers to the questions are based on up-to-date international **research**. In the last two decades there has been an ever increasing supply of research on bilingualism and bilingual education. The results of this research are contained in this book and can be followed up by reading various references given at the end of the final section.

At the end of the book, information is given about **extended reading**, about the *Bilingual Family Newsletter*, and importantly about establishing a **network** with like minded parents who wish to raise their children bilingually.

The author

Some readers will want to know about the background and qualifications of the **author** in writing this book. The perceived validity of the answers needs judging against the degree of experience and expertise that an author brings to the task. First, the author specializes academically in bilingualism and bilingual education. He has published four **books** alongside over 30 other publications on the subject. The books are: *Aspects of Bilingualism in Wales* (1985), *Key Issues in Bilingualism and Bilingual Education* (1988), *Attitudes and Language* (1992) and *Foundations of Bilingual Education and Bilingualism* (1993). With Professor Ofelia García of the City College of New York, he has edited a book of readings: *Policy and Practice in Bilingual Education: A Reader Extending the Foundations* (1995). The author is currently writing an *Encyclopedia of Bilingualism and Bilingual Education*. Therefore, this book is informed by a knowledge of international research, and several decades of academic writing and research on bilingualism and bilingual education. The book also contains insights gained through lecturing in this area for over a decade to undergraduate and postgraduate students, teachers and parents. The author was elected a Fellow of the British Psychological Society in 1994 for his work on bilingualism.

Second, the author and his wife, Anwen, have successfully raised **three bilingual children**. During sixteen years of varied experience, discussions between parents, and with the children, have constantly taken place. Problems have been met, and still arise. No journey to bilingualism is trouble free. Our three children, Sara, Rhodri and Arwel are currently fully and functionally bilingual in English and Welsh. Anwen (the mother) has always spoken Welsh to the children, while I have usually spoken English. The children normally speak Welsh to each other. Each has experienced bilingual education from kindergarten (age three or four) into secondary education. However, their routes to bilingualism have been varied, different and not trouble-free.

Third, the author works in a School of Education in a **University that specializes in bilingualism and bilingual education**. Hence, there is a constant dialogue with colleagues about bilingualism, plus engagement in research in bilingual schools. Currently, the author is one of a small team of professional advisers to the UK Government's Curriculum and

Assessment Council in Wales (ACAC). He has also been involved in a Council of Europe project on bilingual education.

There is a **fourth** experience that influenced the writing of this book. When giving formal talks and in informal conversations, the author has frequently discussed bilingual family issues with **other parents**. In the indigenous minority language situation in Wales, among Asian, Turkish and Greek language minority parents in England, with several Spanish–English families in the United States, and with parents raising their children in two and sometimes three European languages, experiences have been shared and ideas swapped. This book has been informed by observing, listening and talking to parents in different bilingual situations.

The style of the book

Readers need to be aware that the **style and approach** are different from an academic text book. When writing the textbook *Foundations of Bilingual Education and Bilingualism* (1993), every effort was made to represent a variety of viewpoints so that readers could make up their own minds on difficult issues. Often options are presented in such an academic book without a firm conclusion about 'best bets' or 'successful recipes'.

This book has a different approach. While alternatives are often given, an attempt has been made, using whatever expertise and experience exists, to give some kind of lead and strategic advice. Parents and teachers often don't want prevarication. They usually seek informed help and direction. Such practical advice will reveal what academics often keep well hidden! Such advice in this book will reveal personal values, personal convictions and preferences alongside information from international research and academic writing.

Not everyone will agree with the **advice**, nor should they. Specific circumstances, particular attitudes, cultural life styles, varying convictions and motivations will lead parents to disagree with some viewpoints. No advice can cover all circumstances. Real situations are very complex, such that no single recipe will be possible.

In writing this book, I have been aware that there will be disagreements, sometimes differing advice and residual uncertainty. No book for parents can provide perfect recipes, give totally authoritative and successful advice for all circumstances, or hope to convince every reader.

I do not wish readers to follow the advice slavishly as if the book presents the ten commandments of bilingualism written on tablets of stone. My hope is that the book stimulates thinking, opens up new ideas, helps parents discuss issues, and work out what is, for them in their specific circumstances, an optimal **strategy**. Such a book aims to inform and 'enable' the journey through childhood bilingualism, stimulate deeper thought and reflection, provide a variety of ideas and encourage.

Bon voyage.

Section A

Family Questions

A1 What are the advantages of my child becoming bilingual?

Bringing up children to be bilingual is an important decision. It will **affect the rest of their lives and the lives of their parents**. For children, being bilingual or monolingual may affect their identity, social arrangements, schooling, employment, marriage, area of residence, travel and thinking. Becoming bilingual is more than owning two languages. Bilingualism has educational, social, economic, cultural and political consequences.

There are many advantages and very few disadvantages in becoming bilingual. A bilingual has the chance of **communicating** with a wider variety of people than a monolingual. When traveling in a country, in neighboring countries and in international travel, bilingual children have the distinct advantage that their languages provide bridges to new relationships. While a monolingual is able to communicate to a variety of people in one language, that language sometimes becomes a barrier to building relationships with people of other nationalities and ethnic groups.

One of the advantages of a bilingual child and adult is having **two or more worlds of experience**. Bilingualism provides the opportunity to experience two or more cultures. With each language goes different systems of behavior, folk sayings, stories, histories, traditions, ways of meeting and greeting, rituals of birth, marriage and death, ways of conversing (compare Italians, Arabs and English people when they are speaking), different literatures, music, forms of entertainment, religious traditions, ways of understanding and interpreting the world, ideas and beliefs, ways of thinking and drinking, crying and loving, eating and caring, ways of joking and mourning. With two languages goes a wider cultural experience.

The monolingual also experiences a variety of **cultures** — from different neighbors and communities, who use the same language but have different ways of life. The monolingual can also travel to neighboring countries and, in a more passive way, experience other cultures. But to penetrate different cultures requires the language of that culture. To participate and become involved in the core of a culture requires knowing the language of that culture. The bilingual has an improved chance of actively penetrating the two language cultures.

Within any language, there is a kaleidoscope of cultures. Monolinguals may be able to experience the periphery of the kaleidoscope of a different culture. To experience fully the inner colors and excitement of the kaleidoscope of culture of a language requires a knowledge of that language.

Being a bilingual not only enables a person to bridge between cultures. It also allows someone to **bridge between generations**. When grandparents, uncles and aunts and other relatives in another region speak one language that is different from the local language, the monolingual child may be unable to communicate with such relations. The bilingual child has the chance of bridging that generation gap, building relationships in the extended family, and feel a sense of belonging and rootedness within the extended family. The monolingual child without the heritage language of the family (sometimes also called the ancestral or native language) may feel a sense of distance from relations and from the past. Bilingualism often enables a sense of continuity of a family across generations.

There are potential **economic advantages** (indeed increasing economic advantages) of being bilingual. A person with two languages may have a wider portfolio of jobs available in the future. As economic trade barriers fall, as international relationships become closer, as Unions and partnerships across nations become more widespread, ever more jobs are likely to require a person to be bilingual or multilingual. Jobs in multinational companies, jobs selling and exporting, and employment prospects generated by the European Union make the future of employment more versatile for bilinguals than monolinguals. In Wales and Catalonia for example, knowledge of the minority language in particular geographical areas is required to obtain teaching and administrative posts, and is of prime value in business and commerce. Bilingualism does not guarantee a meal ticket or future affluence. However, as the global village rises and trade barriers fall, bilinguals and multilinguals may be in a relatively strong position in the race for employment.

Apart from social, cultural, economic, personal relationship and communication advantages, research has shown that bilinguals have the chance of some advantages in **thinking**. Bilingual children have two or more words for each object and idea (e.g. 'kitchen' in English and '*cuisine*' in French). This means that the link between a word and its concept is usually looser. Sometimes corresponding words in different languages have different connotations. For example, 'kitchen' in English has traditionally been a place of hard work (as in the phrase 'tied to the kitchen sink'). '*Cuisine*' in French has different connotations. The French concept of '*cuisine*' is a place for creativity, a place where the family congregate, not only to eat, but also to socialize.

When slightly different associations are attached to each word, the bilingual may be able to **think more flexibly** and creatively. Therefore, a bilingual child has the possibility of more fluency, flexibility and elaboration in thinking. Being able to move between two languages may lead to more awareness of language and more sensitivity in communication. This is considered in detail later in the book.

Where parents have differing first languages, the advantage of children becoming bilingual is that they will be able to **communicate** in each parent's preferred language. This may enable a subtle, finer texture of relationship with the parent. Alternatively, they will be able to communicate with parents in one language and with their friends and in the community in a different language.

For many mothers and fathers, it is important for them to be able to speak to the child in their first language. Many parents can only communicate with full intimacy, naturally and expressively in their first (or preferred or dominant) language. A child who speaks to one parent in one language and the other parent in another language may be enabling a maximally **close relationship** with the parents. At the same time, both parents are passing to that child part of their past, part of their heritage.

Children in families who speak a minority language (with the majority language being used outside the home), have the advantage of carrying forward the **heritage language** of the family and all the intimacy and rootedness involved. Also, bilingual children will be able to communicate in the wider community and with school and street friends without problems. When meeting those who do not speak their language particularly well, bilinguals may be more patient listeners than monolinguals.

Language separates human beings from beasts. One major difference between animals and humans is language. Through language, a child is cared for, cherished, cultivated and cultured. One barrier between nations and ethnic groups tends to be language. Language is sometimes a barrier to communication and to creating friendly relationships. Bilinguals in the home, in the community and in society can lower such barriers. Bilinguals can be **bridges** within the nuclear and extended family, within the community and across societies. Those who speak one language symbolize that essential difference between animals and people. Those who speak two languages symbolize the essential humanity of building bridges between peoples of different color, creed, culture and language.

A2 Are some families better placed than others to produce bilingual children?

The honest answer is 'yes'. For a child to become fully bilingual, there needs to be plenty of **stimulating language experience** (listening and speaking, and reading and writing) in both languages. Some families enable this to happen better than others. In some families, there is a natural and straightforward dual language pattern enabling both languages to flower. For example, when one parent speaks one language, the other parent a different language, and when the father and mother are both at home interacting with the children for considerable periods of time, the child may have plenty of exposure to both languages. Another example is where the child is learning one language at home, the other language in a playgroup, school or community. Here there may also be plenty of stimulating experience in both languages. Both these examples (and others considered later in the book) may lead to successful bilingualism.

There are other situations that are sometimes less likely to promote bilingualism. For example, if the father is away from the home for long periods and he is the source of minority language experience for the child, uneven growth in language may occur. When the child is in nursery school all day, and only hears the home language for a short time in the evening and at weekends, parents will find creating bilingualism a challenge requiring effort and enterprise.

In families where bilingualism seems more of a challenge than cloudless sunshine, **language engineering** is important. Careful decisions about **family language planning** need making. How can the language menu of the family be arranged to create the conditions for the long-term growth of bilingualism? This does not mean equal amounts of stimulation in each language. It is almost impossible to achieve a perfect balance in exposure to both languages. The minority language may need stimulating more in the home to counteract the dominance of the majority language outside the home.

Where bilingualism is more difficult to achieve in particular family situations, a well thought out **plan of action** is needed. It is important for parents to talk about their child's language development not only before, or as soon as the child is born, but also for constant discussion and monitoring to occur. Bilingualism will flourish even in difficult circumstances when there is a plan of how, when and where a child will be exposed to both languages to ensure both languages develop well.

When a child has insufficient experience in listening and speaking a language, miracles of bilingual development will not occur. A **strategy** is needed. The strategy needs to include a consideration of the quantity of exposure to each language and the quality. A child who hears one language for half an hour a day, particularly at the end of the day when she or he is tired, is unlikely to grow competent in that language. When a child is deliberately exposed to an ever increasing variety of language in different contexts (e.g. books, listening to cassette tapes, visits to the zoo and park), a realistic chance of bilingualism exists.

The **quality of language** interaction is important, as different from quantity. Parents who talk at their children, rather than with their children may not best stimulate progress in language. In some homes, there is a paucity of **communication between parents and children**. There is also the other extreme. Some parents bombard their children with a never ending stream of language. The child receives but is not encouraged to give. Interesting questions to the child, asking the child to relate a story rather than always listen to a story, nursery rhymes and songs said together, language games (e.g. 'I Spy', simulated telephone conversations), using role play (e.g. playing doctors and nurses, puppets, cops and robbers) are just some examples of ensuring that language development is active, alive and appreciated by the attentive child.

Bilingual language development is aided when parents have a child oriented conversation strategy. Some parents' language seems to focus on orders and messages, control and discipline. A **conversation strategy** ensures parent language:

- is not too complex;
- expands a child's attempts to communicate (e.g. 'me out house' 'Yes, it's time we went to the park');
- has plenty of open questions (i.e. questions where there are plenty of possible answers rather than a simple 'right and 'wrong' answer);
- includes plenty of encouragement and approval for the child's language attempts;
- values the child's contribution;
- is attentive to the child; the parent is a good listener;
- connects words with objects to convey meaning and aid memorization, plus plenty of gesturing.

The 'bottom line' question is whether there are circumstances where bilingual development is nearly impossible? The answer is that bilingualism is possible in many different situations, if thought and care, pleasure and purpose are injected. It requires motivation and a positive attitude from parents, often considerable perseverance to achieve a distant goal, and a willingness not to expect too much too soon. Children's **bilingual skills constantly change**. They become stronger in one language or the other, as geographical and socioeconomic movement of families, changes in friends and school, and relationships within families all develop. There will be periods of darkness in the valley. For example, an adolescent child may stop using their minority language at home. At other times, there will be top-of-the-mountain experiences. For example, when a child translates or interprets to help a monolingual listener, there is that feeling of pride in the eye of the child and the parents.

The **factors** that are likely to affect the ability of a family to produce bilingual children include: geographical stability and mobility, changing relationships within the nuclear and extended family (e.g. the father's and mother's working conditions), the language situation and attitudes of the local community, being a recent or established in-migrant, changing priorities in the family (how important is language development compared with other developmental issues in the family), the attitudes and motivations of the child itself, the influence of brothers and sisters, friends and 'significant others' outside in the community and the effects of the child's school.

In some situations, producing bilingual children is easy and natural. In other situations it is a struggle. Where the family is isolated and has doubts, there may be a struggle. However, if producing bilingual children is high enough a priority in the **family's personal balance sheet**, the advice of this book, constant discussion and careful family language planning are likely to make the journey possible and the destination reachable.

A3 Is the mother more important than the father in the child's language development?

In families where the father goes out to work and the mother raises the children, it is not surprising that the term **'mother tongue'** is used. In such a situation, the amount of time a mother spends with the child will clearly affect the nature and speed of the child's language development. It is not surprising that many mothers whose first language is different from the language of the community or region, still prefer to talk to their child in their **first language**. For such mothers, it is natural, vital and appropriate to use their dominant language with the child. To speak in a different language, even if it is the language of the father, the local community or the majority language of the nation, can feel artificial, impersonal, distant, even distasteful.

One important example of the value of the mother using her **minority language** is when her children are in their teenage years. If such a language minority mother speaks the majority language with a 'foreign' accent (and if her language is sometimes incorrect), the teenager may be embarrassed, the parent ridiculed. If such a language minority mother speaks her minority language, she may retain more authority and credibility, and be more valued by the teenager.

Some mothers choose not to use their heritage language with the child. To them it feels sound and sensible, important and educative to use the local language, the language of the father or the language of the school. Parents who are **in-migrants** sometimes strive to integrate into the host nation. For some families, this means language change.

The danger is in thinking that the mother's language interaction with the child is all-important. Research in language development has shown the important contribution of the **father**. The danger is in undervaluing the role of fathers. This also implies that fathers need to be aware of the important role they play in child language development. Some fathers have relatively fewer hours of employment, or are unemployed. Leisure time has grown in this century. In such situations, the role of the father in language development has become more important. Some fathers stay at home to raise the children while the mother goes out to work.

In many societies, mothers are often responsible for housekeeping and child-rearing. Research has shown that much of mothers' language interaction with their children is about basic housekeeping functions (e.g. feeding, bathing, dressing, discipline). Fathers often have opportunities to play with their children, allowing considerable language stimulation. Many fathers interact with their children in child-centered ways. Thus a father's contribution to a child's language development is sometimes underemphasized.

In some families (e.g. where one parent speaks one language, the other parent a different language), both parents promote bilingualism. In this situation, fathers and mothers need to be conscious and aware of their important role in the child's language development. **Fathers** can be encouraged to take pride in their conversations with the child, even at the babbling and cooing stage. Even before the child says its first word, the baby picks up the sounds of the second language from the father as well as the mother. As the baby grows to a young child, the father plays an important role in the quantity of language interaction. Fathers as well as mothers need to vary the contexts in which language is used to give that child a wider language experience.

Fathers also influence the attitudes of their children to languages. Whether the father is positive or negative about bilingualism will considerably affect the child. For example, if the father is skeptical about bilingualism, or doesn't like the mother using her 'own' language, the child will soon pick up these negative vibrations and language behavior will be affected. On the other hand, if a father encourages his children's bilingualism, applauds them speaking to their mother in her 'own' language, the effect on the child's language confidence and attitudes will be substantial.

An important decision between husband and wife concerns **what language to use with each other when the child is present**. Sometimes that language is naturally the one always used in the partnership. Yet for the child's sake, consideration needs giving to achieving a rough **balance** within the family between the two languages. If, for example, the child hears one language for 80% of the time, and a second language for only 20% from the father, then the husband and wife may consciously choose to use the lesser heard language in front of the child. This may help promote both languages approximately equally.

Therefore, the answer to the question is that **both parents** are very important in the child's language development. Both parents need to be aware of the importance of the language that the child hears and uses with each parent. There is a need for **engineering of the language environment** in the home. Just as the dietary balance of meals is increasingly of interest and debate in families, so it is important that the diet of language in the home is also open to discussion.

The language diet of the home (taking into account the language of the community and school) needs considering. A recipe needs formulating and testing. The language ingredients of the meal need to show variety and color if the child is to enjoy being a bilingual. As experience with the recipe grows, additional ingredients may be included, the balance between ingredients may change and adjustments will be made to suit different tastes and palates. Both mothers and fathers are important chefs in the language kitchen.

A4 What happens if parents don't agree that their children should become bilingual?

There are many families who have raised bilingual children without discussion or disagreement. For some parents, raising bilingual children is **natural**, normal and nothing to be discussed. In many economically developing countries of the world, bilingual, trilingual and multilingual children are often the norm rather than the exception. In such areas, there is nothing peculiar or exceptional about bilingual children. Bilingualism is accepted and expected.

In other families, **debates** about the languages in which a child should grow take place before birth, after birth, during childhood, adolescence and into adulthood. If you are one of these families, consider yourselves typical and not different; normal and not deviant. The most positive thing is that children's bilingualism is being discussed and debated. Just as many parents discuss the manners, television viewing habits, hair styles and clothes of their children, so language is an important area for a family to consider openly.

Discussion about a child's languages can be about the pattern of relationships that exist in the family, about relationships with grand-parents and uncles and aunts, about schooling, about interaction with the community, about future employment and job prospects, and importantly about a child's self-concept, self-esteem and self-enhancement. Discussion about raising a child bilingually or monolingually is not just about language. It is very much about the whole child. It is about the sense of security and status that a child will have, a child's self-identity and identity with a community and language group.

When there is **disagreement**, consider language as just one part of a child's whole development. Discussion about bilingualism in the child is not just about two languages. It's about personality, potential and the pleasure of a secure and stimulating period of childhood. Bilingualism in the child cannot be considered in total isolation. Bilingualism is one major part of the jigsaw of the child's total development. The fit of the bilingualism part of the jigsaw into the total picture of the child's development requires dialogue between parents.

If there is disagreement in the family, consider writing down the advantages and disadvantages. Consider the pluses and minuses on a **'balance sheet'**. Rather than argue about one or two points and let emotions sway, consider the widest variety of factors mentioned in this book. There needs to be a long-term view of the development of the child and not just a short-term, 'here and now' viewpoint. In the final balance sheet, who counts most? Consider the interests of the child and not just the short-term preferences of the parents. One danger is that one parent may insist on a personal strongly felt language opinion, without adequate consideration of what is in the best interests of the child.

With care and consideration, a parent may sometimes feel it possible to sacrifice an opinion in the **best interests of the child**. For example, if the father worries that he cannot understand what the mother is saying to the child in her heritage language, is a child's bilingualism to be sacrificed because of the father's concern? With diplomacy, love and meeting problems as challenges to be overcome, solutions and understandings can be gained. A father in this example may find it possible to forgo understanding conversations between mother and child in order for the child to become fluently bilingual. The challenge may be for the father to change rather than the child. Can the father at least gain a passive understanding of the minority language rather than a child lose out on bilingualism?

In short, disagreements need tactfully resolving. Open and frank, positive and empathic discussion is the route to resolution. The most important destination to discuss is the long-term interests of the child.

A5 If we raise our child to be bilingual, will it affect our marriage?

There is an instant answer to this question. If raising the child to be bilingual doesn't affect the marriage, there is something odd about the marriage! However, the way the question is posed hints that it will have a negative effect. The hint in the question may be that a bilingual child could be disruptive. For example, if a child is able to say things about the mother to the father in a language the mother does not understand, the child may be undermining the husband–wife relationship. A second example is when parents have to consider what language to speak to each other in front of the child; whether to switch languages when grandparents, relations, friends and others come into the home. When a minority language is used at home, and majority language monolinguals come into the home, do parents **switch** their languages when speaking to their children?

Bilingualism in the family opens up extra areas for discussion and decisions. Just as there are policy decisions within the family on the distribution of money across various headings, so also there needs to be discussion about the **distribution of language in family situations**. Such discussions are not once and for all. Just as family income changes across years leading to changes in spending, so language situations change across years (e.g. as friends, school and the prestige of languages change) leading to constant decisions about the **language economy**. Are the child's two languages in profit? Is there a growing debit account in one language? Can this be rectified? When new and different people enter the family situation, how can this be used to raise the profit of languages?

In raising children, there are constant **mountains and valleys**, periods of pleasure and occasions of worry and pain. There are times in a child's physical development when there is the glory of crawling, walking, running, winning races, learning to swim. There are also periods of illness, pain and discomfort. In social development, there is the joy of new friendships, of warm relationships with close friends and meeting new and exciting people. There is also the pain of arguments and fights, bullying and disloyalty. In intellectual development, there are the mountain-tops of learning: manipulating numbers, understanding new concepts, passing examinations. There are also the troughs of forgetting, not understanding and failing.

Therefore, in bilingual language development, there are also going to be mountains and valleys, peaks and troughs. There are the **joys** of hearing a child speak two languages to different people, of being able to break down barriers and build bridges with their two languages, of having two worlds of experience. There are also the **anxieties** and self-doubts about whether a child's two languages will develop to proficient bilingualism, of apparent interference between the two languages, and of people being excluded when a child is using one of their languages.

The answer is therefore that a child's bilingual development will affect a marriage and it should do. There will be highs and lows, **moments of glory and moments of grief**. This is no different from physical, social or intellectual development. Just as the vast majority of children turn out to be physically mature, socially effective and intellectually well developed adults, so children's dual language development also tends to have more glories than griefs. Just as parents care for a child's social, emotional, physical and intellectual development, so two languages need to be cared for. In the vast majority of cases, if problems become challenges, then long-term bilingual development is usually successful.

A6 What happens if grandparents and the extended family disapprove of bilingualism?

There are many situations when **grandparents** and the **extended family** have a vested interest in the bilingualism of children. Where the grandparents live in another country, for example, a monolingual child may be unable to communicate with grandparents, uncles and aunts, cousins and distant relatives. When a family is in-migrant, guest-worker or refugee, bilingualism in the child may help secure close family relationships with those left behind.

Disapproval of bilingualism may be found among monolingual grandparents and monolingual extended family members. For example, if an English speaker marries a French speaker, grandparents who are rooted in a tradition of monolingualism and monoculturalism may express a distaste for bilingual grandchildren. For such grandparents, their strong monolingual culture is seemingly being usurped and replaced by a diluted bilingual and bicultural experience.

There is also the historical legacy of bilingualism being identified with less intelligence, language under-development, problems of personal identity, and school under-performance. None of these attributions has been found fair or correct by research. Nevertheless, **prejudices** about bilingualism still abound, particularly among Western monolinguals.

Such disapproval, if based on prejudice, needs meeting with more up-to-date and **better informed evidence**. Information found in this book and other books (see a list at the end of this book) may be used to counteract misjudgements by grandparents, uncles and aunts and others. Where bilinguals are characterized negatively, there needs to be a clear assertion that bilingualism tends to have advantages and raises individual potential.

A different type of disapproval occurs when grandparents or others feel personally **excluded**. Research and evidence are unlikely to affect such inner feelings of alienation. Therefore, parents of bilingual children need to be **social as well as language engineers**. There is a need to explain to children and grandparents alike how communication can best be facilitated. It is possible to explain even to young children that grandma and grandad may not understand them talking English and therefore they need to use Spanish. Young children become amazingly adept at switching to the appropriate language and have everything to gain from communication with grandparents in the latter's preferred language.

Grandparents and others also need an **explanation**. Grandparents can be helped to understand the advantages of the child being bilingual, of the naturalness of the child switching between two languages, and that no loss of love or care is implied when a language is spoken that is not understood by grandparents. Where disapproval exists, diplomacy is needed. Bilingual parents and bilingual children are often relatively well equipped (language-wise and socially) to act diplomatically in cases of disapproval. The very act of having to deal diplomatically with languages only adds positively to a bilingual's life experiences and enhances their portfolio of skills and accomplishments.

If grandparents live in the same house, street or community, there is a wealth of language experience that can benefit the child. Grandparents, and other members of the extended family, provide an opportunity to learn or practice one language. For example, if parents speak one language to the child and the grandparents don't speak that language, the grandparents (and other extended family members) can be used to introduce and extend a second language. Their objection can be 'turned on its head' to foster bilingualism. Grandparents become the second language model for the child. Not only is the child taught a second language, but the wise and pithy sayings, nursery rhymes, songs, folk stories and traditions of that language can be passed on to the new generation.

A7 I'm a one-parent family. How can I raise my child bilingually?

Almost all books and case studies of bilingual children assume a two parent family. By accident and not by intention, this tends to lead to the assumption that a one-parent family has much less chance, or no chance of raising a child bilingually. A seemingly sympathetic view may be that a one-parent family has enough problems without taking on board the additional 'problem' of raising a bilingual child.

One-parent families are usually good at meeting challenges. Having often overcome or accommodated a variety of financial, social, moral and interpersonal obstacles, a one-parent family may take on the idea of raising a child bilingually without flinching. It is possible to raise a child bilingually inside a one-parent family. This is simply because a child's bilingualism may be acquired outside the mother–child or father–child relationship. What languages do the brothers and sisters speak? What language do the uncles and aunts, neighbors and friends speak to the child? Does the child go to a nursery school or a school where a different language is spoken from the home? What is the dominant language of the community? If a child has sufficient experience of a different language from that of the home, such a child may become bilingual with unsuspected ease.

For the one-parent family, will the child obtain **sufficient experience in two languages** for that child to develop fluency in both languages? If, for example, the mother speaks one language continuously to the child, the child may receive sufficient experience of a second language in a nursery school, in the street and in school to ensure dual language development.

A less likely and a more difficult option, but not an impossible one, is for the parent to use two languages on different occasions. If the parent uses two languages during the day to the same child, the problem is separation within the child of those two languages. Some mixing of languages is likely, with an immediate and short-term problem of separation. If a single parent feels it important to use two languages with the child, then there need to be clear **boundaries** of separation between the two languages.

For example, speaking to the child in one language on four days a week and in another language on three days of the week is unusual but possible. Speaking to a child in one language at mealtimes and playtimes, and reading to the child and educating the child in the preschool years in a different language may be an alternative. However, this strategy tends to be rather artificial, difficult to maintain naturally and would need clear explanation to the child in his or her own terms.

For the one-parent family, one important decision must be how to separate the child's two languages. How will it be possible for the child to recognize the differences between the languages? The answer lies in using each language in different contexts or with different people. A second decision concerns engineering a very rough and approximate balance of experience between the two languages over time (e.g. throughout childhood and the teenage years). A positive decision on these two points can enable one parent families to produce two language children.

A8 Neither of us speak a second language. How can we help our child become bilingual?

If you are keen on your child becoming bilingual, there are many other routes than within the family. Some children pick up a second language by attending a nursery school, play group or with a childminder, babysitter or *au-pair*. If a child has a continuity of second language experience outside the home, the child can become bilingual. There are many successful case histories of children speaking one language at home, and through regular attendance at nursery school, quickly becoming fluent in a second language. If that experience is consolidated in formal schooling, a highly competent bilingual may result.

Children can also be successful in acquiring a **conversational second language** in the street. Playing with friends over successive years in the evening, during holidays and at weekends, provides the opportunity to acquire a second language painlessly and effortlessly. Other children attend Saturday schools or Sunday schools sponsored by religious organizations and ethnic minority groups. For example, children have learned Arabic, Hebrew, Spanish, Italian, French and German through Saturday and Sunday language classes. Such 'conversational competence' in a second language may not be enough to cope in all language situations (e.g. the classroom). How a child can best learn a second language through school is left until later in this book when education questions are considered.

The dangerous conclusion would be that the first language should be learned in the home and the second language can be acquired outside the home. This is a false and dangerous position because parents' attitudes, encouragement and interest are vital in a child's second language development. Gentle inquiries about the child's second language development may indicate to the child that the parent is positively interested. **Praising** the child when they hear the child speaking the second language may do wonders for the child's language ego. **Visiting** the nursery school or childminder and showing interest in the language development of the child in that context may both encourage the teacher or carer. It will also signal to the child the parents' interest and awareness.

There is a danger in allowing interest to become concern, and enthusiasm to boil over into anxiety. A smile, a 'well done', a pat on the back and kindly praise do wonders for a child's motivation. If the parent thinks that second language development is important, the child will soon regard it as important as well. If the parent thinks that second language learning is of high status, the child will grow in status by identifying with the parents' wishes.

Second language support may also be provided by parents in the form of cassettes, videos, books, posters and comics. One limitation of bilingualism learned in the street is that the level of language development is restricted. The relatively simple conversational skills required to communicate in the street and playground need to blossom further. The language level of the classroom and office is more advanced.

The child ideally needs to grow from listening and speaking a second language to **literacy** in that language. The full flowering of the second language comes with reading and writing in a second language. Parents can encourage literacy in the second language in two ways. First, parents can provide stimulating material in the second language (e.g. books and magazines). Second, they can listen to the child read in the second language even if they are 'encouragers' rather than 'correctors'. Research has shown that even if a parent doesn't understand what a child is reading, the child engaging in reading practice (plus the visible encouragement and interest of the parent) facilitates development in reading in a second language.

While parents in such a situation may not be able to give language help, **the language of support and encouragement** is definitely needed.

A9 My children get little practice in speaking one of their languages outside the family. What should I do?

When one language is not used in the community, the only constant source of language practice may be inside the home. In this situation, parents need to consider how to establish a **richness of language experience** for their children in that particular language. It is important to arrange for the children to extend their language in a variety of situations. In order for the language of the child to extend beyond food, bedtime, and family chores, it is important to arrange language experiences in a variety of contexts.

New vocabulary needs developing alongside a wider and deeper understanding of the shared meanings of words. Appropriate use of language in **different situations**, holding a sustained conversation, pronunciation, an awareness of language and a love of language, accuracy of grammatical structure are all enhanced when language frontiers are continuously pushed back. Visits to the park may allow the absorption of the vocabulary of the natural world. Visits to beaches, banks and bookshops, swimming pool and sports events, carnivals and circuses mean that new experiences stimulate language growth. Meeting different people who can speak the home language (on trips abroad or within the region), allows the experience of different styles of speaking and pronunciation to be absorbed by the child. Obtaining cassette tapes (or parents creating their own tapes of family stories and old traditions), video tapes, books and comics from the home country will give opportunities for extending the child's language experience. Listening to nursery rhymes, songs, jokes and wise sayings in the home language will allow the child's language canvas to be painted with a wider variety of colors.

The examples given above emphasize that richness of language experience must not become 'homework'. Language practice means **pleasurable participation** and not deadly drills; inspiration rather than perspiration. A motivating challenge rather than an imposition.

When one language seems like a small island inside the home, it is important to fill that island with a richness of language experience. New situations and new experiences inject a freshness into the child's language. A child's language needs stimulating outside the home in a **variety of situations**. However, the danger is that the child sees the language as a small island. It may be important for the child to realize early on that the nuclear family's language island connects with language territory and language communities elsewhere. The child needs the experience of speaking the home language to relatives and people in a native country. The danger is that the language becomes isolated within the house, so it needs to break through the walls of the house and grow in a variety of environments outside. When this occurs, exploration replaces isolation.

A10 When watching television, should my child be encouraged to listen to one language or both languages?

To a very limited extent, parents can arrange for language experience by the child through listening to the **television and other mass media**. When there is insufficient exposure to one language, the use of video tapes and television programs may be a helpful supplement to a child's language diet. Minority language parents often buy language minority video tapes to encourage their children to grow in the minority language. They feel it important that the minority language and not just the majority language is identified with high status mass media images. Another example is when French speakers in English-speaking areas buy in French videos or obtain French television channels by satellite. Not only does a child receive language experience by such enjoyable and captivating means, the language itself may be raised in status inside the child's eyes by being attached to this important modern image.

There are limits to parental power concerning television choice. Children at a very early age become adept at tuning to the channel of their (and not their parent's) choice. Watching a favorite cartoon becomes more important than the attempted language engineering of the parent. This occasionally works to the advantage of bilingualism. Watching Mickey Mouse or Bugs Bunny is important, watching it in German, French, Japanese or English can become relatively unimportant to the child. I have spotted my own children watching German language television — particularly sports and children's programs — even though they have not been taught that language. So, in most family situations, the child votes for their television language experience with their finger on the remote control rather than via the guiding hand of the parent.

Since languages are not mixed on television, there seems an advantage for children to watch television in either of their languages. Watching one program in German and the next in French seems to be valuable since there is no confusing of the two languages. There is definite **separation** of languages.

However, the value of television in children's language development should not be exaggerated. While it may help to a limited extent in extending the language versatility of the child, television is essentially a **passive medium**. A child does not practice or use their language with a television set — only in rare situations. The child is the recipient of language rather than the producer of language. A child's listening vocabulary may be extended. Television does not usually produce opportunities to extend speaking performance. At the same time, television has some input in a child's literacy, however small. Titles and subtitles, lists of football teams, teletext, subtitles with the news may give the child language experience that is small but valuable.

Another danger with television is that it extends a child's stronger language rather than their weaker one. If a child obtains plenty of practice in the experience of one language, it is more important for television to be in the weaker language. The tendency of children is to watch television in majority languages — particularly English. Lesser-used languages in the mass media have relatively few hours of television prime time. Therefore, the danger is that the television diet does not provide the appropriate language vitamins to encourage fluent bilingualism.

A11 My children can speak two languages. How can I help them belong to two cultures?

In one sense, merely speaking a language to a child conveys **culture** to that child. Within a language, there are wise sayings, folk stories and ways of describing that carry the culture of that language. As a child learns a language, the child learns the emotive and 'accumulated meaning' associations of each word. Embedded in the meanings of words and phrases is always a culture. In acquiring a language, a child is also acquiring a particular way of seeing the world. Through language, a child learns a **whole way of life**, ways of perceiving and organizing experience, ways of anticipating the world, forms of social relationship, rules and conventions about behavior, moral values and ideals, the culture of technology and science as well as poetry, music and history. Listening, speaking, reading and writing a language essentially means the transmission of culture. Culture is reproduced in the child through the fertilization and growth of language.

However, it is possible to speak a language fluently yet not really understand, fully experience or fully participate in the culture that goes with a particular language. This is like saying about a person 'they speak Italian but don't act Italian'. In Wales, there are people who speak Welsh, yet do not engage in specific Welsh cultural forms or even feel themselves to be Welsh. It is paradoxically possible to be bilingual yet relatively monocultural. How can we lead a child on to **identify** themselves with a particular language culture? How can we help them belong to a particular language group?

Many adults and children who are bilingual do not belong to two language cultures as a monolingual belongs to a one language culture. A person who speaks English and French, for example, may partly share and identify with English language culture, and partly identify with French language culture (or better put — cultures). Being **bicultural** is different from being two monoculturals glued together. It is not a question of adding together two single language-based cultures to make two cultures. A bilingual tends to be bicultural in a unique sense. There is a complex but integrated combination of both cultures inside one person. It is like the overlapping of two circles rather than two circles side by side.

With considerable differences from person to person, and considerable changes over a time within a person, an individual may feel more French or more English but neither to the exclusion of the other. In this **hyphenated variety**, there is a separation of cultures and integration, distinct French and English varieties yet also a unique combination. To be Anglo-French is to be neither English nor French. There is more discussion about this later.

As bilingual children get older, they decide mostly for themselves to enhance one or both their cultures. **Parents** can only act as **gardeners**, showing their children the variety of cultures that go within each language. Gardeners can aid growth but not cause growth. The language seeds sown need planting, watering, tending and fertilizing. Some language flowers need extra care and protection by parents. Other flowers will grow quickly and effortlessly. Sometimes reseeding is necessary. Growth will vary with climatic conditions outside the control of the language gardener. Parents nevertheless have to be language garden landscape engineers, providing conditions for maximal growth inside those climatic variations.

Through meeting speakers of their two languages, visiting a variety of cultural events — from markets to sports matches, from religious meetings to rustic festivals — parents can introduce their children to the cultures that surround each language. Where first hand experience is not possible, television and video tapes allow second-hand experience. Introduction to the broadest range of cultures that goes with each language will potentially broaden the **horizons of the child**, open up more and new opportunities, and give a world view where there are fewer barriers and more bridges.

A12 How important is it that the child's two languages are practiced and supported outside the home?

This question particularly reflects the concerns of those parents who speak their heritage language to the child in isolation. Where families are **guest-workers, in-migrants or refugees**, there may be little support for the home language in the community or in formal schooling. When such parents feel **isolated**, there is sometimes the tendency to feel like giving up the heritage language and speaking the regional majority language to the child. The pressure in the community tends to be to speak in the language of the region rather than a foreign language.

The answer is that bilingualism inside the child can be effectively **sustained** through the language of the home being different from the language of the community. However, this will be a challenge and a constant journey that moves across bright mountain tops and dark valleys. If the child learns the community language via the school and the street, there is sufficient support for that language outside the home for the child to become fully bilingual.

The problem is not usually with learning the majority language of the region, but in maintaining the language of the home. Determined parents should not be deterred by their language being an island in the home. The answer to the ninth question in this section provides the information about what support is important to sustain that language island.

A13 What kind of community support is valuable for bilingualism?

This question particularly concerns those who live in different types of minority language or **'language island'** situations. For example, where only a small proportion of a community speak a language and the majority language is all pervading, how does one react? In a minority language situation, the danger is that the home minority language will wither and fade as the child increasingly grows stronger in the majority language by experiences outside the home and with the mass media. Also, this question concerns those families who feel isolated; for example, a German-speaking mother in an English language environment.

When a child is being brought up bilingually, any possibility of similar parents and toddlers **getting together** needs encouragement. Sometimes this is impossible due to geographical distance. Yet with mother and toddler groups, small nursery groups or compulsory schooling, groups of same-language speakers can each help a language minority family feel less isolated, and less of a minority. This includes two different types of situation.

First, there is the example of local mothers, fathers and children meeting and using their common minority language. In some mothers and toddlers' groups for example, the language of playing and conversation will be the minority language only. In a **second** situation, bilingual parents with bilingual children of different combinations of languages may meet to exchange ideas, hunt out answers to problems, swap information and literature, and importantly, encourage each other. If you feel that you are an isolated language island, try to find other similar islands near you and develop links between them. If those different islands speak the same language, there can be an exchange of materials as well as interaction in the home language. If the islands use different languages, there is still the opportunity to reduce isolation and feel part of the community of islands. **Sharing needs to replace isolation**.

A14 My neighbors think we should integrate more which means using a different language from the home. Should we keep separate or integrate?

Such neighbors are usually monolinguals. The monolingual view of the world tends to be that languages keep nations and people apart. Having a common language is the only way to integrate. The problem is that the word integration tends really to mean **assimilation**. Monolingual neighbors really want you to become the same as them. Instead of being bilingual and bicultural, they want you to be like them, monolingual and monocultural. Such neighbors do not like **variety in the language garden**. (This is an analogy that is intentionally pursued and expanded throughout the book.) They want everybody to be daffodils, or everybody to be tulips, or everybody to be English red roses.

Neighbors who are bilingual themselves and bicultural are not only usually more happy with the idea of language variety. They also tend to admire a variety of flowers in the language garden. Bilinguals seem more adept at accepting people as they are, and not feeling challenged or excluded when they hear different languages being spoken. Monolinguals tend more to want uniformity and similarity.

Sometimes neighbors need to be educated. When neighbors believe that integration means monolingualism, kind and gentle education of such neighbors may be desirable. If neighbors believe that local assimilation demands monolingualism in their language, the price of friendship needs weighing against the wealth gained from **language preservation**.

One issue raised by this question is whether children should be kept away from neighbors so that they do not develop superior performance in one language rather than another. The answer is that one language does not usually develop at the cost of another. Languages do not develop like a balance: the more one side rises, the lower the other descends. **Languages grow interdependently** and with no long-term cost to each other. Therefore, it is sensible and natural that children should have language practice with people around them who matter, and who are important in a local network of relationships. To stop a child talking to neighbors for fear of language pollution is taking language engineering to unreasonable limits. Making a child anxious or neurotic about language life can be the death knell of bilingualism and not its salvation.

Language is essentially about **communication**. Who better to communicate to, and build relationships with than local neighbors? However, this does not mean that there should be a free language economy in the locality. When an 'isolated' language is used in the home, parents will have to engineer situations and visits for children to use their minority 'island' language. There is a cost to bilingualism in such situations — financial as well as time-wise. There are also great benefits for children.

A15 Can I learn a second language alongside my child?

This is not as unusual as it sounds. There are many examples of a parent learning a language from the other parent alongside their first-born or second-born child. For example, a father may pick up a minority language spoken by the mother while listening to the mother speaking to the child. The father will be able to understand many minority language conversations in the family. At the same time, he may continue to speak in the majority language. In this example, the father may find it artificial and unnatural to speak to the child in anything except his first language.

In other cases, a parent will attend a language learning class as soon as a child is born, keeping a few months ahead of the child. One aim is to establish some kind of language uniformity inside the house so that all the occupants are speaking the same language to each other, or at least, understand each other speaking. In a minority language situation, particularly where that minority language is not strong in the local community, there is value in this. The child will later become bilingual outside the home.

One danger is where language standardization or uniformity exists in the home that parallels the same language uniformity in the community. For example, **in-migrant** parents decide to lose their heritage language and speak the language of the host country instead. In such cases, the chance of bilingualism will be lost and monolingualism may result. Another danger in this 'in-migrant' situation is that the parent speaks an incorrect or pidgin form of the majority language to the child. If the parent learning the second language is a poor **language model** for the child, then the child may be placed at a disadvantage. If the parent learning the second language is inaccurate in vocabulary, wrong in sentence construction and provides inexact meanings, the child is learning to speak the language in a less correct and sophisticated manner than may be preferred. Children may also come to despise and show dissatisfaction towards the parent who they later realize speaks a second (majority) language 'incorrectly'.

A16 We have just moved to a different country. Should we speak the host country's language in the home to help our children?

Since there has recently been more movement from one country to another, this question is increasingly being asked. **First**, if one or both parents can speak the host country's language, it still often feels unnatural and stilted to speak that (second) language to the children. In this sense, the **artificiality** of changing the language spoken by the parents will not help the settling down period. Indeed, an abrupt language change may hinder the settling down phase. **Second**, if children already have **confidence** in a language, suddenly to switch languages at the same time as switching country, home, family and friends can be psychologically disruptive for the child. Some continuity and reassurance for the child may be gained by continuing to speak the language of the home. **Third**, speaking the host language to children already **competent** in a language, means that the level of conversation will change. The language will have to be simple and the conversation sometimes tedious. Importantly, the conceptual growth of children may be hindered by their being spoken to in a new language.

Nevertheless, many parents want their children to become fluent quickly in the host country's language. Therefore, they automatically want to provide the environment where quick acquisition of that language occurs. If the children are very young, they will usually pick up the **host country's language** in the street, shops and particularly in nursery or kindergarten schooling. Generally, children pick up a new language when they are young with some degree of ease. Since the vocabulary and complexity of language structure required in young children's conversation is much less than adults, and since young children acquire language almost accidentally and painlessly, young children are often more adept at adjusting to a new language than most adults.

The specific advice is that children (when infants and quite young) do not need parents to speak the host country's language in the home. They will usually pick up that language easily outside the home. It is usually better for the heritage language to be taught in the home, giving the child the chance of bilingualism, biculturalism and a sense of continuity.

In later childhood and teenage years, children may be expected to operate in the host country's language in the school. Even if simple conversational proficiency is acquired relatively easily by such children, the level of language competence and confidence needed to work in the school curriculum is much harder to attain. A child learning algebra, gravity, world climatic variations, the history of the Renaissance plus Roman Catholic doctrine will often find that the **gap** between simple conversational skills learned quickly and the language required in the curriculum is many kilometers apart.

When children are in the middle childhood and teenage years, advice from 'experts' differs. When competence in school work becomes important to the child, and where there is no choice in the language of the curriculum, parents may feel it their duty to provide **extra support** in the host country's language for their child. On such occasions, a family may decide to switch the language of the home to the school language after discussion and agreement with the child so that the child gains maximally from education. Other 'experts' argue for the **continuity** of language and culture in the home. Therefore, no language switch is needed or necessary. This argument is rooted in keeping family traditions alive, maintaining heritage language culture, and retaining a sense of the past in the present.

There occasionally arises a circumstance when minority language preservation, bilingualism itself, may need sacrificing for the greater good of the child. There are occasions when bilingualism cannot be the highest priority within the family. On such occasions, following discussion with the child, supporting the language the child requires in education and employment may be relatively important and a higher priority than preserving the heritage language. Fortunately, in many cases this is not required. Bilingualism can be maintained. Ultimately, bilingualism has to be a pleasure and not a pain, a means of enhancing the quality of life and not an end in itself. A belief in bilingualism is based on a belief about what is best for children. Bilingualism is supported because it supports children.

Section B
Language Development Questions

B1 What are the most important factors in raising a bilingual child?

Children are **born ready to become bilinguals** and multilinguals. Too many are restricted to becoming monolinguals. Children are born with the equipment to run and play, to laugh and to learn. No caring parent or teacher denies children the chance to develop physically, socially, educationally or emotionally. Yet we deny many children the chance to develop bilingually and multilingually.

The most important factor in the language development of a bilingual child is nothing to do with language. It is about **making language enjoyable**, fun and a thoroughly happy experience for children. Parents of bilingual children are often anxious about the correctness of their children's language, their ability to separate the two languages, how the development of thinking is affected by two languages, the self-identity problems that may face their children, and all the positive and negative things other adults will say or think about their children.

Language is about **communication**. We need language to communicate information, to build relationships, to play games and tell stories, to make new friends and work in groups. Some bilingual parents fuss endlessly about **correctness** of grammar, accuracy of vocabulary, not mixing two languages, and skilled interpreting and translating. Instead, the most important factor in raising a bilingual child is to make their language development a pleasure, a positive and enjoyable experience. Children need to value their two languages, two cultures and in a modest way, become aware of the advantages of being bilingual and bicultural.

Parents who make the development of proficiency in two languages a **crusade**, a source of conflict, a series of mini crises, a competition against monolinguals are likely to work against themselves. A language castle is simultaneously built and attacked. Even if children exist in such a negative language situation, language development will still occur in two languages. A child may be able to speak, even learn to read and write fluently in two languages. What the child has also learned is that bilingualism is not beautiful. The child has learned that bilingualism is associated with pressure, anxiety and constant correction.

It is important that children's attitude towards their two languages (and their motivation to extend their two languages) is **encouraged continuously**. Show delight at small steps forward in bilingual development. Without being patronizing, or making the child overly conscious, praise your child for speaking two languages. The occasional pat on the back, a quiet 'well done', a wink or a smile works wonders for a child's **language ego**. For example, when a child has correctly switched languages in front of grandma so she understands, or automatically translated something for a friend to help relationships in a group, gently show your delight. We all need encouragement to carry on learning and refining our skills. Encouragement and aptly directed praise will provide the positive ambience, the caring ethos and helpful family atmosphere to surround the development of bilingualism.

When the child speaks a minority language, encouraging use of that **minority language** may need to be more rather than less. When there is discouragement in the street, little reinforcement on the screen and in the school playground for minority language usage, parents are often pivotal in fostering favorability of attitude among the children to that minority language. When the child speaks a minority language, it is important to amplify that minority language rather than the majority language, especially in the early years. The winds of influence usually blow in the direction of the majority language: mass media, employment, communication with bureaucracy, for example. Therefore, the balance of language experience needs tilting in favor of the minority language. While ensuring the child becomes fully fluent in the majority language, some **sheltering** from incessant blasts of the pervasive majority language is important.

A most important factor in raising a bilingual child is **the language that surrounds language**. The gardener cannot make the language seeds grow. All the gardener can do is to provide certain conditions: a rich soil, ensuring the light falls in the right places, watering and tending in a caring way. Language growth in children requires the minimum of pruning — these are tender, young plants. Correcting language continuously, formally getting the child to repeat sentences is the kind of pruning that research shows to have almost no effect, even a negative effect on language growth. The role of the language gardener is to provide a stimulating soil — a variety of pleasurable environments for language growth.

This does not mean that all that is needed is encouragement and care. The **language gardener** needs to plan, to prepare the soil, to water, fertilize and sometimes weed. Other parts of this book provide ideas about language irrigation and intervention. Language growth can be slow. There will be many anxious days when tender young shoots are wilting in the heat of the majority language and in danger of breaking among the strong winds of peer pressure. The parent as language gardener can help maximize those conditions that are open to influence, but parents cannot control the growth of language.

B2 Do some children find it easier than others to become bilingual?

Do some children have more aptitude for language learning? Do more able and more intelligent children learn languages much more easily than others? A **first** answer is that children develop at slightly **different speeds** in their bilingual language development. Just as some children learn to crawl earlier than others, walk earlier than others and say their first words earlier than others, so the speed of language development varies between children. This is even more so in the development of two languages.

The speed of language acquisition is only partly due to the child's **ability**. Indeed, some children who turn out to be very able in academic terms are slow in their language development. There is generally little relationship between how quickly someone learns to speak one or two languages and eventual school success. Early language developers are not likely to be more successful in adult life — be success defined in terms of work, marriage, affluence or self-enhancement.

A **second** answer is that a child's **interest** in language is also important and is partly separate from ability and aptitude for language learning.

When a child is encouraged and stimulated in language development, an interest in reading, for example, will be increased. Parents who listen with attention to what the child is saying, answer the child in a child-centered way, make language fun by rhymes and songs, will tend to aid language development. A child's interest in language and motivation to engage in lots of conversation will affect their speed of development.

As with monolinguals, very few bilingual children do not become proficient in at least one language. Given adequate encouragement, practice and a stimulating environment for language growth, **children** find the acquisition of two languages relatively straightforward, painless and effortless. In contrast, many Western **parents** locate the bends in the road, develop worries, and debate whether the effort to encourage bilingualism in their children is worthwhile. Some parents (in similar circumstances) find bilingualism easier to achieve than others. Their children tend to reflect parents' attitudes, behavior, expectations and beliefs. A positive parent tends to breed a successful child. Parents who expect failure tend to breed less success. This is particularly true of a child's bilingual development.

There are **many hurdles but few insurmountable barriers** to children reaching whatever bilingual language destination is possible. However, routes to dual language proficiency are long. This is one reason for undue concern by destination-seeking parents. Early acquisition of two languages for some parents seems like slow motoring. For other parents, the journey in later childhood and the teenage years seems troublesome, even like backpedaling. Such concerns seem usual and prevalent among parents of bilingual children. However, if safety in numbers doesn't satisfy, consider comparing your bilingual child against other bilinguals and not against the fastest moving monolingual who sets the pace. Many bilinguals show similar language performance to monolinguals in one of their languages. Some, but not all, develop considerable competence in a second language. Rarely are bilinguals equally at ease in all situations in both their languages.

Not all bilingual children will reach the same **language destination**. Family, community and education circumstances sometimes mean the journey halts at passive bilingualism (that is, understanding but not speaking a second language). Such a halt is a temporary resting stop. Partial or passive bilingualism is not a finishing line. Given a need to become an active bilingual (e.g. by visiting the country where the hitherto 'passive' language is dominant), the journey can be continued to more complete bilingualism.

There is no simple reason why some children are quicker than others in dual language development or find it easier to become bilingual. For each individual child, there is a **complex equation affecting the rate of bilingual development**. Into the equation go factors such as the child's personality, the child's ability and aptitude for language learning, the child's social development, the quality and quantity of interaction with parents and peers, neighbors and extended family, the variety of language inputs and a stimulating environment for language development, the perceived attitudes of significant other people around the family and the child's own attitudes about bilingualism. The child's own priorities, the family language balance sheet, and the place of languages in the child's community life are also important.

It is usual that **some children tend to be faster than others** in their bilingual language development. Just as monolingual children vary in their language development, and very few monolinguals fail to become fluent in their language, so with bilinguals. Given a stimulating language environment and a positive atmosphere in the home to bilingualism, dual language development will usually occur successfully if sometimes slowly. Separate questions in this book deal with language disorders (see Sections C and E).

If the analogy will stand, language development is like distance running. Some people complete the course with speed, others go at a slower pace but still successfully manage to complete the language distance. For some, the distance is relatively easy. For others, completion takes time, patience and effort. Parents as spectators sometimes become agitated by the slow speed of the bilingual course. Parents want adult-like language performance while the child is in the early and middle stages of the marathon. Becoming fluent in two languages is a slower process for everybody than learning to run.

B3 Is it easier to become bilingual as a young child?

The answer is both yes and no. The answer is 'yes' in that **young children** pick up language so easily. Language is acquired unwittingly, subconsciously, without the effort of secondary school language classes, without the pressure of 101 other important matters to consider (as in adolescence and adulthood). Young children learn through play and concrete situations. They are not worried by their language mistakes, nor about not finding the exact words. They are only interested in getting their message across and receiving needed information. Young children learn languages as **naturally** as they learn to run and jump, paint and play.

The young child has less to learn compared with the older child to reach a level expected of young children. The process is not learning but **acquisition** when children are young. Language among young children is caught rather than taught. Language acquisition is a by-product of playing and interacting with people. There is plenty of time to acquire the language. The pressure and competing opportunities that exist among older children are not present. Language for a young child needs not to be forced, pressured, an imposition or a dirge. Competence in language from the 'one word' baby stage to the fun of the five-year-old is a pleasure without pain.

When children are very young, they pick up accurate **pronunciation** quickly. Children easily learn the distinct sounds of two languages and local dialects. Compare such young children pronouncing their languages with adults learning a second language. Adults often struggle with correct pronunciation. For adults, rolling the 'r', tonging a 'th', guttural sounds and nasal sounds are more difficult, seemingly impossible to master perfectly. Even when adults become perfectly fluent in a second language, often their pronunciation in French or German, Arabic or Japanese still carries the ring of the first language. Compare mainland Europeans, Africans, Arabs and Asians who have learned to speak English fluently. Rarely do they pronounce English like an American or British person. The sounds and pronunciation of their first language affect the way English is intoned. Research has found that young children have an advantage in learning languages in that they are more likely to pick up appropriate pronunciation of their two languages compared with those who learn a second language later.

The second part of the answer is 'no'. Very young bilingual children tend to learn a language relatively slowly. Their rate of development and progress is not fast compared with a teenager or an adult learning a second language. Because **older children and adults** have better developed thinking, information handling, analytical and memorization capacities, they tend to learn languages faster than very young children. So, if efficiency is defined by the amount of time it takes to learn a second language, teenagers and adults tend to be superior to young children. Adults will be able to run the language course quicker than young children.

The **speed** with which adults become bilingual through learning a second language will vary according to: the amount of time for lessons and practice, attitude and motivation, aptitude and ability for language learning, and persistence in using the second language when there are incorrect utterances. As a generalization, most adults learn a second language faster than most children. However, as previously indicated, while adults may become fluent and literate in a second language, their pronunciation of that second language is unlikely to be as good as a young child. There is sometimes resistance to learning a new language, particularly in the teenage years. This can be part of a general resistance to a variety of things, no perceived need to learn a language, even a narrow monoculturalism.

The answer given so far mustn't be seen as a competition. It is possible for both young children, teenagers and adults to become fluently bilingual. Many routes can produce an equally successful outcome. The routes on the language course may be different, the timing to complete may be varied. But if this is a fun language run, success is possible among both young and old.

B4 Will my child become equally fluent in two languages?

The answer is usually a definite 'NO'. There are only a few exceptions to this answer. One idealistic and unrealistic notion of some parents about incipient bilingual children is that they are going to finish with a perfectly bilingual child. The hopes of many parents are that their child will be two monolinguals inside the one bilingual person. For example, the expectation is that the child's French and German will be equivalent to French and German monolinguals. This idea of balanced bilinguals, perfectly balanced in both their languages, is one muddled myth that surrounds bilingualism. This myth is part of a monolingual view of the world. The monolingual views the language world as someone totally fluent in a language. The monolingual view of bilinguals is that they should be perfectly fluent in two languages.

The reality that surrounds most bilinguals is very different. Languages have purposes. For a bilingual, **each language tends to have different purposes, different functions and different uses**. Bilinguals tend to use their two languages in different places at different times with different people. For example, a person speaks English at work and when playing a particular sport. That person uses the other language at home, in church or chapel, mosque or temple, and with neighbors and friends in the community. The two languages are mostly different tools for different jobs.

Many bilinguals are 'stronger' in one language than another. The problem is what 'stronger' means. Take an example. If one language is used much of the time, and the person has been educated in that language, it may have a width of vocabulary and complexity of structure not found in the other language. However, this other language may be the one that is naturally used in the nuclear and extended family. That family language is developed to meet the needs of home life and is thoroughly sufficient for that situation.

Such **varying strength in two languages** is unlikely to be stable and consistent over time. As children and adults move house, move school, move employment, go for long or short trips abroad, have new friends and extend their personal culture, so the balance and strength of the languages change. Children who were passive bilinguals (able to understand but not speak a second language), once in a region that demands use of that language, often quickly become speakers, readers and writers in that hitherto weaker language. The only certainty about a bilingual's future dual language use is uncertainty.

Even children brought up by the **one parent–one language** method rarely show equal proficiency in both languages. Rarely does that unequal balance between the two languages stay the same. For example, as brothers and sisters arrive and develop, the balance between the two languages may change. As the child gathers a group of friends inside and outside school, proficiency in the two languages may change and fluctuate. As the child moves through school and into college or employment, the balance between those languages may change again.

It is important **not to compare bilinguals with monolinguals** in their language development. Bilinguals should be compared with bilinguals. Bilinguals are not two monolinguals inside one person. They own a unique combination of two languages that are both separate and integrated within the thinking system. While two languages are visible in production (e.g. speaking), in the thinking quarters of the brain, one feeds the other. One language helps the other to grow. In this sense, there is integration between the two languages. Ideas and concepts learned in one language can be easily transferred into the other language. Mathematical multiplication and division learned in one language do not have to be relearned in the second language. Once the idea of multiplication and division is complete in the child, that understanding is immediately available in the second language.

Since bilinguals use their different languages in different circumstances and with different people, it is unnatural to expect them to have the same linguistic repertoire as two monolinguals. For example, children's religious vocabulary may be strong in one language and not in the other as they attend church or chapel, mosque or temple in one language only. The child may be strong in scientific vocabulary in one language only, having been taught solely in that language. However, there will be transfer in thinking from one language to another (e.g. in religious ideas and scientific concepts).

Another **danger** is to compare bilinguals with monolingual 'native country' speakers. Take, for example, the case of a child who has learned German in a country outside Germany. In the country of residence, German is rarely heard by the child. It is false to expect the child to speak German like a native German child. Width of vocabulary, complexity of language structure and pronunciation, for example, may be different. However, communication with other Germans is very probable. The language competence the child has in German enables both the gaining of information and the gaining of friendships — two key aspects of communication. From that base, when the child visits Germany, there will be adaptation to the German spoken in Germany, and a growth in 'native' language skills.

The bilingual is a different language creation from the monolingual. For many bilinguals, **bilingualism is their language**. For those who acquire two languages from birth, bilingualism is their first language. Two monolinguals they are not.

Parents of bilingual children should therefore not expect their children to become as language competent as two monolinguals. Rather, bilinguals have the advantage and flexibility of being able to move between two languages, two or more cultures in a way that monolinguals cannot. There is no deficit or disadvantage implied when there is an imbalance between the languages. Such an imbalance only reflects the reality of the circumstances in which bilinguals live, and their ability to be decathletes rather than specialists in one event only. However, the difficulty arises in school and employment markets where bilinguals are sometimes compared with monolinguals. This can work both for, and admittedly, sometimes against bilinguals.

B5 Is it better to develop two languages together or one language later than the other?

The answer is that neither is better or preferable. Developing two languages at the same time or learning one language later than another are **both successful routes to bilingualism**. As expressed in this section already, there are many cases of older children and adults successfully learning a second language. Through language learning classes in school, adult language learning classes, immersion in a new community and occasionally a change in the language pattern of the home, older children and adults can be quicker and more efficient in learning a second language than very young children. There are examples of adults learning Hebrew and Welsh when they were aged sixty, seventy and eighty. Success in becoming bilingual is possible whatever the age.

However, if the home conditions allow it, there is much value in developing children's bilingualism **earlier rather than later**. Because of the ease with which young children acquire language, the uncluttered nature of early childhood, and the tendency to acquire pronunciation better when very young, early bilingualism needs encouragement wherever possible. Such early bilingualism gives immediate cognitive and social advantages, and possible longer-term economic, interpersonal and cultural advantages. If the family situation allows bilingualism early on in the child's life, the best current advice is to start as soon as possible, ideally on the first day.

Teenagers and adults learn to swim by attending swimming instruction lessons. They learn the breast stroke, front crawl, back stroke and butterfly through practice, watching examples and through thinking about their physical movements in the water. Young children seem to learn swimming much more easily and naturally. They may be slower in perfecting their swimming strokes, but there is the joy of seeing the young child move through the water and enjoy all the fun of the pool. The same occurs with language. When learning the four language strokes (listening, speaking, reading and writing), both children and adults can become good language swimmers. If a bilingual language pool is available for the very young child, it seems sensible to give the child a chance to swim in two languages as early as possible.

There are situations where learning one language thoroughly first, the other language later is possibly preferable. This occurs in minority language **'subtractive'** situations. Where the majority language dominates in the community and country, it may be preferable to concentrate on full development in the minority language first. Once a child is in the street, school, supermarket, swimming pool, and socializing at discos and parties, the majority language usually develops at great speed.

The **danger for minority language parents** who introduce the majority language early on is that the child increasingly uses the majority language. When playing in the street and school, the common language is the majority language. The majority language is perceived by even young children as of higher status, more prestigious and having more uses and purposes. Therefore, developing a deep-rooted minority language and culture is important. A child who learns the majority language later (e.g. at age five when attending school), learns quickly. There is such a transfer of language learning skills, awareness of majority language status and an availability of experience in the majority language that learning the majority language later rather than earlier is rarely a problem.

B6 How do I know my child's language development in each language is normal and acceptable?

While it is possible to provide guidelines (and these are given later) as to a typical child's language development, it is **firstly** important to stress that **children vary** considerably in the speed of their language development. Early bloomers in language are not necessarily those who will be the great linguists of the future. In the same way, those children whose language development seems slow early on, may be those who catch up very quickly later. Einstein did not speak to the age of three. Many other famous people started speaking later than customary.

Secondly, there is great variety in the range and type of experiences that a child receives in both of their languages. For example, in some families French and English may receive roughly equal input. In other families, the balance may be more towards, for example, 80% English and 20% French. It is unrealistic to expect these two families to show similar development in their children in French.

Thirdly, when a child's language is definitely not developing normally, it is important to seek professional advice. For example, speech therapists, audiologists, clinical psychologists, educational psychologists, counselors and doctors may be contacted for advice and treatment. It is important that such professionals have some training regarding bilingualism, and preferably experience of bilingual children. In Sections C and E of this book, there is a discussion of language disorders and bilingualism. It is worthwhile reading appropriate answers to questions on **language delay**, language disorders, assessment and special education for bilinguals before consulting medical and psychological professionals.

Set out below is an average **pattern of development for bilingual children**. Children in families where both languages are approximately equally developed will be close to these norms. However, it must be stressed that many children differ from these general averages and will show perfectly normal language development later in childhood. It is only when children approach formal schooling (and require sufficient language development in one of their languages to be able to understand the curriculum), that most developmental language concerns should begin.

A separate question later in the book deals with language delayed children.

Age	Language
First Year	Babbling, cooing, laughing (dada, mama, gaga)
Around 1 year old	First understandable words
During second year	Two-word combinations, moving slowly to three- and four-word combinations. Three-element sentences (e.g. 'Daddy come now'; 'That my book'; 'Teddy gone bye-byes').
3 to 4 years	Dramatic changes. Simple but increasingly longer sentences. Grammar and sentence structuring starts to develop. Conversations show turn taking
4 years onwards	Increasingly complex sentences, structure and ordered conversation. Use of pronouns and auxiliary verbs.

If a personal experience is allowed, one of my children was very slow in learning to speak. One grandparent immediately ascribed this to his bilingualism. A lack of clarity of the speech in those early years was also obvious. Since no problems of hearing were found, no action was necessary. Three years on, both languages were well developed, with appropriate vocabularies, complexity in sentence structure and a standard of work in school that made those early years no predictor at all. At meal times, play times and at bedtime, anybody listening to him would be more likely to suggest that he now suffers from language overdevelopment!

B7 Will learning a second language interfere with development in the first language?

The answer is no, definitely not. There may sometimes be some very minor knots on the wood that are easily planed off over time. For example, mixing words from the two languages often temporarily occurs among children. Generally, the effects from one language to another are positive. Research suggests that becoming bilingual has positive effects on language development, including on the first language. For example, when learning two languages, the child may become more sensitive and aware of language itself. There may be more sensitivity in communication and more awareness of the needs of listeners. Having two (or more) words for each object, idea or concept will **expand** rather than contract **the mind**.

Above is a picture of bilinguals that is **incorrect**. This picture of bilinguals is of someone with two **language balloons** in the head. In the picture below, this incorrect idea of two languages is that they are stored within two separate language areas in the brain. The apparent assumption is that God made just enough room for one language inside the head. If one language is poured into that balloon, the mind will work maximally efficiently. If two languages are poured into the thinking quarters, the result will be two half-filled language balloons. Such under-filled language balloons in the bilingual will create an inefficient brain.

This 'two balloon' concept is wrong. First, there is more than enough room inside the thinking quarters for two or more languages. It seems impossible to set limits on the amount of learning, understanding and knowledge that a person can hold within their thinking quarters. Second, the picture is wrong because there is **transfer** between the two languages. As in the example of a child taught mathematical multiplication and division in one language, those concepts do not have to be retaught in the second language. They immediately transfer as an idea and an understanding into another language (so long as the child has the vocabulary to reproduce it in that second language). Thus, the two language balloons

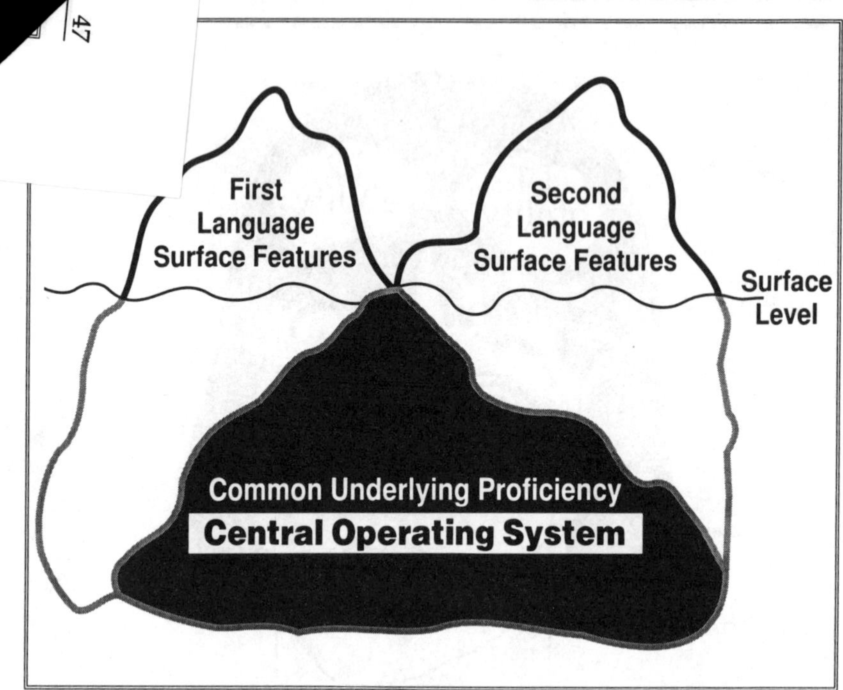

The Iceberg Analogy

merge inside the thinking quarters. There is a common thinking area that can be serviced and supplied by both languages.

The incorrect balloon picture can be replaced by the picture of a dual **iceberg**. Two icebergs are separate above the water line. A bilingual's two languages are separate when speaking (and on the 'exterior', separate when reading and writing). Below the surface of the water, the two icebergs are fused. A bilingual's two languages are joined together beneath the surface in the operating area of the brain.

So, rather than a second language interfering with the development of the first language, it is more likely to provide thinking advantages, social and cultural advantages, even economic advantages in the long term.

B8 What effect will bilingualism have on my child's intelligence?

One misguided legacy of over a hundred years writing on bilingualism is that children's intelligence will suffer if they are bilingual. Some of the earliest research into bilingualism examined whether bilingual children were ahead or behind monolingual children on **IQ tests**. From the 1920s through to the 1960s, the tendency was to find monolingual children ahead of bilinguals on IQ tests. The conclusion was that bilingual children were mentally confused. Having two languages in the brain it was said, disrupted efficient thinking. Thinking was better conducted through one well developed language. It was argued that having one well developed language was superior to having two half developed languages.

The idea that bilinguals may have a lower IQ still exists among many people, particularly monolinguals. However, we now know that this early research was misconceived and incorrect. First, such research often gave bilinguals an IQ test in their weaker language — usually English. Had bilinguals been tested in Welsh or Spanish or Hebrew, a different result may have been found. The **testing** of bilinguals was thus **unfair**. Second, like was not compared with like. Bilinguals tended to come from, for example, impoverished New York or rural Welsh backgrounds. The monolinguals tended to come from more middle class, urban families. Working class bilinguals were often compared with middle class monolinguals. So the results were more likely to be due to social class differences than language differences. The **comparison** of monolinguals and bilinguals was unfair.

The most recent research from Canada, the United States and Wales suggests that bilinguals are, at the least, equal to monolinguals on IQ tests. When bilinguals have **two well developed languages** (in the research literature called balanced bilinguals), bilinguals tend to show a slight superiority in IQ scores compared with monolinguals. This is the received psychological wisdom of the moment and is the good news for raising bilingual children. Take for example, a child who can operate in either language in the curriculum in the school. That child is likely to be ahead on IQ tests compared with similar (same gender, social class and age) monolinguals. Far from making people mentally confused, bilingualism is now associated with a mild degree of **intellectual superiority**.

One note of **caution** needs to be sounded. IQ tests probably do not measure intelligence. IQ tests measure a small sample of the broadest concept of intelligence. IQ tests are simply paper and pencil tests where only 'right and wrong' answers are allowed. Is all intelligence summed up in such simple right and wrong, pencil and paper tests? Isn't there a wider variety of intelligences that are important in everyday functioning and everyday life? Do we only define an intelligent person as somebody who obtains a high score on an IQ test? Are the only intelligent people those who belong to high IQ organizations such as MENSA? Is a famous football coach whose team wins the cup intelligent? If someone is poor and becomes a billionaire, are they intelligent? Was Don Juan intelligent?

Is a chairperson who manipulates members of a board intelligent? Is a thief who cracks a bank vault intelligent? Is there social intelligence, musical intelligence, military intelligence, marketing intelligence, motoring intelligence, political intelligence? Are all, or indeed any of these forms of intelligence measured by a simple pencil and paper IQ test which demands a single, acceptable, correct solution to each question? Defining what constitutes intelligent behavior requires a personal value judgement as to what type of behavior, and what kind of person is of more worth.

The current state of psychological wisdom about bilingual children is that, where two languages are relatively well developed, bilinguals have **thinking advantages** over monolinguals. Take an example. A child is asked a simple question: How many uses can you think of for a brick? Some children give two or three answers only. They can think of building walls, building a house and perhaps that is all. Another child scribbles away, pouring out ideas one after the other: blocking up a rabbit hole, breaking a window, using as a bird bath, as a plumb line, as an abstract sculpture in an art exhibition.

Research across different continents of the world shows that bilinguals tend to be more fluent, flexible, original and elaborate in their answers to this type of open-ended question. The person who can think of a few answers tends to be termed a convergent thinker. They converge onto a few acceptable conventional answers. People who think of lots of different uses for unusual objects (e.g. a brick, tin can, cardboard box) are called **divergers**. Divergers like a variety of answers to a question and are imaginative and fluent in their thinking.

While many monolinguals are divergers, there is a tendency for bilinguals to be ahead of monolinguals on such tests of divergent thinking. There is a slight tendency for bilinguals to be more creative and divergent in their thinking, more fluent and flexible. Having two or more words for each object and idea may mean there is more **elasticity in thinking**. A child may have different associations for the word 'brick' in each language. Having two or more words for a concept may give the bilingual a wider range of meanings attached to that concept. For example, a Welsh/English bilingual has the word 'school' and its Welsh equivalent '*ysgol*'. '*Ysgol*' also means ladder. The idea of school is thus extended to an image of schooling being a ladder. There is a sequential climb through school learning with the aim of getting to the top rung.

There are other dimensions in thinking where approximately 'balanced' bilinguals may have temporary and occasionally permanent advantages over monolinguals: increased **sensitivity to communication**, a slightly speedier movement through the stages of **cognitive development**, and being less fixed on the sound of words and more centered on the meaning of words. For example, imagine young children are asked: what is more like the word 'cap', 'cat' or 'hat'? There is a tendency for bilinguals to center more on similarity of meaning (i.e. the word 'hat') than similarity of sound (i.e. the word 'cat'). Such ability to move away from the sound of words and to fix on the **meaning of words** tends to be a (temporary) advantage for bilinguals around the ages four to six. This advantage may mean an initial head start in learning to read and learning to think about language. More details about the advantages in thinking shared by bilinguals can be found in references given at the end of this book.

Only when a child's two languages are both definitely under-developed (this rarely occurs), are there possible cognitive or thinking disadvantages for the bilingual child. When a child is functioning in two languages well below age expectations, and in situations (e.g. the classroom) where more complex language forms are demanded, thinking disadvantages may be present. When one language is well developed and the other language is catching up, bilinguals and monolinguals may be no different in their cognitive development. Where a bilingual has two reasonably well developed languages, there can be some temporary and a few permanent thinking advantages for the bilingual. This is illustrated in the picture of the three floor house.

Up the sides of the house are placed two language ladders, indicating that a bilingual child will usually be moving upward and is not stationary on a floor. On the **bottom floor** of the house will be those whose current competence in both their languages is insufficiently developed, especially compared with their school age group. When there is a low level of competence in both languages, there may be detrimental cognitive effects. For example, a child who is unable to cope in the classroom in either language may suffer when processing instructional information.

At the **middle level**, the second floor of the house, will be those with age-appropriate competence in one of their languages but not in both. For example, children who can operate in the classroom in one of their languages but not in their second language may reside in this second level. At this level, partly bilingual children will be little different in thinking from monolingual children. They are unlikely to have any significant positive or negative cognitive differences compared with a monolingual.

At the top of the house, **the third floor**, reside children who approximate 'balanced' bilinguals. At this level, children will have

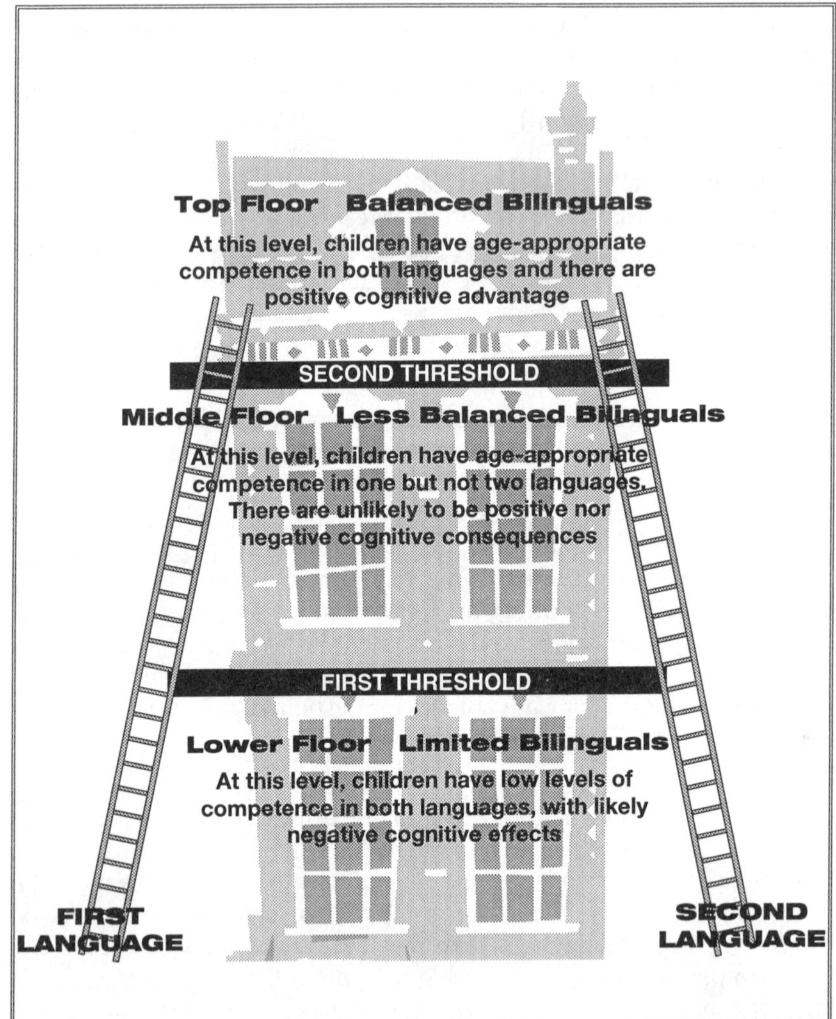

age-appropriate competence in two or more languages. For example, they can cope with curriculum material in either of their languages. It is at this level that the positive cognitive advantages of bilingualism may appear. When a child has age-appropriate ability in both their languages, they may have cognitive advantages over monolinguals.

Research tends to provide good news for the raising of children bilingually as far as thinking is concerned. There seem advantages for those where both languages are relatively well developed. This good news still needs to pervade the legacy of prejudice about the intelligence of bilingual children.

B9 I want my children to be successful. Should I concentrate on developing their first/majority language skills?

Parents usually want their children to be **successful**. Parents differ in the particular skills they expect their children to master. Some parents want their children to be musicians, entrepreneurs, athletes, airhosts/hostesses or fashion models. Other parents hope their children will become devoutly religious, scientifically expert or socially skilled. Many parents want their children to excel academically at school and show examination success. So the answer to the question partly depends in what way you want your child to be successful.

The positive answer is that bilingualism is favorably connected with many of these aims and goals. **Bilingualism** is **valuable** for musicians, entrepreneurs, sports people, airline personnel and many other areas of 'success'. In the twenty-first century, it is likely that employment will increasingly demand language skills. So in the long term, children raised bilingually may receive an extra boost to their employment prospects, economic success and chances of affluence.

For those parents who want their children to be **skilled interpersonally and socially**, bilinguals are often the ones that are sensitive and sympathetic in communication. Bilinguals can break down barriers and build bridges, and are often more open-minded about racial and ethnic group differences. Research shows that many bilinguals perform as well as monolinguals in the school situation — and sometimes better. This is considered and explained in Section E. Academic success is not usually impeded by a child being bilingual. On the contrary, it may lead to greater success.

However, there are many parents in minority language situations where **minority language bilingualism** connects with poverty, unemployment, deprivation, subordination and less political power. In the ghettos of inner cities, bilinguals are often the ones with less security, less status and less chances of success in life. Therefore, it is natural for minority language parents to focus on the importance of fluency in the majority language to increase the chances of success.

In such a minority language situation, there is little to gain by moving from bilingualism to majority language monolingualism. To deny one's heritage and to lose one's home language may create a loss of identity, even rootlessness (*anomie*), a lack of clear purpose and disruption in the family. It is possible to preserve the minority language and still to become fully fluent in the majority language. The idea of the balance, the majority language going down as the minority language rises, is incorrect. Rather, gaining **competence in the minority language** may allow the later development of the majority language to proceed with more ease.

Suddenly to submerge someone who can speak a minority language in the majority language may not only cause psychological dislocation, it also denies the language abilities the child already owns. Such language abilities **transfer** easily into the majority language. The majority language can be successfully learned alongside the minority language. Bilingualism is just as viable as monolingualism.

Supporters of bilingualism do not usually deny the importance, economically, politically and socially, of a high level of **competence in the majority language**. To compete for jobs, economic advance and political power, fluency in the majority language is often required and demanded. To deprive someone of majority language competence is to deprive them of chances of success in later life. However, ensuring a high degree of competence in the majority language need not be at the cost of minority language skills. Bilingualism is usually a case of addition and not subtraction; multiplication and not division.

B10 Should my child keep the two languages separate in different situations and with different people (e.g. visitors)?

One key idea in raising children bilingually is that of **language boundaries**. Experts on bilingualism place considerable stress on the importance of keeping the context of children's languages compartmentalized. For example, this will occur when one parent speaks one language and the other parent speaks a different language to the child. For this child, there is a clear division when listening to those two languages. Language separation makes it easy for children to recognize when they should speak which language to which parent.

A similar example with clear separation between two languages is dual language schools in the United States. In such schools, there is a set alternation of language. For example, on one day, curriculum content is taught through Spanish, the next day through English, rotating alternately to ensure both languages receive equal treatment in the curriculum. The central idea of alternate days with different languages is to maintain **clear**

language boundaries. Rather than have a Tower of Babel confusion and a jumble of language production, language compartmentalization aids bilingual development.

The value of **consistent language separation** becomes more obvious when we consider a lack of partition. Imagine a parent who speaks both French and English to their child (called Strategy 3 in the Introduction to this book). This parent changes languages inside a sentence and across sentences. One outcome may be that the child will emulate the parent, mixing the languages inside a sentence. Very early on in a child's bilingual development, this is natural and to be tolerated. The older the child grows, the more important separation becomes. If a parent jumbles two languages, the child may consider that there is one overall language system. Therefore, mixing languages may become normal and natural to that child. Parents of bilingual children usually want to avoid such mixing (unless switching languages is used for a particular effect).

Keeping languages separate with **clear demarcation and boundaries** between them is important. This advice will tend to make bilingual development more efficient, more socially acceptable and feed the child's language memory and language repertoire in a more appropriate way. How is such separation achievable? What **strategies** can be employed?

(1) There is the '**one language–one parent**' separation strategy. Each parent speaks a different language to the child who responds in that language.
(2) Inside the home, minority language parents often speak the **minority language only**, ensuring that everything they say is in that minority language. Outside the home, the child will experience the majority language.
(3) Another strategy is to speak the second language on certain days of the week — for example on weekends or **alternate** days. This has been achieved by bilingual families. The residual question is about its naturalness or artificiality.
(4) Language compartmentalization also naturally occurs when a different language from the home is used at school or in another **institution**. For example, when a child learns most or all of the curriculum in a different language, or uses Hebrew or Arabic in the synagogue or mosque, there is clear language demarcation. Other children go to Saturday schools and Sunday schools for language experience, giving clear allocation of times and places where different languages are spoken and acquired (although not necessarily making children bilingual due to the brevity of language experience).

Children also tend to create their own language boundaries, particularly when they are very young. Here are some examples: (1) in the one parent, one language situation, a child may get used to speaking one language to the father only. The expected language boundary is that all men speak that language. All women are expected to speak a different language. (2) A better example is when a child hears older people speaking one language (often a minority language) and young people speaking a different language (often a majority language). If the young child suddenly hears a person not fitting that stereotype, there may be a bemused or frightened reaction. (3) If children only hear one of their two languages inside the home, and then hear it when traveling abroad, a similar startled reaction may occur. Each example illustrates that children operate their own language boundaries. These perceptions develop, become more sophisticated and conscious. Part of bilingual development is accepting and manipulating these language boundaries.

Family life is not always sufficiently simple to make **language compartmentalization** easy, particularly if a balance between languages is attempted. In the 'one language–one parent' situation, there is the issue of which language parents speak to each other. Which language does a family speak when together (e.g. mealtimes)? Such a decision may tilt the balance towards one language rather than the other in the family. The guiding principle is for parents to try to achieve an **approximate balance** in the quality and quantity of the two languages as experienced by the child. This cannot be achieved mathematically, with equal percentages of time or stimulation. However, the balance needs careful thought and consideration. When brothers and sisters are part of the nuclear family, language interaction between siblings cannot be programmed so easily.

The approximate **balance** between languages needs discussion and decisions. The discussion of balance needs to include the dominance and status of the languages in the community, in school as well as in family life. For example, when one language is of lower prestige, that language may be given much more prominence in the home. Such prominence will attempt to counterbalance the dominance of the second language outside the home. A case in point is a father who speaks a majority language to the child, the mother speaking a minority language. The father needs to consider speaking the minority language in the home to raise its status in the eyes of the child.

Where both parents speak one language to their children, there are occasions when visitors, strangers, guests and friends who only speak a different language enter the home. The question for parents is **what language to speak to their children when visitors are present**. Do the parents stick to, for example, the minority language (which is customary), or do they switch to the majority language so as not to exclude the visitors? Alternatively, as some experts advise, do parents carry on as usual, not disrupt normal language patterns, but translate for guests?

If no change is made, visitors need an explanation of the 'language rules of the home' out of courtesy. So as to not exclude visitors, someone may interpret for the visitor when needed. If all members of the family temporarily switch to the visitor's language, it is possible to signal to the child that this is an occasion where social etiquette requires a switch in family language. Children are usually quick at catching on which language to speak to whom in which situation.

A mid-way solution is to switch to the visitors' language when talking to them directly. When the family are talking to each other, they use their normal language pattern.

There is no simple answer about what to do when normal language patterns are disrupted. Issues about language development become entwined with etiquette and manners, social engineering and personal relationships, tolerance and habit. Answers will naturally vary from culture to culture, subculture to subculture, family to family. However, some guidelines are possible. First, it is desirable for parents to **discuss** in prospect or retrospect the different situations that occur. It is advantageous to plan ahead the language that will be used with strangers and with each other. An understanding in the family will give language strength to that family and present a common and stable situation for the visitor. Yet, and in paradox to this, it is important to be natural and well mannered, making language life enjoyable and not a burden.

As will be explained in detail in a later section, it is part of a bilingual's natural and usual repertoire to switch languages purposefully. After an initial period (during which a child learns that there are two different languages and is reasonably aware of that duality), there are many occasions when bilinguals validly and valuably switch their languages in conversation: to emphasize ideas, convey important messages, relay jokes and conversations, even to exclude people from conversations. So **switching language** after the two languages are securely separated is a valuable part of a bilingual's language accomplishments that has function and purpose.

B11 Should my child use two languages with the same person?

In the early stages of bilingual development, it tends to be more helpful if the child consistently speaks **only one language with a particular**

person. For the young child, it is often confusing when anything different from 'one language per person' is apparent. Imagine the situation where a child speaks French to the father who answers in English. The child attempts a reply in English and then the father switches to French. The child may become insecure and muddled. The younger child requires some security and stability when speaking and listening. As discussed in the previous section, it is also valuable to set out clear language boundaries and language compartmentalization.

A typical situation is the child moving away from the language boundaries that have been established. For example, in the one parent–one language situation, the father may find the child starts to speak to him in the language hitherto reserved for the mother. To maintain the language boundaries, the parent can use polite and gracious 'reorienting' tactics such as:

'I'm sorry. What did you say?'
'What did you say you wanted?'
'Please say that in our language'.
'Tell me again, please'.
'I didn't quite understand. Can you repeat it in [French]'.

If such **tactics** are consistently applied, the child soon learns that language boundaries are fixed and enduring.

However, once the child has achieved reasonable language separation and does know the differences between the languages, it is not uncommon that older children will use both languages with the same person. In a one to one situation, the older child's use of languages with a particular person will usually be stable and relatively invariant. Once other people enter the conversation, the older child may **switch languages**. For example, if a mother and child naturally speak French to each other and the father enters the conversation, and if the father can only speak English, the child will naturally switch to English so that both father and mother are included in the conversation. Children are amazingly adroit at knowing when to switch languages. Partly for this reason, bilinguals seem to have some degree of social sensitivity that monolinguals do not have to have in a language situation.

Such language adjustment carries with it the danger of one language becoming stronger. If experience and stimulation of the other language diminishes, then that language may not develop as fully as the other language. Parents thus have to steer a **compromise** between (1) a 'free market language economy' where chance events partly dictate the flow of the two languages and, (2) a highly structured and rule-bound language strategy.

Early on in language development, it is important that some measure of language **stability** is present for the young child (e.g. one language is identified with each person). As the child grows older, it is part of a bilingual's social and language repertoire to be able to switch languages. This needs no encouragement; it is natural. The encouragement needed is early on, to move a child through that stage where the two languages increasingly develop and are perceived as two different systems.

B12 Will my child's attitudes affect the learning of a second language?

A parent can provide a stimulating language environment, but that is not enough. A parent can take a child on lots of trips, provide plentiful resources and materials in the home for language practice and variation. A parent can ensure that a child meets other speakers of a minority language. All this is valuable and will give the child a good chance of becoming bilingual. Yet, if children's **attitude, motivation and interest** in their languages are not inspired, the parent may find that hopes about bilingual development are not fulfilled.

Consider this question with an analogy. Some parents buy lots of books for their children. Such parents often believe that, by providing a vast library of books, their children will develop literacy. While creating the right physical reading environment is important, it is clearly not enough. Children need to be encouraged to read. Another cluster of parents tend to think of (and teach) reading as a skill. Religiously, every evening there is half an hour's practice for the child to learn to read. The parent picks out a book and patiently listens to the child reading, ensuring that the child's reading skills develop continuously. That is excellent, but not enough. Such parents may find that when such children are able to read by themselves, they are no longer interested in books. Reading has been taught as a skill and not as a pleasurable activity of value in itself.

Encouraging a positive attitude to reading, making books an enjoyable experience for children, and encouraging them when learning to read is important in the long-term development of reading habits. It is possible to have a home library and advanced reading skills, but never pick up a book. Yet, occasionally the child who has fewer books, less skill but loves reading may be the person that flourishes in literacy in the future.

The same idea holds with bilingual language development. Providing a stimulating and varied environment for vocabulary and linguistic structures to evolve, ensuring that a child's linguistic skills become well developed is important. It is not enough. Without being patronizing and without growth of arrogance in the child, it is also important for the child to have a **positive self-concept about their two languages**. Parents are only one source of language encouragement for the child. For example, the perceived status of a minority language in society will affect the child's language self-concept. To a rebellious teenager, parental approval can have the opposite effect to that intended. Before and during these pivotal teenage years, parents can engineer an appropriate language environment for the child. Examples of parental language engineering include: wisely choosing secondary schooling, taking children to enjoyable events where the minority language is used and inviting friends who speak the minority language to the house.

The **language self-esteem** of children can be raised by admiring and not just observing their skills in two languages. The occasional gentle word of praise, the smile, the 'pat on the back' for their bilingualism will encourage a favorable attitude towards two languages. This is nowhere more important than with minority languages. When in adolescence and adult life there may be pressures to drop the minority language, establishing and maintaining a positive motivation towards the minority language is important. A parent needs to convey regularly their delight in their child's bilingualism with warmth and sincerity. A positive attitude to bilingualism is a long-term preserver of bilingualism in a child.

B13 Is it sensible to raise my child in three languages?

In different parts of the world, there are children who learn two or more local languages and learn a national language as well. For example, in parts of India, Africa and Asia, there are children who become trilingual and multilingual. In some parts of the globe, **trilingualism** is a fairly usual and natural occurrence. Such trilingualism tends to be at the oral rather than the literary level. In Western society, trilingualism is less common, but certainly present (e.g. in Scandinavia).

There is little research on trilingualism and multilingualism in the family to provide clear advice. However, in Canada there has been research on children becoming trilingual in English, French and Hebrew (and in English, French and an indigenous North American Indian language). In mainland Europe, there are many children who become fluent in three languages (e.g. Swedish, Finnish, English; German, French, English). The **Scandinavians** seem particularly experienced and successful in producing trilingual children. Many Scandinavian children learn two languages in school (e.g. English, German) as well as being fluent in their home language. Language learning has relatively high status in Scandinavian countries. In parts of Africa, Asia and India, trilingualism is also relatively frequent and accepted. Trilingualism is possible and valuable.

One documented route to trilingualism is **parents** speaking two different languages to their children at home. The children then take their **education** through a third language. The majority language of the community will influence the relative strength of the three languages. The relative proficiency of the three languages will change over time. Stable trilingualism seems less likely than stable bilingualism. Establishing trilingualism early on is slightly easier than successfully maintaining trilingualism over the teenage years. A school that is positive towards multilingualism and multiculturalism is needed to ensure children's attitude to their language agility is favorable.

At the bottom of this section, specific references are given to those who want to follow up case studies of raising trilingual children. One case study (Charlotte Hoffmann) concerns Spanish (acquired mostly from the father and *au-pairs*), German (acquired mostly from the mother and visits), and English (acquired mostly among peers and in school). The one parent, one language 'rule' was followed. English came to be dominant as school experience and peer relationships developed. Equal facility in all three languages is much less likely than less competence in one or two of the languages (e.g. in grammar, width of vocabulary).

One proviso about trilingualism is that at least one language needs developing fully. It is important in a child's cognitive development that at least one language develops at age-appropriate levels. For example, the child will need sufficient language competence to operate in the increasingly abstract nature of the school curriculum. The danger (that parents of trilingual children do usually avoid) is a low level of development in all three languages. This would impede the child's cognitive development. This need not happen in a trilingual family, but it does require extra **vigilance**, extra commitment and thoughtfulness within the family.

References for further reading

Christine Helot, 'Bringing up Children in English, French and Irish: Two Case Studies'. In *Language, Culture and Curriculum*, Vol. 1, No. 3, pp. 281–287 (1988).

Charlotte Hoffmann, 'Language Acquisition in Two Trilingual Children'. In *Journal of Multilingual and Multicultural Development*, Vol. 6, No. 6, pp. 479–495 (1985)

B14 Do girls and boys differ in their progress towards bilingualism and biliteracy?

The first thing to note is that children differ widely in their rate of progress in acquiring two languages. Girls differ widely amongst themselves, as do boys. Such **differences** may be related to personality, the quality and quantity of language interaction with parents and other people, contexts, environments and the atmosphere in which language flourishes, and the pressures on, and motivations of the child. However, as a broad generalization with many exceptions, girls tend to show slightly faster bilingual development than boys. This may be partly due to parent expectations which differ for girls and boys. For example, many parents expect girls to become fluent readers earlier than boys. The gender difference may be due to the type of language interaction that occurs between parents and girls and boys, gender stereotypes, and the expectations and behaviors of teachers.

Gender differences in becoming bilingual need not exist. They are likely to result from **environmental** rather than genetic influences. Environmental effects can be changed. For example, there is research that shows that when teachers expect girls to read at an earlier age than boys, that situation occurs. When teachers expect there to be no difference between girls and boys in the rate of learning to read, then that also tends to occur. So gender differences in language development may reflect cultural expectations, different behaviors towards girls and boys, and nothing that is unalterable or worrying.

There is no reason to believe that girls are better equipped to become bilinguals than boys. There is no reason why girls should be treated differently from boys (or vice versa) with regard to the childhood development of bilingualism. The attitudes of the two genders to minority languages, particularly in the **teenage** years, may become a problem. In Wales, for example, there is evidence to show that boys tend to develop less favorable attitudes to the minority language compared with girls. Girls tend to retain their bilingualism and boys veer slightly more to English monolingualism in the teens and twenties. This partly reflects what behavior gives status and peer approval, as well as mass media influences, and continuing parental and 'heritage culture' influence. There are many exceptions to this gender pattern. Also, trends in the teenage years are not permanent.

B15 Are first-borns different to later-borns in developing bilingualism?

There is plentiful research from the 1950s onwards to show that the pattern of relationships between brothers and sisters has an **under-estimated effect** on child development. Only borns, first borns, later borns tend to show slightly different personality and motivation characteristics, different levels of achievement in school and in later life. How siblings affect the language environment of the home, particularly in bilingual families, is almost unexplored research territory. One area of research that is likely to develop in the next two decades is how brothers and sisters affect the language environment in a bilingual family.

When the second-born arrives, the language pattern of the household tends to be relatively well established. Who speaks what language to whom on which occasions is fairly well established by the arrival of the second-born and the third-born child. With the birth of the second-born, decisions about **language interaction** in the home have already been **established**. The language the first-born child speaks to each parent will have been standardized, with the likelihood that later-born children will follow a similar pattern.

What is new is the language interaction between older and younger siblings. If the mother is the full time carer, her language may be replicated in the interaction between siblings (particularly when the children are young, and if she speaks a majority language). For example, if the mother speaks Spanish to her children, the children may speak Spanish to each other. What is novel is that the language balance may change within the home when new borns arrive. The **balance** of languages heard and spoken may be different for the younger than the older child. The younger child may learn much language through listening and talking to older-born children. The older child provides a **language model** for younger siblings. Thus, younger siblings are sometimes slightly slower in their bilingual language development partly because they are excluded from the more advanced language interaction between mother and older siblings, and partly through copying older siblings. Older siblings also tend to answer for their younger brothers and sisters!

What tends to be an advantage for later borns is that **parents** have accumulated valuable **experience** in the language life of the home. Parents have acquired craft and competence in raising bilingual children. The anxiety that accompanies the development of the first-born is less. Discussion and decisions about bilingualism in the family have taken place. Decisions will have already been made about which languages to use in which circumstances with which people. Alternatively, there is a latently agreed and accepted **pattern of language interaction** within the family (and with 'outsiders') already established by the arrival of second-born and later-borns. The second- and third-borns fit into a well established language routine. Thus, there will sometimes be less nervousness and anxiety about the bilingual development of later-born children.

There is every reason why later-borns can become bilingual within the family. Nevertheless, in reality, **later-borns** often show **different language histories** over time compared with first-borns. As family circumstances change, as patterns of friendship vary, geographical and social and vocational mobility occur, so may the varying opportunities for bilingual development. For example, first-borns will bring their friends home. In a language minority home, the welcomed friends may be majority language speakers. The language of play will switch to the majority language. The later-born may thus experience relatively more exposure to the majority language.

Another example is when parents emigrate early in the life of the second-born. The language of the host country may come to play a more dominant place in the life of the later-born than the first-born. In this case, first-borns may become more active bilinguals and later borns more passive bilinguals. However, the reverse can also occur. Published case histories of bilingual families rarely show parallel bilingual development in first-borns and later-borns. Language variety is found within bilingual families and not just in the wider world.

B16 Does switching between languages have any value or purpose?

Appropriate language switching has some powerful and positive advantages. When both or all participants in a conversation understand both languages, mixing has a purpose. It's almost as if a third language is introduced. The table below provides some examples of the major uses of switching between languages. To make a point, stress an argument, report something somebody else said more authentically, highlight warmth of friendship, and sometimes exclude people from a private conversation, code switching isn't interference between languages. It is a third subtle language that bilinguals use to good effect.

(1) Code switches may be used to **emphasize** a particular point in a conversation. If one word needs to be stressed or is central in a sentence, then a switch may be made.

(2) If a people do not know a word or a phrase in a language, they may **substitute** a word in another language.
(3) Code switching may be used to **express more adequately** an idea. In discussing computers, mathematics or science, children may switch from their home language to the language used in school to increase expression and enhance understanding.
(4) Code switching may be used to **repeat** a phrase or a command. For example, a mother may repeat a demand (e.g. go to bed. *Dos i'r gwely*) to accent and underline a demand. Repetition may also be used to clarify a point. Some teachers in classrooms explain a concept in one language, and then will explain it again in another language believing that repetition adds reinforcement of understanding.
(5) Code switching may be used to communicate **friendship**. For example, moving from the common majority language to the home language or minority language both listener and speaker understand well, may communicate friendship, common identity. Similarly people may deliberately use code switching to indicate their need to be accepted by a peer group. Someone with a rudimentary knowledge of a language may inject words of that new language into sentences to indicate a need to identify and affiliate. The use of the listener's stronger language in part of the conversation may indicate deference, wanting to belong or be accepted.
(6) In **relating a conversation** held previously, the person may report the conversation in the language or languages used. For example, two people may be speaking Spanish together. When one reports a conversation with an English monolingual, that conversation is reported authentically — in English as it occurred.
(7) Code switching is sometimes used as a way of **interjecting** into a conversation. A person attempting to break into a conversation politely may use a different language to that occurring. Alternatively, interrupting a conversation may be signaled by changing language. The message to the speakers from the listener is that 'I would like to become involved in this conversation'.
(8) Code switching may be used to **ease tension and inject humor** into a conversation. If in a committee, discussions are becoming tense, the use of a second language may signal a change in the tune being played. Just as in an orchestra, different instruments may be brought in during a piece to signal a change of mood and pace, so a switch in language may indicate a need to change mood within the conversation.
(9) Code switching often relates to **social distance**. For example, when two people meet, they may use the common majority language (e.g.

Swahili or English in Kenya). As the conversation unravels, roles, status and tribal identity are revealed, a change to a regional language may indicate that boundaries are being broken down, there is less social distance, with expressions of solidarity and growing rapport indicated by the switch.

(10) Code switching can also be used for more Machiavellian purposes. It can be used to **exclude** people from a conversation. For example when traveling on the Metro (subway, underground), two people having been speaking English, may switch to their minority language to talk about private matters, or other people on the Metro, thus excluding others from the conversation. One example of this occurred in a London theater. A very tall and wide professor was sitting in a London theater. Behind him were two ladies who had been talking English. Before the curtain rose, they switched to Welsh and protested to each other that their view was blocked by this large male. The amused professor said nothing. At the end of the play he simply turned round to the two ladies and, in their minority language, expressed his hope that they had enjoyed the play.

(11) Code switching may be used to indicate a **change of attitude** during the conversation. For example greetings may be expressed in the home, minority language. But when one person asks to borrow money or asks a favor of the other, the moneylender may change to the majority language. To indicate a change of relationship and a change of attitude, code switching occurs. Greetings in the native language; business in the majority language. At the end of the business conversation, farewells may revert to the native language. A change in relationship, on a temporary basis, is indicated by code switching.

In one research in a minority language hospital, nurses were found to switch from the minority language to English to repeat a request or give directions. Nurses perceived the language of authority as English, and code switched for that purpose. Familiarity, projected status and the ethos of the context as well as the perceived linguistic skills of the listeners affect the nature and process of code switching. This suggests that code switching is not just linguistic; it indicates important social and power relationships.

B17 When will my bilingual child be able to interpret and translate from one language to another?

Children around the age of three and four begin to be able (if their two languages are both relatively well developed) to **translate** simple words and sentences from one language to another. Children sometimes do this automatically, much to the amusement, enjoyment and delight of their parents. For example, if one parent is unable to speak a language, the child may quickly advise the parent what has been said in another language. Situations include the doctor's surgery, with sales representatives on the doorstep, at parents' meetings in school, with electricity, gas and water officials, and in shops.

There is a very **positive side** to children translating and interpreting. It gives children a position of privilege and power. In conveying a message from one person to another, children can add their own slant, take part in a decision, gain praise from a parent, give status and self-esteem, be of increased value to the family, even work a message to their own advantage! Children may become close to their parents when they have a 'translator' value. There is reciprocal dependency. The act of being an interpreter is an act of empathy, an act of bridge building. Such an act may lead to increased maturity, sensitivity, shrewdness and self-reliance.

However, translation can become a **burden** for children. Being the middle person between one adult and another often means translating language that is at a higher level than is customary. For example, if the bilingual child or teenager accompanies the mother to a doctor and the mother cannot understand the language of the doctor, translating the medical language may place a strain on the child. The information from the doctor may also disturb the child. A child may be placed under emotional stress by being party to private information. If there is constant pressure to translate when parents do not understand the majority language of the area, the pleasure and fun of childhood may be lost in providing a language bridge between parents and outside society.

There is a second occasion when a child is placed under **pressure** in translating. When parents expect children to perform on the spot, showing off their ease of movement from one language to another, the child is in danger of acting as a performing monkey in a circus. Children sometimes resist attempts to make them perform bilingually. For them, language is something that is natural, ordinary and subconscious. Performing language tricks in two languages seems strange to many children. Translating as a game is artificial, patronizing and embarrassing.

There is thus a thin line between encouraging a child's bilingualism, celebrating their ability in two languages and their performing language tricks to a captive audience. The **child's self-esteem** and attitude to their languages is all important in such a situation. Ensuring a favorability of attitude and a delight in their bilingualism is the guiding principle.

B18 How much will experience of majority language mass media affect the development of bilingualism in my child?

One key question often raised by minority language parents is about the effect of the mass media on their children. Parents who wish to maintain the minority language of their children often worry when their children watch endless cartoons in the majority language. The **concerns** are twofold. First, such parents are concerned about the language diet that television, video tapes, radios, cassettes and compact disks provide. Since many children consume large amounts of television, the passive reception of the majority language may affect both skills in the minority language and productive use (speaking and writing) in both the minority and majority language.

Some **minority languages** (and most languages other than English) have tended to respond to a diet of Anglo-American children's television by producing television programs in the minority language or dubbing cartoons and children's films. This is much to be applauded. Also, it is important that the minority language **culture** is spread through the mass media. The danger is that dubbed films and minority language cartoons still contain majority language or particularly Anglo-American culture. The cultural elements in television broadcasts and videos are as important as the language content in conveying the status of a language community to the child.

It is usually important for parents raising bilingual children to try to obtain videos and audio cassettes in the child's minority or weaker language. Parents who want their children to acquire a non-local language will need to obtain as much variety of mass media material as possible for their children. A diet of minority or 'foreign' language mass media input is important, not only to enhance language competence, but also in the implied **prestige** value of the language.

At the same time, parents need to be wary of too much language input by mass media. The mass media provide **receptive language** only. Rarely does the child speak a language when watching television or listening to a record. Records, cassettes and compact disks that invite children to join in are more valuable in providing language practice. Language participation is of paramount importance.

As children move through middle childhood, and particularly when they enter their teenage years, there is often a pressure towards mass media in the dominant, majority language. The peer group listens to high-status Anglo-American pop music, films and television programs.

The **influential images** in the pre-teenage and teenage years are too rarely from the minority language and too often via the English language. During these years, children's bilingualism may be at risk due to their conformity to peer group norms which stress majority culture.

The **prestige of a language**, or its negative image, is quickly picked up outside the home. When children join street groups, clubs and teams, at a tender age (e.g. seven years onwards) they perceive the pecking order of languages. This is reinforced and extended by the media. Parents thus need to monitor and sometimes be creative in language arrangements to ensure the language diet is not becoming stale in one language and a feast in the other.

Research shows that children who **maintain their minority language** are the ones who, in their teenage years in particular, participate in out-of-school events in their minority language. (A discussion of the teenage years follows later in this section.) Research from Wales suggests that it is not majority language mass media in and by itself that is a threat to the minority language in teenage children. Rather it is movement away from the minority language, to less participation in out-of-school events in the minority language, that causes language decline in teenagers. The culture of the teenager becomes a most important element in the language life of that teenager.

B19 Can music and drama help my child's bilingual development?

For a language to live within the child, there needs to be **active participation** in that language. That language needs to be valuable and useful to that child, enjoyable and pleasurable in a variety of events. Music and drama are just two of a whole variety of activities through which children can enjoy using their language. In such events, language is a means and not only an end in itself. In music and drama, language growth occurs almost unnoticed by the child in an enjoyable way.

For example, imagine young children in a nursery school **dancing** vigorously in an action song, shouting the words while moving enthusiastically around the floor. The child is subconsciously learning the language, connecting words with actions, being exhilarated and educated — all at the same time. Children **singing** nursery rhymes or acting out a folk tale are not only learning language, enjoying the drama and having fun. They are also picking up part of the culture allied to that language. The language is becoming anchored.

Contrast this with children being taught grammar and given spelling tests and drills in language. Imagine children at desks going through a dull, repetitive exercise or **learning by rote** some rules of language structure. In the drama and music situation, language has bounce and beauty. Learning language by rote is often boring and banal. When language is learned through activities that are intrinsically motivating to the child (e.g. shopping, cooking, singing, acting, as well as authentic and lively desk work), then languages inside a child may live. When language is turned into a war with many battles, bilingualism may be a burden.

In the **teenage** years, it is important, wherever possible, that children have stimulating activities — activities that are intrinsically motivating for teenagers — to maintain their languages. This is particularly so in the 'weaker' or minority language. If rock music and reggae, pop music and parties, laughing and loving is in the minority language, bilingualism may advance in these difficult years.

In Wales, youth Eisteddfodau provide the means whereby Welsh-speaking children, teenagers and young adults congregate together at local, county and national level. Not only do they sing and dance, but also listen to Welsh pop music, and drink beer through the Welsh language! Such provision in the teenage years for language life has to be **engineered by the community**, through language activist parents, through effort and enthusiasm. Unless teenagers are given the opportunity to participate in their minority language, all the good work achieved in the home in producing early bilingualism may wither and fade.

B20 Will computers and Information Technology affect my child's bilingualism?

Our present age is sometimes called the Information Society. With the growth of computers and microcomputers, electronic mail and library databases, computers in schools and Information Technology, the majority language (particularly English) has been promoted at **the expense of minority languages**. When children use their Amiga, Super Nintendo, IBM-compatible microcomputer or their Apple Macintosh in school or at home, the language is so often in English. Vast amounts of software are only available in the English language. When children access a computer, they are likely to work through the medium of English. It also means that this high status electronic equipment is aligned with the high status

English language. The prestige of English tends to be exalted at the expense of the minority language that seems more old fashioned, more traditional and more historical.

For the eager parent, there is computer software in other majority and minority languages. In Wales, there has been an active movement for over a decade to translate English language software so that children experience it through the Welsh language. There has also been the occasional production of Welsh language software.

We cannot run away, bury our heads in the sand and imagine that computers are not going to be an important part of future existence. The Information Society is going to demand that almost all children gain some knowledge of the value and use of computers in the home, in school, in business and in society. The English language dominance of computers means that parents have to take this into account in working out the **language equation of their family**. It may become even more imperative that certain activities take place in a language other than English (e.g. going to church, clubs and societies, living in particular neighborhoods so that the child can regularly practice their weaker language). The bilingual language software that runs a child's thinking system needs a multimedia experience that extends beyond captivating computers.

B21 How important are employment prospects to preserve my child's languages into adulthood?

In the life of a language, there are **two** very **important factors**. (1) A language needs to be **reproduced within the family**. Bilingualism exists because of its place in the life of the mother and father, in the community, and the relationship of language with culture and heritage. (2) A language also must have **utility** for its owner. Language life within the individual and within society is considerably strengthened when that language has economic value. Take the case of a child who speaks a minority language and is taught through that language in school. If there are no jobs in that language, the value of that language will be considerably reduced, even undermined. When languages have **utilitarian value** in the employment and promotion market, then language learning and bilingualism will have extra drive and vigor.

In the literature on bilingualism during this century, the importance of the **economy** in the language life of a person (and the future of a language in society) has been understated. Like everyone else, bilinguals need access to the employment market and to affluence. Bilinguals will first and foremost wish to avoid poverty, deprivation and disadvantage. The quality of home, community and cultural language life is partly based on finance. Language and the family economy are not separate.

In present and future employment markets, some bilinguals will have an **advantage** as they can move between markets among different language groups. Bilinguals can act as bridges and brokers, sales staff and shop sellers with more flexibility and mobility. Those who can speak French and English, German and English, German and French, Japanese and French, and lots of other combinations may be well placed in future international jobs markets. The European Union is attempting to give status to the different languages of Europe. This includes full recognition of major international languages such as German, French, Italian, Spanish and English, of indigenous 'first' languages such as Irish, and through the European Bureau of Lesser Used Languages, to the 'lesser used languages' of Europe such as Luxembourgish, Occitan and Frisian.

What of the plight of those whose one language is a **minority language**? It is certainly important for those to be fluent in a majority language. As Spanish-speaking Americans will testify, access to power and employment usually demands full English fluency. Minority language speakers need to be bilingual to maximize their chances of economic success.

Wherever possible, **employment** in and through the minority language needs to be encouraged for that minority language to survive. For a minority language to be seen to have utility and value in society, there needs to be employment prospects which demand and value the minority language. For example, in the county of Gwynedd in North Wales, becoming a teacher, civil servant, or local business person, demands fluency in both Welsh and English. In Catalonia, fluency in Spanish and Catalan is often demanded for economic advancement. In the Basque Country, having both Basque and Spanish is helpful in security and status of employment. Helmut Schmidt, Former Chancellor of the old Federal Republic of Germany once said: 'If you wish to buy from us, you can talk any language you like, for we shall try to understand you. If you want to sell to us, then you must speak our language'.

Where employment prospects demand or prefer bilinguals, there is a much greater incentive for bilinguals to retain their two languages well into adulthood. For a language to have no economic value, there may be less **incentive** to retain that language during adulthood. Language preservation then depends on social and cultural life.

B22 I need to change the language(s) I've used with my children. How will it affect them?

This question is typically asked when parents, through choice or necessity, **move from one country to another**. Parents will often contemplate using the language of that region inside the home so that the child quickly achieves plenty of experience and practice in that new language. This is particularly likely if parents intend to stay in that new country for a long period.

This kind of question also occurs when a **family lifestyle changes**. For example, when there is divorce, one parent dies, one or more grandparents join the nuclear family relatively permanently, or other relations join to create an extended family. Established language patterns may need to change.

The first debate needs to be about whether it is vital to change languages or not. Is there sufficient reason to sacrifice the mother tongue or the language of the home? Will the child's **emotional and personality development** be affected by a sudden change in language? Will a child in a new country who already feels dislocated and initially isolated feel further upset by a change in the language of the home? Isn't language stability in the home an important rock on which the child can build new relationships and a new pattern of life?

Sometimes the circumstances are not so constrained. The mother for example, may want to switch to the language of the husband, providing a monolingual environment in the home rather than a bilingual environment. This is likely to be less traumatic for the child. Nevertheless, the change is likely to provide (at least initially) some complications. If a decision has been made, it is important to **discuss the matter with the child** at a level the child can understand. A child deserves and needs an explanation. Wherever possible, the child should become part of the decision making process.

Children are often able to express in their own way their worries and concerns, their preferences and priorities. **Sensitivity to the child's needs** is highly important in this 'change' situation. If the child is vehemently against change, it is probably wise to put off any change or introduce it very slowly. Sometimes, a slow transition may be preferable to a sudden abrupt change. If the child is willing for change to occur, it is still vitally necessary to **monitor** that change, to discuss it with the child, to be extra supportive of the child and provide extra love and care.

Children tend to manage language change faster than adults. Children often have the ability to make new relationships, make smoother transitions and adjust quickly to new circumstances in a way that inflexible adults find difficult. Given support and care, children are amazingly resilient. However, it is important at the outset of this transition to discuss the needs and problems of the child with his or her carers, teachers and any others who support that child during the day. While total protection is impossible, a **supportive environment** is possible so that temporary psychological problems disappear. Protection and support can gradually be reduced as the child adapts and adjusts.

A slightly different case occurs with younger children. When children aged two, three and four are involved in this change situation, explanations and adult problems and needs may be more difficult to translate into child language and understanding. Certainly with very young children, a **transition period** will be important. Very young children may not notice this transition where one language is slowly decreased in usage and another language is increased. With loving support, care and sensitivity, such transition may be relatively smooth. A sudden overnight switch may not be understood by the young child and may lead to a sense of rejection, distrust and nervousness.

Questions about Problems

Section C

C1 What are the disadvantages of my child becoming bilingual?

Some parents who raise their children bilingually seem to search for language problems in their children. Some parents fear there will be negative consequences of bilingualism. Too few families hunt for the advantages and celebrate the many positive consequences of their child's bilingualism. In this section, the major worries that bilingual parents tend to experience are considered.

There are always trials and tribulations, incidents and problems, worries and anxieties in a child's physical, social, personality and health development. There is no such a thing as a trouble-free child. Therefore, raising children to speak two languages is not going to be trouble free. There are going to be times when parents will worry about the language development of their children. For example, parents may worry about one language being weaker or a negative attitude developing to one language.

Whenever there is a language, educational or social problem (e.g. low self-esteem, concerns about self-identity, bullying), many parents of bilingual children tend to think of bilingualism as a possible cause of the problem. If a child lacks success at school, the parent of the monolingual child may lay the blame with the child's motivation, intelligence, personality, the standard of teaching, or the school itself. The parent of the bilingual child may think of all these causes, but add on the child's bilingualism as another major potential cause.

If a child does have social, motivational, educational or personal problems, don't immediately focus on bilingualism or biculturalism as the first cause. Rarely will this be so. When the child has problems, try to **hunt** down a variety of possible causes and not just highlight language. Discuss the problems with friends, the child's teacher, the child itself, and all too often, bilingualism will be wrongly blamed for whatever problem occurs.

It would be false and misleading to suggest that there are never any disadvantages to bilingualism. In the real world, ownership of two languages is not trouble free. First, there will be a disadvantage if a child's two languages are both **underdeveloped**. The most crucial definition of underdevelopment is that a child is unable to cope in the curriculum in the school in either language. This rarely occurs, but it is important to avoid. Details about such avoidance are given in the next two sections. The more usual situation is that bilingualism gives the child marginal advantages over the monolingual child in the curriculum.

A second potential problem parents experience is the **amount of effort** often required to raise bilingual children. Parents need to engineer thoughtfully and creatively their child's bilingual development. It is not like scattering a few seeds on the ground and expecting swift, strong and simple growth. The tender language shoots need to be nourished, the garden well fertilized in order for later blossoming and color to occur. As the seasons of language development change, the parent has constantly to tend the language garden.

For some parents, the route children take to full bilingualism is relatively straightforward and uncomplicated. For others, there are moments of concern, where challenges seem more like problems. Just as the hard work of digging, manuring and weeding in the garden eventually produce beautiful blooms, so with the language garden. There is an ultimate goal, of the blossoming of the child into full bilingualism. The individual, cognitive, social, cultural, intellectual and economic advantages given to the child via bilingualism make the spade work and effort spent in sowing and cultivating all worthwhile.

A third problem area tends to be with the **identity** of the child. If the child speaks English and French fluently, are they French, English or Anglo-French? If a child speaks English and a minority language such as Welsh, are they Welsh, English, British, European, Anglo-Welsh or what?

For many parents and children, identity is not a problem. While speaking two languages, they are resolutely identified with one ethnic or cultural group. For example, many bilinguals in Wales see themselves as Welsh first, possibly British next but not English. Being able to speak the English language is important. However, it is anathema to be considered 'English'.

At the other end of the spectrum is the **in-migrant**. Sometimes, the first or second generation in-migrant desperately wants to identify with majority language people and culture. They may actively want to lose the identity of their home or heritage language. For example, in the United States, Spanish speakers from Mexico or Cuba or Puerto Rico, sometimes want to assimilate and become monolingual English-speaking Americans. They want to lose the identity of their native country, and be as American as any monolingual, monocultural American.

Between the two opposites presented above, there are potential cases of identity crisis and conflict. There are some bilinguals who feel both English and French, Spanish and Catalan, Mexican and American. There are some people who feel quite happy being culturally hyphenated (e.g. Swedish-Finns, Anglo-French, Chinese-Malaysians, Italian-Americans). There will be others who feel uncomfortable moving between two identities. Bilinguals may ask: Am I Asian or am I British or am I Asian-British? Am I Swedish, am I Finnish or am I Swedish-Finnish? Am I Chinese from China, like the Chinese scattered throughout the world, or a Malaysian? Am I Italian, American or some integrated or uneasy **combination** of these?

Such identity conflicts are not inevitably the result of language. It is possible to own two languages and not have such identity conflicts. However, languages are clearly a contributor. Languages provide the potentiality of mingling in two or more cultures, of thinking and acting in two different ethnic groups, of identifying with each group or neither group. Language is a vehicle through which an **identity conflict** may arise. Such identity problems will be further discussed later under different questions in this section. For the moment, it is important to be honest and not to suggest that everything in the garden is perfect. Self-identity, cultural identity and ethnic identity can be a problem for some bilinguals.

C2 My child mixes the two languages. What should I do?

Consider yourself a **very typical** family. There is probably no bilingual family where the child does not mix the two languages, at the very least in the early stages. Language mixing is given other labels:

transference (i.e. transfer between two languages);
code switching (a term regularly used by researchers); and
a related term, **interference** between languages.

There are many people who are concerned about the purity of a language — language standardization. Listening to a person mixing two languages is anathema to the purist. While the purity of a language is an important issue, from the child's point of view (and not from a 'standard language' point of view), the language mixing results in the message being communicated and usually understood. From the perspective of the child, mixing is usually suitable and workable. The listener accepts the style of expression; the meaning is understood. While hybrid languages (e.g. mixing Spanish and English) may be temporary (e.g. in early childhood), they can also be relatively stable and shared by a large group (e.g. the mixing of Spanish and English in certain parts of New York).

Mixing is very **typical** and to be expected in the **early stages** of bilingual development. However, many parents see mixing languages as a problem. Except in a few language communities (such as the Puerto Ricans in New York), parents do not like to hear children mixing two languages. Parents expect the two languages to become separate.

In the very early **stages** of learning two languages simultaneously, as the table below reveals, children seem to employ their two languages as just one language system. In the very early stages, children do not seem able, nor need to distinguish between the two languages. Both languages appear stored together. After this, children learn to separate their two languages. This does not occur miraculously, overnight or suddenly. There is a gradual process of compartmentalization and separation of the two languages.

Some authors have described this process as moving through **three stages**. While bilingual development in the early years is gradual and not like three steps, these stages help to understand such changes. The three stages are given in the table below. They refer mostly to the one parent, one language situation.

When do these stages occur? The age and speed through the stages varies greatly from child to child. The age of moving from one stage to another differs due to: amount of separation a child experiences in listening to the two languages (by people and context); the balance of the two languages in the child's life; the quantity of language experience in both languages; the quality of language experience; parents acceptance (or not) of mixing the two languages; and the experience of mixing in the community. As a very approximate guide, Stage 1 (Amalgamation) occurs

Stages of Early Bilingual Development

Stage 1: Amalgamation

There is no separation between the two languages. The two languages are mixed when talking. Only one word seems to be known for each object or action. Some words and phrases are a mixture from two languages. Many parents of bilingual children worry during this stage about mixing languages. However, such mixing is only temporary. Children speak their mixed language to different people. The two languages appear to be stored as a single system in the thinking quarters.

Stage 2: Differentiation

There is a growing separation of languages. Children will increasingly use a different language to each parent. Equivalent words in the two languages are known. However, phrases and sentences may reflect just one grammar system (e.g. saying 'This is brush Mummy' rather than 'This is Mummy's brush'). Also, there will be some mixing of languages as the child will not have equivalents for all words.

Stage 3: Separation

While there is still a little mixing of the two languages, separation has mostly been achieved. The child is aware of which language to speak to which person. Awareness of having two languages begins. The child increasingly observes the different grammar of the two languages. Such differentiation is gradual.

between 0 and three years; Stage 2 (Differentiation) after two years of age; and Stage 3 (Separation) often after three years (but it can occur earlier), and throughout life!

Parents can help in this process of language separation by various do's and don'ts. The most important 'don't' is to avoid criticizing, or constantly pointing out mistakes, revealing anxiety and concern. This is unlikely to have a positive effect on a child's language development. On the contrary, it is more likely to make the child inhibited in language, anxious about their bilingualism and may slow down language development. Don't constantly correct the child, showing the child what to say and how to say it. A constant focus on language correctness and form is unnatural for the child, who is more interested in facts and ideas, stories and activities. For the child, **language is a means to an end**, not an end in itself. Language is a vehicle to help move along the road of information exchange and social communication.

To help language switching, parents can ensure that **language boundaries** are kept. Languages spoken by a parent need to be separate wherever possible. A parent who speaks one sentence in French to a child, the next sentence in English, is latently teaching the child that languages can be mixed. Parents who put German words in French sentences, for example, are teaching their child that language mixing is allowable.

One form of language separation is the **one parent...one language strategy**. Each parent speaks a different language to the child. An alternative is if both parents only use one particular language, with the other language used in different contexts (e.g. in the school, for religion, in the mass media, in the community). When language is separated along divisions of different people, different contexts, even different times of the week or day, a child is learning that language compartmentalization exists. Mixing will still occur early on. Rather boundaries enable a smooth transition to a stage where children keep their languages relatively separate.

C3 My child refuses to use one of his/her languages. What should I do?

Within all bilinguals, there is language shift and movement. Languages do not stay static and equal. In the teenage years, particularly among minority languages, there is often movement towards the majority language. This is a typical source of concern, even desperation for some parents. Having worked so long and so hard to produce bilingual children and gained a measure of success, parents find their teenage children are turning towards one language rather than another. Children in their teenage years sometimes **reject** using one language. A child may refuse to speak one language in the home, prefering to operate in the higher status language used in the peer group. This is quite customary among language minorities.

The locally felt status and prestige of a language plays a major part in acceptance or rejection of a language. Irrespective of one of the child's languages being a 'non-native' majority language or a minority language ('native' or 'non-native'), and irrespective of the international status of a language (not understood by many children), even young children feel 'vibes' about their two languages. Before the teenage years, children pick up the pecking order of languages in the family and the community.

There can also be **rejection of the majority language** by language minority activists. This occurs to a small extent in Wales among older teenagers and young adults. Such activists see bilingualism as a half-way house to majority language supremacy. Bilingualism is seen as a mid-point location on a map, somewhere in between minority language vitality and majority language dominance. This creates a movement towards minority language monolingualism. Where the language minority is strong, economically and culturally, this separatism becomes possible. Whether the move to monolingualism (and monoculturalism) in a minority language is enlightened or not is hotly debated and depends on life-style preferences, personal values and needs. It is part of a mosaic of life-patterns that expresses language individuality and language alternatives.

Sometimes, rejection is short-lived. Just as teenagers go through fads and fashions with clothes, eating habits, sleep, so there are language fashions. Language change may be temporary, reflecting peer group culture, a symbol of growing emotional and social independence from parents and family life, growing self-assertiveness and the need for a distinct, independent self-identity from the family. Children often don't want to appear different. They want to conform to the status-giving behavior of the peer group. This may entail a temporary non-use of one of their languages. **Teenagers** also feel sensitive towards those who are excluded from conversations. When non-speakers of a language are present, they want to include them in all conversations. This is discussed further in the next question.

C4 My teenage child is speaking the majority language more and more. What can I do?

During the **teenage years**, language engineering is much less in the power of parents, and much more in the hands of the teenagers. During the teenage years, conformity to the norms of the parents usually begins to disappear. If teenagers are to maintain both of their languages, it has to come from conviction rather than conformity. If pressure is placed by the parents on the teenager to speak a language, the danger is that the child will react with hostility (in the long or the short term). When teenagers begin to assert their language preference, parents can only act as **gentle gardeners**. They can encourage, irrigate the language garden when possible, tend and care for the young but now sturdy language plants, offer opportunities and possibilities, but rarely decide, direct or drive the language life of the teenager. During the teenage years, the right of the individual to his or her own language life becomes more conscious.

The **short-lived rejection** (bound for example, by particular occasions and situation, other persons present and changing identity in adolescence), needs to be separated from longer-term rejection. What happens to bilingualism during the teenage years, even if problematic, may not be long term. When teenagers reject one language, often they come back to it later in life. There is **change** and movement in language life in early and middle adulthood. As opportunities for travel, employment and new relationships develop, so may changes in language preference. What was regarded during the teenage years as a language millstone round the neck, in later years may be seen as a life buoy that provides new opportunities and new possibilities. As teenagers move further into adulthood, there is often the desire to find out about the heritage, the rootedness of the family. Those who temporarily abandoned one language in teenage years may pick up the language again later (e.g. to develop links with the past and establish continuity with the present).

To increase the chances of reversing the rejection of one language, parents can talk to the teenager in that language. The teenager may insist on responding in a different language, but at least 'passive' or 'receptive' bilingualism will be maintained by the teenager **consistently hearing** the other language. This maintains the language experience of childhood. It also makes it easier for the teenager to speak that language again, later in life. Familiarity with, and exposure to that language has been maintained.

So in times of language despair, parents need to have faith, hope and love. All parents can do is to **provide the conditions** in which an individual makes up their own mind about the future of their language existence. The gardener can prepare the ground, sow the seeds, provide an optimal environment for language growth. The parent as language gardener cannot force the growth, change the color of the language flower or have control over its final blossoming.

C5 Will my child learn two languages only half as well as a monolingual child?

The answer to this question is a definite 'no'. There is no known limit to a child's language learning capacity. It is not the case that the monolingual has one well filled language balloon and the bilingual two half filled language balloons. As we have seen in Section B, this picture is totally wrong. The child has enough capacity in the brain for learning two or more

languages. Some two thirds of people in the world are bilingual and most of these show that bilingualism and trilingualism are perfectly possible.

It is likely that the bilingual child will not have as large a **vocabulary** in each language as the monolingual child. Generally, a child's total vocabulary in two languages will far exceed the monolingual's in one language. Bilingual children usually have enough vocabulary to express themselves easily and fluently in either language. There may be occasional periods when the bilingual child seems a little behind the monolingual in learning a language. However, this **lag** is usually temporary. With sufficient exposure and practice, the bilingual child will go through the same language development stages as the monolingual child. Occasionally, the speed of the journey may be slightly slower, but the route through the developmental stages is the same.

C6 Will my child's thinking be affected by being bilingual?

The answer is yes, and probably for the better. The presence of two languages in the operating system of the brain is likely to produce a more richly fed thinking engine. There are various reasons for this. **First,** a bilingual child is less centered on the sound and form of a word. The bilingual tends to be more aware of the arbitrary nature of language. For example, the concept of the moon is not the same as the word 'moon'. Having two languages or more seems to **free** the child from constraints of a single language, enabling the child to see that ideas, concepts, meanings and thoughts are separate from language itself.

Second, a bilingual child can look at an issue or a problem through either language. The different associations of vocabulary in either language, the variety of meanings may give the child an extra **breadth** of understanding. Take a simple example of a child who has two different words for 'folk dancing'. Different associations and understandings accompany the word in each language. The connotations of folk dancing in Finnish are different from 'American' or 'British' English. The associations about 'folk dancing' are different again in Swahili, Swedish, Scots Gaelic or Spanish. This wider set of associations provides the child with a broader vision and a more comprehensive understanding.

Third, a bilingual child may be more sensitive in communication, more sensitive to the needs of listeners than a monolingual child. Since bilinguals have to know when to speak which language, have to separate out languages, constantly monitoring which language to use with which person in which situation, they appear to be slightly more sensitive to the needs of listeners than monolinguals. Being slightly more conscious about language may make the bilingual more interested in efficient and **empathic** communication. If the bilingual is slightly more aware of what is going on beneath, above and inside language, the bilingual may be more in harmony with the needs of the listener in conveying exact meaning sympathetically.

Fourth, there is evidence to suggest that bilinguals are relatively more **creative** and more imaginative in their thinking. Having two or more words for each object and idea tends to mean that many bilinguals are more flexible and fluent in their thinking, more creative and divergent thinkers. Bilinguals appear more able to move outside the boundaries of words and establish a wider variety of connections and meanings. The proviso is that a bilinguals' languages are both relatively well developed.

Fifth, research evidence from Canadian, Basque, Catalan and Welsh bilingual education reveals that some children who operate in two languages in the curriculum tend to show superior **performance**. Children who operate in the curriculum in either and both of their languages tend to show slightly higher educational performance. This is probably related to the thinking advantages of bilingualism mentioned above.

Some parents believe that bilingualism will have negative thinking effects. Such problems will only arise in a small minority of cases, when a child's two languages are both underdeveloped. When a child cannot cope in the **curriculum** in either language, a child's thinking may be disadvantaged. When a child has one language that is well developed and the other language that is less well developed, it is likely that the child will show no difference in thinking or educational achievement from the monolingual child.

The good news for bilingual parents is that when two languages are well developed, there are **advantages** rather than disadvantages in thinking. This is the good news of bilingualism, the figurative new testament and not the old testament that highlighted problems of bilingualism. The Old Testament idea of the Tower of Babel, of confusion of tongues, is replaced by the New Testament idea that speaking in tongues is a gift. In the Biblical New Testament, at that central moment of Jesus on the cross, the inscription was written in three languages, Hebrew, Latin and Greek. At that pivotal moment of history, there is a celebration of trilingualism. The early Apostles were given a gift of God — the speaking of tongues — a celebration of the diversity of language. The new testament of bilingual research at the end of the twentieth century is that bilingualism has thinking advantages for children and does not produce mental confusion.

C7 Does bilingualism have an effect on the functioning of the brain?

A variety of studies have examined the brains of bilinguals. A frequently asked question is whether a bilingual's brain functions differently compared with a monolingual's brain? How is language organized and processed in the brain of a bilingual compared with a monolingual? Research is at a very early stage and recent reviews show that **few conclusions** are warranted. For example, in one study, a man was regressed by hypnosis to the age of seven. Under hypnosis, the man spoke fluent Japanese. When he returned to his adult self, he could not speak Japanese. This indicated that a language learned early, but not maintained, is dormant in the brain. However, other studies have not replicated this finding. Therefore, no conclusion is currently possible.

In most right-handed adults, the left hemisphere of the brain is dominant for language processing. The question is whether bilinguals are different from monolinguals in this left lateralization? Some authors have suggested that bilinguals may use the right hemisphere more than monolinguals for first and second language processing. The idea is that the second language of a bilingual will use the right hemisphere of the brain for language processing more than the first language. However, as proficiency in the second language grows, right hemisphere involvement might decrease and left hemisphere involvement increase. This assumes that the right hemisphere is concerned with more immediate, pragmatic and emotional aspects of language. In contrast, the core aspects of language processing are assumed to reside more in the left hemisphere.

However, recent reviews tend to suggest that monolinguals and bilinguals are little different from each other in lateralization (use of right and left hemisphere of the brain). The left hemisphere tends to dominate strongly language processing for both monolinguals and bilinguals. Differences between monolinguals and bilinguals are the exception rather than the rule.

There is currently no strong evidence that bilingualism has negative effects on the everyday functioning of the brain. In terms of efficient and effective use of the brain, storage in the brain and processing in the brain, bilinguals do not seem particularly different from monolinguals.

C8 Will my bilingual children have a problem of identity with two different cultures? (My children speak French and English. Is there a danger that they won't know whether they are French or English?)

In the second question of this section, this area of **identity** was raised as one potentially important and sometimes problematic issue in the raising of a bilingual child. It was suggested that there is a dimension. At one end of the dimension are children who learn to switch between two cultures as easily as they switch between two languages. Such children and adults celebrate their fluency and ability in moving between two worlds: being French in France and English in England; being a Hebrew-speaking Jew in Israel, a Yiddish-speaking Jew in the home in New York and an English-speaking American at school. For some, there are few problems of cultural compatibility or identity crisis. Theirs is **biculturalism** fully flowered, easily exhibited and much admired by all who view.

Close to this are those (for example, from a language minority), whose identity is securely rooted within their **minority language culture**. Welsh speakers for example, primarily belong to their language minority and belong to a larger group (e.g. British or European) sometimes with reluctance, sometimes marginally. Welsh speakers often regard themselves as Welsh first and foremost, English definitely not, British possibly and European reluctantly but increasingly. For such people there is little identity crisis as there are strong roots in a minority language garden.

At the other end of the dimension, there are those who experience rootlessness or **dislocation** between two cultures. For example, with older in-migrants, there is sometimes a passive reaction, **isolation**, numbness and loss of a rooted identity. In younger in-migrants, there is sometimes an aggressive reaction, having lost the identity of home and heritage, and finding it difficult to penetrate the thick walls to enter the new host culture. For some in-migrants, there may be a sense of rootlessness, confusion of identity, feeling neither one ethnic identity nor the other. This can lead to hopelessness, an ambiguity of cultural existence, or feeling lost in a cultural wilderness.

Reactions among in-migrants include (sometimes in approximately this order):

- a brief honeymoon period when there is great **optimism**, pleasure in new surroundings and much hope for the future;
- a period of **frustration**, when optimism and hope are dashed and barriers to integration seem overwhelming'
- a period of **anger**, when the wrong decisions seem to have been made (internalized anger) or other people are preventing access to jobs, integration, friendships and success (externalized anger). Followed by
- a period of **isolation**, when pessimism and gloom are dominant. The in-migrant may become a marginalized person. Or
- rejection of the 'old' language and culture and wanting total **assimilation** and identification with a new language and culture. A person may suppress the home country, concentrating solely on being a true citizen of the new country. Or
- **integration** which means retaining all that is best from the past and adding on all that is good in the new way of life. Or
- **conforming without conviction** to the call for allegiance to a new language and culture.

Adjustment among in-migrants thus takes many different forms: happy integration, uncomfortable assimilation, isolation, rejection and anomie. Bilingualism is greatly affected by the outcomes of adjustment.

Among in-migrants, ethnic identity begins around three to five years of age, and by the age of seven or eight, is well established but continues to develop. In the teenage years, ethnic differences may become increasingly conscious and considered. Overt and covert racial discrimination, racial abuse and harassment, color, religion, dress and dietary differences surface to increasingly focus ethnic awareness, ethnic identity and ethnic inequity.

It is important to be constructive and suggest what can be positively achieved to minimize an identity crisis. This is a problem that some parents of bilingual children will have to face. There are no final solutions but there are positive strategies to attempt to establish a positive self-identity and self-esteem.

It is natural for a child or adult to have **different identities in different contexts**. We are all like actors and actresses on a stage. As the script changes, the co-actors and actresses change, the props and scenery and audience changes, so does the role we play. Fathers and mothers have to take on different identities in different situations with different people. There is the identity of the home, at work, in church or mosque, in the cafe or bar, as a parent and when acting in an official public capacity.

As we move in and out of **different roles**, we naturally have different identities. The child assumes different identities (and role-playing behavior) in school with teachers, in the playground with friends, in the street in the evening and at weekends, in church or the mosque, being Granny's little girl or little boy, being the sophisticated socialite at parties or the young raver at discos. With different people and in different situations, the child, particularly the teenager, learns to play different roles, wear different 'costumes' and harmonize with a different set of players. It is important that such roles and resultant **sub identities** integrate into a satisfactory harmonized whole. We all need coherence and wholeness around those sub identities. From this consideration, something important can be said about bilingualism and self-identity.

This discussion of sub identities and playing different roles suggests two things. First, that a child needs experience of, and exposure to playing different roles successfully. Acting on a new stage with different people with unusual props is difficult for any of us. The more exposure and experience to changing scenery, changing actors and actresses and a different play, the more harmonized with a role we become. Therefore, a child needs plenty of exposure and **experience of the cultures that go with the two languages**. For the Anglo-French child, living in Britain, this may mean regular trips to France, mingling with a group of French people in Britain, having a feast of French culture at home — video tapes, nursery rhymes and books with plenty of historical, literary, social and cultural information about French-speaking people.

Second, in a **minority language situation**, it seems important that children obtain a continuous (including through the teenage years) experience of minority language culture. If the minority language culture is to be retained within the child, there has to be **continuous participation through that minority language**. Otherwise, in the teenage years in particular, there may be a break away from that language and culture. In such a minority language situation, there is usually plenty of exposure to the majority language culture. Cinemas and television, newspapers and visits to English-speaking areas, sport and pop music all contain powerful, pervading influences that ensure Anglo-American culture is experienced.

For the **recent in-migrant**, there is the dual task. There is the need to retain a **continuity of cultural experience** within the heritage language culture. For the Asian family recently settled in a host country, harsh dislocation from the home and the heritage culture for the child may mean an identity crisis is unwittingly contrived. Throwing off all vestiges of the drama one has enacted in the home language in the past is like denying the past, denying the value of the home language, killing a part of the Self.

At the same time, a **gradual transition** needs making into the host culture. To open up economic, employment and equality of opportunity prospects in the short and long term, the in-migrant family often needs to learn the lines of a new play, attempt to play alongside new actors and actresses, and become comfortable with a new script, different props and scenery. This is rarely easy. Sometimes, the host actors and actresses do not want to let newcomers in on their drama. To preserve their economic and social advantages, to establish clear racial and ethnic boundaries, in-migrant actors and actresses may find it difficult to penetrate an established theatrical company. As much as the in-migrants may want to assimilate and integrate, they will often be barred from entry into privileged circles. Of all the different bilingual situations, this is the most frustrating, fearsome and resistant to harmonization.

In the situation described above, **conflicts of identity** may well arise. Wearing different dress (e.g. saris), speaking a different tongue, having a different color, ethnic identity and religion, may make the establishment of a new identity, (or adding onto the existing repertoire) a difficult drama. There are no rehearsals; only a stage with a potentially skeptical or hostile audience. There is a danger that children will not know who they are, from whence they came, nor whither they are going.

To help, parents may wish to look for opportunities for their children to **integrate** into the host culture while retaining the home culture. If there are particular playgroups, evening activities, churches and mosques where harmonization can occur without sacrificing the heritage language and heritage culture, a child may be encouraged to take on new identities. The **school** has an important role in helping resolution of this paradox: retaining the child's heritage language and identity and culture, while allowing that child entry into the host language and culture. The school has the task of ensuring that there is addition and not subtraction (i.e. losing the heritage language and culture). The school has the responsibility of developing a harmonic multiplication of identities within the child and not a division of identities that makes a child feel lost or in despair. Too few schools take this responsibility seriously. The better schools do.

Parents need to face the issue of whether experiencing two different cultures means the watering down of one culture while the other culture gains. At its best, the Anglo-French, Swedish-Finn, Chinese-Malaysian bilingual child will be a fresh and valuable species in a colorful language garden. This hyphenated variety is neither purely French nor English, nor solely Finnish or Swedish, neither mainland Chinese nor purely Malaysian. The bilingual, bicultural child needs a dual repertoire of custom and culture that allows high self-esteem, a positive self-concept, an optimistic outlook on the future and a potential for choosing for oneself which cultures to accent in the future.

C9 Will bilingualism have any adverse effect on my child's personality?

A variety of research in the past has tried to locate **personality differences** between bilinguals and monolinguals. Overall, research has not found particular differences. It appears that bilinguals and monolinguals do not generally differ (because of their language differences) in their neuroticism, extroversion, introversion, self-confidence, anxiety, self-esteem, shyness, sociability, need for power, need for achievement, conscientiousness or cheerfulness. Quite simply, bilingualism or monolingualism is not the cause of personality differences.

Where personality differences between bilinguals and monolinguals do exist, they will be due to factors other than language. For example, where bilinguals are in-migrants suffering problems of hostility and racial abuse, it is not language but ethnicity and hostility surrounding in-migrancy that are likely to be a major cause.

At the other end of the spectrum, where bilinguals appear more confident or accepted, this is not usually due to their dual language advantage. Rather such bilinguals may come from elite groups (e.g. from geographically mobile upper middle class parents) or homes with successful child rearing practices. A stable and well adjusted personality tends to be the outcome of many other family characteristics than an approach to bilingualism. **Bilingualism**, in and by itself, does **not** seem **a major cause of different personality characteristics**.

If advice is needed on what does affect a child's personality, there are the wise words of Dorothy Nolte:

If a child lives with criticism, he learns to condemn.
If a child lives with hostility, he learns to fight.
If a child lives with ridicule, he learns to be shy.
If a child lives with shame, he learns to feel guilty.
If a child lives with tolerance, he learns to be patient.
If a child lives with encouragement, he learns confidence.
If a child lives with praise, he learns to appreciate.
If a child lives with fairness, he learns justice.
If a child lives with security, he learns to have faith.
If a child lives with approval, he learns to like himself.
If a child lives with acceptance and friendship, he learns to find love in the world.

C10 Will bilingualism have any adverse effect on my child's friendships and social development?

Overall, bilingualism is likely to be an **advantage** in social relationships. If children have two or more languages, they have the potential of being able to make more friends rather than less. They will also be able to increase the variety of their friendships being able to make bridges with children from different language groups. One joy of a bilingual parent is seeing their child interact with different sets of children from different language groups, using either language to form friendships.

When visiting grandparents, uncles and aunts and cousins in a different country, one of the joys of bilingual children and their parents is seeing such children **communicate** so **easily**. They are at home in foreign parts. Having traveled a long distance, there is no distance to be traveled in language. With the speed of Concorde, the child moves from one language to another, one language community to another language community.

One advantage of childhood bilingualism is that it dismantles social barriers, enables more fluent growth of friendships with children from two or more language communities, widening the child's social, cultural and educational horizons.

The type of problem that sometimes arises is when a minority language child, for example, is confronted by majority language children. If that child's majority language skills are still developing, other children may deride the child's language skills and show **hostility** to the child. That a child is not fluent in one language does not seem a problem in young children's friendship formation. Through non-verbal communication, body language, plenty of pointing and gesticulating, young children rarely seem conscious of language barriers. As children enter middle childhood and the teenage years, rivalries and competition, sometimes prejudice and peer group conformity contrive to make language a barrier. This is an argument for early bilingual development.

When language becomes a barrier to friendship, or when **prejudice** and hostility arise due to language communication problems, the parent and teacher need to strike a very delicate balance between protection, facilitating transition into a new friendship group, maintaining a child's dignity and self-esteem, while slowly pushing forward the frontiers of cooperation and conciliation. Overprotection of the child, and overexposure to negative experiences are both to be avoided by the child, the parent and the teacher.

There is an increasing responsibility for educationalists, teachers as well as **curriculum** planners, to ensure that majority (and minority) language children, monolinguals especially, are given courses in language awareness. The responsibility for breaking down barriers to friendship which language and cultural differences might create, lies partly within a school curriculum. Through role playing, language awareness lessons, discussions in the classroom, the naturalness and value of language diversity in the world needs teaching in schools as much as any curriculum subject.

In helping a child choose friends, create new friendships and deal with problems of friendships, the parent needs to be a friendly listening ear, a confidant, a suggester of possibilities, a shoulder to cry on, and occasionally a protector. At the same time, a parent needs to **communicate** with teachers where major problems arise, and gain the support and sustenance of other parents with similar problems. A language problem shared is a bilingual's problem halved.

C11 The balance of my child's two languages seems to be shifting. How can I ensure one language doesn't disappear?

It is often the case that the strengths of a person's two languages tend to **vary** across time. As there is more or less exposure to one language, as different people such as brothers and sisters enter the family situation, as schooling starts and peer group relationships grow, so does the language dominance and preference of children for one of their two languages. In the life history of bilinguals, it is usual for the strength of the two languages to vary across time, across different contexts and in use with different people. A child may find it easier to speak English in some circumstances, French in a different context and this may vary as practice and experience change.

Sometimes the shift will be large. For example, a child may **stop speaking** one of their languages while still being able to understand that language. There are many case histories of bilinguals where there is a move from active bilingualism to passive bilingualism — that is understanding without speaking one language. The teenage years sometimes witness such a change. Some children move towards speaking the majority language or their dominant language more and more, their minority language or less dominant language less and less. This is a naturally worrying event for many parents.

It is often impossible and usually unwise to impel a child speak a language. Sometimes, bilingual parents try to achieve conformity without conviction. For example, a parent may say to their children that they do not understand them speaking the majority language. Unless this is handled tactfully and skillfully, the result is that children learn that language is an imposition, a part of authoritarian power. It is often unwise to control dogmatically children's language preference. This is not to say that one shouldn't try to **influence** it tactfully and more latently. Manipulation rather than domination tends to achieve more in the long term.

When children are younger, one possible solution is to **extend the range of language experiences** in their less preferred language. If a child is becoming weaker or developing a negative attitude to one language, a wider and pleasurable range of language experiences may be needed. For example, staying with grandparents or cousins, visits to enjoyable cultural festivals or occasions, a renewal in the language materials and other language stimuli in the home for that weaker language (e.g. videos, pop records, the visits of cousins) may manipulate a reversal.

Another solution is for one parent to spend more **time** giving the child language experience. If the father (rather than the mother) reads to, or listens to the child reading before bedtime, or if the language of family conversation at the meal table is manipulated to advantage, then subtly the language balance of the home may be readjusted. If the analogy will stand, it is like the gardener experiencing difficult conditions in the garden. Adding more fertilizer, watering, weeding and shielding the tender young plants from strong prevailing winds, may promote their stronger growth.

There need to be both principles and pragmatism. If there is an underlying **principle**, it is to attempt the impossible task of providing a relatively balanced language diet for the child, considering all the different contexts, people and occasions where the two languages are used. If the minority language is being used decreasingly, it may demand decisions about increasing the contexts and occasions where the minority language is spoken. If the child's second language does not seem to be progressing, then decisions need to be made about how best to stimulate further development in that language. **Pragmatism** is also necessary to avoid language life in the home developing into rigid rules. There are always occasions when communication needs, friendships and fun make exceptions justifiable.

There are times in a bilingual's life history that allow little intervention, manipulation or fertilization even by the most experienced gardener. When **adolescents** reject a language, negative reactions by parents will often only harm future bilingual prospects and undermine the good that has already been achieved. Just as in teaching children and teenagers manners and morals, values and beliefs, parents have to let go the reins slowly and trust in an ultimate goodness embedded in their child, so with bilinguals. There comes a point in the teenage years, when parents can have little influence on language usage and dependent children must grow into independent adults.

Should the adolescent reject one language, the parent has still provided sufficient growth in the sturdy young plant for passive bilingualism to change into active bilingualism later. It is surprising how some reluctant teenagers return later in life to bilingualism. In their twenties, thirties and forties, a person who has not actively spoken or read a language for ten or twenty years will still find it relatively easy to **relearn** and become an active bilingual again. The long-term benefits in speaking two languages are not easily visible to teenagers. During early and middle adulthood, the value of two languages and two language cultures can be reawoken. Therefore, a positive message is possible even in the most negative situation. There are long-term possibilities among short-term failure.

The parent has been successful in providing the conditions for later growth. Not all flowers bloom early. Some flowers that bloom late in the summer, even in the autumn, retain all the beauty promised in the sowing of the seed.

C12 My child seems to have learning difficulties. Is this due to bilingualism?

As previously stated, one tendency of parents of bilingual children is that they (and other people) tend to blame varying problems on their child's bilingualism. If a child is slow in learning to read in school, or is placed in the lower half of their class in mathematics, or finds history boring and science difficult, people too quickly latch on to bilingualism as the first **explanation**.

Research tells a very different story. **Rarely is bilingualism a cause of learning difficulties**. Learning difficulties occasionally occur within bilingual children. This is totally different from bilingualism being the cause of their learning difficulties. Learning difficulties are caused by a variety of possibilities, almost none of them aligned to bilingualism. Five examples of causes follow:

(1) The problem may be in the standard of education. A child may be struggling in the classroom due to poor teaching methods, a non-motivating even hostile classroom environment, a dearth of suitable teaching materials, or clashes with the teacher.

(2) The school may be inhibiting or obstructing learning progress. If a child is being taught in a second language and the home language is ignored, then failure and perceived learning difficulties may result. One example, is various Spanish-speaking children in the United States. Such children are often placed in English-only classrooms on entry to school. They must sink or swim in English. Some swim; others sink and may be deemed to have a deficiency. By being assessed in their weaker second language (English) — rather than in their stronger home language (Spanish), such children are labeled as in need of special or remedial education. Thus the monolingual school system is itself responsible for learning failure. A school that celebrated bilingualism would probably enable learning success for the same child.

(3) Another set of causes of learning difficulties lies with little self confidence, low self-esteem, a fear of failure and high anxiety in the classroom.

(4) A fourth possibility is failure caused partly by interactions among children in the classroom. For example, where a group of children reinforce each other for fooling around, have a low motivation to succeed, or where there is bullying, hostility, social division rather than cohesion among children in a classroom, the learning ethos may disrupt the child's development.

(5) Another case is where the child is a slow learner, where there is a mismatch between the gradient of learning expected and the ability level of the child. Some children learn to read more slowly than others, still learning to read well, but after a longer period of time. Less able children can learn two languages within the (unknowable) limits of their ability. Other children experience specific learning difficulties (for example, dyslexia, neurological dysfunction, 'short-term memory' problems, poor physical co-ordination, problems in attention span or motivation). None of these specific learning difficulties or other language disorders are caused by bilingualism. At the same time, bilingual children will not escape from being included in this group. Bilingual families are no less likely to be affected than other families.

This list, neither exhaustive nor comprehensive, shows that bilingualism has almost nothing to do with these problems, either as a secondary or a primary cause. Bilingualism is unlikely to be a direct or indirect cause of a child's learning difficulties.

Almost the only occasion when a learning difficulty of a bilingual child is attached to bilingualism is when a child enters the classroom with **neither language sufficiently developed** to cope with the higher order language skills demanded by the curriculum. In the rare cases where a child has simple conversational skills in two languages but cannot cope in the curriculum in either language, language may be related to learning difficulties. In this case, the problem is not really with bilingualism but with insufficient language practice in the home, in the nursery school or in the outside world. Here we are talking not about bilingual deprivation, but about deprivation in any language. This is a rarity but is the only reason bilingualism appears indirectly connected with learning difficulties.

If a child has lower ability than most in the school, there is evidence to suggest that less able children can acquire two languages within the unknown limits of their abilities. While well meaning friends, teachers and speech therapists sometimes suggest that one language only should be developed, Canadian research tends to show that less able children are surprisingly capable of acquiring two languages early on. Just as their mathematical ability, literacy and scientific development may occur at a slower pace, so the two languages will develop with less speed. The size of vocabulary and accuracy of grammar may be less in both languages than the average bilingual child. Nevertheless, such children acquiring two languages early, will usually be able to communicate in both languages, often as well as they would communicate in one language.

C13 My child seems to have an emotional/behavioral problem. Is this caused by bilingualism?

No. There is no evidence that bilingualism in itself causes emotional or behavioral problems. The ability to speak two languages is usually a valuable accomplishment for a person. Therefore, bilingualism is often associated with an emotional and social **gain** and not a loss. Bilingualism is often an asset and not a debit.

Bilingualism is sometimes wrongly associated with emotional and behavioral difficulties because bilingualism is connected with some economically underprivileged, racially harassed and financially impoverished ethnic groups. The lower status of bilingual in-migrants in Europe and North America, the relative lack of political power among various 'native language' groups in all continents tends to display apparent connections between bilingualism, being a member of rejected, neglected and despised ethnic groups, and individual social and emotional problems. Such **connections are usually false**. While bilingualism is one of the characteristics of such groups, it is not a cause of their problems.

If children from such underprivileged groups experience problems in emotional or social adjustment, the **cause is not language**. Causes of emotional problems need searching for in, for example, the economic, political and financial characteristics of the language minority group, or in the quality of child development experiences provided in the home, community and school. There is nothing emotionally damaging or restricting about owning two languages. On the contrary, bilingualism opens the door to wider emotional experiences from the different language cultures.

However, there are occasions when a child is diagnosed as having a particular problem, the diagnosis and treatment of which involves language. This situation is considered in the next question.

C14 My child has a specific diagnosed problem (e.g. learning difficulty, language disorder, emotional problem). Should we change to speaking one language to the child rather than two languages? What language should I speak to my child?

Parents of bilingual children do not escape the real problems that are found in younger and older children. The bilingual child may, for example, be diagnosed as dyslexic, aphasic, partially hearing or with a low IQ score. Hopefully, the **specialist** making the diagnosis will have both experience with bilingual children and have studied bilingualism in professional training. If so, the diagnosis will include an assurance that bilingualism is not the cause of the problem. The communicative differences of language minority children must be distinguished from communicative disorders. Other answers in this section demonstrate that such problems are too quickly attributed to bilingualism, partly because bilinguals are 'different'. Research tells a very different story. Bilingualism will **co-exist** with, but will **not be the primary cause** of such problems.

A particular problem that illustrates the wrongly attributed link between bilingualism and developmental problems is '**language delay**'. Language delay occurs when a child is very late in beginning to talk, or lags well behind peers in language development. Estimates of young children experiencing language delay vary from 1 in 20 to 1 in 5 of the child population. Such varying estimates partly reflect that some delays are brief and hardly noticeable. Others are more severe. Language delay has a variety of causes (e.g. partial hearing, deafness, autism, severe subnormality, cerebral palsy, physical differences (e.g. cleft palate), psychological disturbance, emotional difficulties). However, in approximately two-thirds of all cases, the precise reason for language delay is not known. Children who are medically normal, with no hearing loss, of normal IQ and memory, are not socially deprived or emotionally disturbed, can be delayed in starting to speak, slow in development or have problems in expressing themselves well. In such cases, specialist, professional help needs seeking. Speech therapists, clinical psychologists, educational psychologists, counselors or doctors may give such advice and treatment.

Parents of bilingual children with such problems should not believe that bilingualism is the cause. Sometimes, well meaning professionals make this diagnosis. As in the example of language delay, if the causes are unknown, bilingualism might seem a likely cause. Having a bilingual background is widely believed to produce language delayed children. The evidence does not support this belief.

A key consideration for a parent is whether removal of one language will improve, worsen or have no affect on the child's bilingualism. Given that the cause of the problem may be partially unknown, intuition and guesswork rather than 'science' often occurs. Research in this area is still in its infancy.

One issue is which language to concentrate on if there is a major diagnosed language or emotional problem? The danger is that parents, teachers and administrators will want to accent the perceived importance of the majority language. In the United States, the advice is often that the child should have a solid diet of English — the language of school and employment. The advice too frequently given is that the home, **minority language** should be replaced by the majority language. Such an overnight switch may well have painful outcomes for the child. The mother tongue is denied, the language of the family is buried, and the child may feel as if thrown from a secure boat into strange waters. The solution in itself is likely to exacerbate the problem.

It is more **important that the anchor language is retained**. The home language gives assurance and a feeling of security when there are stormy seas. Even if the child is slow in sailing in that language, with progress delayed, even painful, it is the boat known to the child. Being forced to switch to the majority language will not make the journey faster or less problematic. It is more important to learn to sail in a familiar boat (the home language) in **minority language** situations.

Even when parents and professionals accept that bilingualism is not the cause of a child's problem, moving from bilingualism to **monolingualism** is seen by some as a way to help improve the problem. The reasoning is usually that the 'extra demands' of bilingualism, if removed, will lighten the burden for the child. For example, if the child has an emotional or language delay problem, simplifying the language demands on the child may be seen as one way of solving or reducing the problem. The apparent complexity of a two language life is relieved by monolingualism. While the cause of the problem is not addressed (often because the cause is unknown), one part of the context (i.e. bilingualism) where the problem occurs is changed to attempt a solution. Is this right?

There are many occasions when changing from bilingualism to monolingualism will have **no effect** on the problem. For example, if the child is exhibiting temper tantrums, seems slow to speak without an obvious cause or seems low in self-esteem, dropping one language is unlikely to have any effect. On the contrary, the sudden change in family life may exacerbate the problem. The stability of a child's language life is disrupted, with possible negative consequences. In most cases, it is inappropriate to move from bilingualism to monolingualism. However, it is dangerous to make this advice absolute and unequivocal.

To give only 'stick with bilingualism' advice is unwise and too simplistic. When there is **language delay**, for example, there will be a few family situations where maximal experience in one language is preferable. For example, where one language of a child is more secure and better developed than another, it may be sensible to concentrate on developing the stronger language. If, for example, the child only hears one language from one parent and that parent is often away, a short term of concentration on the stronger language may help in a language delay period.

This does not mean that the chance of bilingualism is lost forever. If, or when, language delay disappears, the other language can be reintroduced. If a child with **emotional problems** really detests using (even being spoken to in a particular language), as part of a solution, the family may sensibly decide to accede to the child's preference. Again, once problems have been resolved, the 'dropped' language may be reintroduced, so long as it is immediately associated with pleasurable experiences. Stuttering (stammering) is also an example where occasionally the temporary dropping of a weaker language may help to move the child through a transitory stage of cognitive 'difficulty'. This issue is dealt with more fully in a separate question on stuttering.

Any **temporary move** from bilingualism to monolingualism should not be seen as the only solution needed. A focus on such a language change as the sole remedy to the child's problem is naive and dangerous. For example, emotional problems may require other rearrangements in the family's pattern of relationships (as discussed with a counselor or psychologist). Language delay may require visits to a speech therapist for advice about language interaction between parents and child. **Temporary monolingualism** should only be seen as one component in a package of attempted changes to solve the child's language or emotional problem.

There are other occasions where changing from bilingualism to monolingualism is unnecessary and wrong. There are times when such a radical change will make matters worse and not better. The child may be further confused, even upset, if there is a **dramatic change** in the language of the family. If someone who has loved, cared for and played with the child in one language (e.g. a minority language) suddenly only uses another language (e.g. the majority language), the emotional well-being of the child may well be negatively affected. The language used to express love and caring disappears. Simultaneously, and by association, the child may feel that the love and care is also not as before. Such a language change is often drastic with its own negative after-effects and consequences.

To **conclude**. When major language or emotional problems arise :

(1) Don't rush to **blame** bilingualism. Bilingualism is very unlikely to be a cause. Don't rush to change to monolingualism as a solution. You may only make matters worse.

(2) **Discuss** the problem with trusted friends, particularly those who may have experienced a similar problem. This may result in some advice. It also helps to clarify one's own thinking.
(3) **Consult** professionals, particularly if they have training and experience in dealing with bilingual children. Speech therapists, psychologists and counselors may be able to give an expert diagnosis and suggest possible treatment of the problem.
(4) If you do adopt monolingualism as a solution to a child's problem, think about this as a **temporary** solution. Bilingualism can be reintroduced later. To deny a child the chance to become bilingual may be denying the child another world of experience.
(5) If bilingualism is continued through the problem, be extra **vigilant** that language doesn't become associated in the child's mind with anxiety, complications or unhappiness.

C15 My child stutters. Is this caused by bilingualism?

For a short period, many children stutter (stammer). This includes repeating sounds or words (e.g. p-p-p-play with m-m-me; I've got to – got to – got to go now); lengthening sounds (e.g. ffffish); time gaps between words (e.g. I'm going ... home now); and unfinished words or phrases. Around three and four years of age, such stuttering is particularly common. Many older children and adults under pressure lose fluency. In addressing a large audience, the speaker may be so tense as to lose customary fluency.

The causes of stuttering are not well understood and seem varied. Some **neurophysiological** theories locate the problem in brain activity, others in a feedback problem between the ear and the brain. Further theories attempt a **psychological** explanation in terms of personality traits, and particularly anxiety (e.g. caused by impatient, over-corrective parents). None of these theories can explain all cases of stuttering.

One **linguistic** theory sees the cause as a difference between the language that is available (potential) and control over speech apparatus (production). Another linguistic theory sees 'cognitive overload' as the cause (e.g. the child is experiencing a difficulty in producing required complex sentences; the child's capacity for fluency exceeds the demands placed on the child). Such linguistic theories may have implications for a few young bilinguals. Some researchers have argued that coping with two languages around the age of two to four may cause a few children 'cognitive overload'. Such researchers argue that bilingualism causes a few children to require additional processing time (i.e. increasing the difference between 'potential' and 'production'). The evidence for this is based on single cases, and is not strong. Overall, bilinguals appear no more likely to stutter than monolinguals. Bilingual and multilingual countries do not appear to have a greater incidence of stuttering than monolingual countries.

The case studies suggest that any problems due to 'cognitive overload' are **temporary** in bilingual children. As language competence in the two languages increases, stammering usually disappears. It is also not clear from such research whether the causes were purely cognitive. Emotional problems (e.g. anxiety) may have been a prime cause; such anxiety derived from sources other than bilingualism. The conclusion seems to be that stuttering is very rarely associated with bilingualism.

Parents of bilingual children tend to focus on bilingualism as the cause of stuttering, rather than looking for other better explanations. Evidence tends to suggest that bilingualism is rarely a direct cause of stuttering. Such evidence as exists also shows that stuttering is no more frequent in bilingual countries than in monolingual countries.

Methods of treatment of stuttering also hint that bilingualism is rarely a cause. Developing a stutter's breath control, learning to speak more slowly, tension reduction and relaxation techniques are examples of treatments. Parents cannot do anything about some potential causes of stuttering (e.g. brain activity). If potential causes of stuttering are more about specific anxieties, nervousness, worries about speaking, or more general worries and fears in the child's life, the parent can help. Parents who criticize a child for stuttering, or who exhibit anxiety when their child stutters, only increase the child's nervousness and frequency of stuttering.

When stuttering first occurs, it is not necessary to seek immediate psychological or clinical advice. The sheer act of highlighting the problem may exacerbate the problem itself. Merely showing and sharing anxiety, highlighting to the child that a problem exists, correcting the child and being impatient may only make the condition worse. Stuttering is frequent in many young children, both monolinguals and bilinguals. It is usually temporary, and reappears when a child (or adult) is particularly agitated and excited. If stuttering continues for a longer period, it may be wise to seek **advice** from experts in child development or clinical psychology.

When the problem first occurs, it is important for parents to surround the child with greater love, greater relaxed care and attention, and more support and encouragement. Be very patient. Focus on what the child wants to convey, not on the language being used. Concentrate on the function of the conversation and not on the form of language. If parents are able to show attention to possible causes of stuttering and seek to remedy those, stuttering may soon disappear. If the sources of tension and anxiety in the child can be located, reduced or swept away, stuttering is quite likely to be a **temporary problem**. For a very small number of children, however, stuttering will be a continuous characteristic.

Stopping children speaking one of their languages will usually be counter productive. It will not change the stuttering. Rather such an act will focus on language. This will increase children's anxiety about their language production. If it is genuinely felt that stuttering is caused by the child's 'potential with language' not matching 'ability in production' or by 'cognitive overload' (see the linguistic theories mentioned above), parents can attempt to:

(1) relax the level of their questions and language demands on the child;
(2) ensure that language expectations are not unrealistic — in both languages;
(3) be extra encouraging and patient when listening to the child, and
(4) in extreme cases, if felt strongly desirable, move to monolingualism for a temporary period.

This discussion of stuttering conveys an important message to parents about their monitoring of their child's dual language development. If parents are anxious, constantly on edge about their child's bilingual development and this is relayed to the child, the child may internalize such anxieties. Stuttering is one possible consequence of the internalization of parental anxiety. It is therefore important that bilingual development is an enjoyable and pleasurable experience for the child. If a happy and positive atmosphere surrounds bilingual language development, bilingualism is very unlikely to cause stuttering.

C16 People make fun of our speaking a minority language. How should I react?

The people who make fun of bilinguals are often monolinguals and not bilinguals. It is the people who can't speak a language who tend to poke fun at those who can speak two or three languages. Therefore the problem is not really with the speakers but with the listeners. The deprivation and disadvantage is the monolingual's and not the bilingual's. Their poking fun may be a sense of their inadequacy in communication, their underlying jealousy, their worries about **exclusion** from the conversation, and meeting a different species from themselves. The problem of bilingualism is not bilinguals — it is often monolinguals — especially those who speak one majority language only.

For bilinguals meeting this situation, it is a matter of diplomacy, building bridges and breaking down barriers, keeping a good sense of humor, trying to be tolerant. Pragmatically rather than idealistically, it is bilinguals who often have to forge improved relationships. It is bilinguals who often, in practice, have to reveal that they are not different creatures from those who make fun of them. Bilinguals are often cast in the role of showing that language diversity does not mean social divisions, that speaking a different language can still mean a harmonious relationship. Since bilinguals often share the same language and the same culture as those who make fun of them, bilinguals can become **diplomats and not dividers**. Ironically, those who are the victims have to become the healers. The moral advantage, the character building nature of such actions is built into many religions and shines forth in the twentieth century examples of Mahatma Gandhi and Martin Luther King.

It is important for speakers of a minority language to have high **self-esteem**. It is important in minority language politics for minority speakers to form a cohesive, self-confident group which takes pride in its language vitality. Language minority speakers must not become islands but gather strength from being part of a language community. Sometimes, such a language community may be geographically close. At other times, the language community may communicate by phone, weekend visits, holiday periods, letters, faxes, swapping material for children's learning and annual festivals. Geographical isolation needs counteracting by creative means of communication to launch a **language community**. If there are self-doubts and derision by outsiders, there is strength to be gained from being part of a language community.

C17 People around me are prejudiced and racist. Should we as a family switch to speaking only the majority language?

There are families whose language difference from surrounding families is joined by ethnic difference, color difference or religious difference. Where language differences accompany differences of color and creed, prejudice and racism so often exist. For many bilinguals in the world, theirs is not an elite bilingualism. In many bilingual situations of the world, bilingualism exists alongside **racism**, deprivation, poverty, unemployment and **disadvantage**. For example, Spanish-speaking Mexicans or Puerto Ricans in the United States, the Tamils in Malaysia, the Bengali speakers in England, the various in-migrant language groups in Germany are united by their minority language status forming part of a cluster of differences in color, culture, creed, economic and social status. The prejudice may be about language, but also very much about color, and a markedly different culture and life style from the host country.

One response by some who experience such a reaction is to want to **switch** to the majority host language. Because they can't change their skin color and they do not want to change their creed, they nevertheless want to share in the economic affluence of the host country. For some, this is interpreted as the need to change language and change culture. Speaking fluent English may become a priority in England and the United States. Speaking German fluently may become a priority for in-migrants into Germany.

The weakness of this position is that it expresses the view that one has to lose a heritage language to gain the majority language. It is as if there has to be denunciation of the home language in order for the majority language to flourish. This is a monolingual position. A bilingual position is much more tenable. It is possible, given the right circumstances, for people in such a minority language position to hold onto their minority language and become fluent in the majority language. There is little reason why the heritage language and culture must be lost, with rootlessness as a possible outcome, rather than becoming bilingual in both languages.

Unfortunately, simply speaking the majority language will not cause a sudden change away from racism, discrimination and prejudice. Such negative attitudes by majority peoples tend to be based on a **fear** of a different ethnic group, a fear of their economic privileged position being overturned, a fear of the unknown culture and a fear about loss of power. Becoming monolingual majority language speakers does not change economic disadvantage nor racial prejudice. Bilingualism that includes a well developed fluency and literacy in the majority language has the equal advantage of allowing potential access to different economic markets and employment as well as retaining all that is good from the past. There is good reason for the family to become fluent in the majority language. This need not be at the cost of the first or minority language.

C18 I'm a recent in-migrant to a country. Should I stop speaking my native language and switch to the first language of that country?

The answer is no. To deny the existence of your first language is to **deny** the **existence** of yourself, your past, your family history and traditions. You will probably want to learn the language of the country to which you have migrated. You will usually hope to communicate in the majority language with neighbors, shopkeepers, teachers and others in the community. You will also usually want your children to become fluent in the majority language of the country. This may occur in the home, in the local nursery school or when the children attend primary schooling.

There is little reason to stop using your native language. Retaining your native language in yourself and your children means retaining the rootedness of the past, maintaining values and beliefs, attitudes and culture that you and your family have held dear. In teaching a child your native language, you are **transmitting** something about **yourself**, your heritage and the extended family. You will be giving your child more rather than less, two languages and cultures rather than just one. As movement of peoples around the world becomes more possible with ease of communications, more likely with economic inter-relationships between countries, so there will be an increasing need for people who can move with ease between countries, adapt to different cultures, make bridges and break down social and economic barriers. Bilinguals are well equipped for such roles.

C19 My second language is not perfect. Should I speak it to my child?

This is a difficult question. It really depends on how perfect or imperfect your second language is. One thing is for sure. If you are a bad **model** of language for your child, you should not speak that language to the child. It would be better to speak your first language to the child. If a child begins to learn incorrect linguistic structures, wrong pronunciation or inexact expression from you speaking a second language, you may be undermining rather than helping the child's language development. Instead, consider speaking the first language to your child knowing that many skills and competences learned in the first language (e.g. ideas, meanings, concepts) transfer easily to the second language.

A second answer is that if you need to speak the second language to the child, why not try to avail yourself of language **practice** to improve your language or attend adult classes? If you feel there is a problem with your second language, why not try to reduce that problem rather than pass the problem on to the child?

A third answer is that the language you speak to the child, particularly when the child is young, may be at the level where correctness is relatively assured. It may be that incorrectness or perceived imperfectness in the second language occurs only when speaking to adults who expect complex grammatical structures and a wide use of vocabulary. In speaking to young children, there is often a simplification of both grammatical structure and vocabulary. So it may be that you have **sufficient language competence** to be a valuable model to the child. Parents may grow in a language along with the child. In that case, the problem is not in language but in your anxiety. As adults, there is still language development and language learning. In middle age there is growing confidence in communication, new vocabulary learnt, more subtle meanings attached to words. Language learning does not stop until death.

A fourth answer is that the language situation of the family and neighborhood. Take two examples. First, a parent speaks a second language to a child in an extended family or neighborhood where that language is used daily. The child has plenty of language models and experiences to improve his or her language. In this case, the parent should have little or no problems in the bilingual development of the child. Second, a parent speaks a second language in a vacuum. Almost nobody else speaks that second language in the locality. In such language isolation, the child may find it difficult to develop age-appropriate competence in that language.

The reality is that it is very difficult for most mothers (and fathers) to speak a second language to their child. It feels restrictive and frustrating. The wealth of wise colloquial sayings, family stories, local jokes and colorful tales, are all stored and can only be authentically conveyed in the first or mother tongue. The transmission of the parents' heritage is best recounted in the mother tongue. That storage of experience in the mother tongue from birth to parenthood seems of low worth if a second language is used with the child.

One example of the pay-off for a parent using a minority language is when the children are in their teenage years. If a language minority mother or father has ignored their first language and speaks the majority language to her children, problems can arise. The majority language may be spoken with a 'foreign' accent, the language used may be perceived by the teenager as incorrect. One outcome is that the teenager is embarrassed, the parent mocked and held in disdain, and the minority language hated. If such a language minority mother speaks her minority language instead, she may retain more prestige and credibility, and be more respected by the teenager.

Adults who have learned a second language often don't learn the language of children in that language. They have no experience of the wonderful world of children in that second language. The appropriate expressions, the intimacy of personal expression may not be present in the second language. For this reason, many mothers and fathers naturally use their first language with their child.

C20 A local professional (e.g. a doctor, psychologist, speech therapist, teacher) advised me against bilingualism. Is this correct?

Such negative advice occurs too often. Parents go to the doctor or to a teacher, and sometimes to a specialist such as a psychologist or speech therapist, and ask about problems with their bilingual children. The doctor or teacher is not usually trained to answer questions about bilingual children. Yet the parent expects the doctor or teacher to be sufficiently professional and skilled to give an expert, highly informed judgement on the situation. Too often, well meaning doctors and teachers tend to reflect in their answers the prejudices and beliefs of much of the public.

Much of the public view is a **monolingual view** — historical and outdated. Such advice is contrary to current research, contrary to expert opinion and contrary to informed debate about bilingualism. All too often, such professionals tend to advise against bilingualism. To them, it is more natural for a child to be monolingual. Learning two languages would seem to exacerbate problems, seem to provide more worries, more of a chance for failure in language development, educational development, identity formation and community integration. As well meaning, as honest and professional as these people are, they are not the ones to consult about bilingual problems. Just as one would not consult a doctor, psychologist, speech therapist or teacher about gardening, growing seeds, use of different fertilizers, watering and pruning, so in the language growth of children. These are not the professionals to consult.

If local **expertise** is sought, it may be found in the local linguistics department of a university or college, among specialist language teachers, amongst those in education specializing in bilingualism and bilingual education, among psychologists who have a special interest in languages or bilingualism, among teachers who have followed courses on bilingualism and bilingual education, and increasingly amongst speech therapists who have taken a course in bilingualism as part of their studies.

Also, if advice is sought about bilingualism, have a look at the **references at the end of this book** for further information. These references provide expert opinions and share information from recent decades of international research into bilingualism.

Section D
Reading and Writing Questions

D1 Should my child learn to read in one language first?

There are cases of children learning to read two languages **simultaneously**. These cases tend to be the exception rather than the rule. Simultaneous dual language reading acquisition from the start is less customary, but still provides a successful route to biliteracy. The more common route is for the child to learn to read in one language first, and learn to read in the second language a little later. **Sequential** rather than simultaneous learning to read in two languages tends to be the norm, and tends to have more successful case histories. This route is preferable when one language is stronger than the other.

When sequential learning to read and write is adopted, it is important in a **language minority** context that the stronger language is used. This will usually build on the child's stronger first (minority) language competence, aid the child's motivation and develop more positive attitudes to literacy. Developing literacy in a child's weaker language is often attempted with in-migrant children. For example, a Spanish-speaking in-migrant in the United States will be taught to read in the majority language of the country — English. Less success and slower development will usually occur than if the child is taught to read in the stronger language (Spanish) first.

In a **language majority** context, children sometimes learn to read in their second language. For example, in Canada, children from English-speaking homes take their early years of education through French. Hence, they may learn to read in French first, and English a little later. This usually results in fully biliterate children. Learning to read in French first will not impede later progress in learning to read English.

Learning to read starts the day a child is born. Learning to read does not start when the child is three to seven years of age. Listening and speaking is a necessary **preparation for learning to read**. The vocabulary and language structures acquired in learning to talk are an essential foundation for reading. As soon as the child becomes aware of toys, it is time for the child to have some simple books to play with. As early as possible, the child needs the concept of a book and to value books in the home. Early in life a child can learn that a book has pictures and objects that are later understood as words. As parents move through the child's first year, it is time to start nursery rhymes and relay pithy sayings. By the time a child has reached the end of the first year, consider starting to read simple books to him or her. Children may not understand every word in the book. They will often understand the story line. They are learning that books are fun and that reading is a pleasure.

Reading can be encouraged before a child can read a single letter. As **parents** read to the very young child, they can gently hold a child's finger and show the movement of the words across the page from left to right, in a rhythmical sequence. As favorite books are read night after night, a child will begin to recognize certain words and begin to associate meaning and word form. How many parents have laughed aloud when a young child picks up a book and pretends to read, having memorized some of the words on the page? How delighted are both the child and the parents at this competence in literacy at a rudimentary stage! The child is learning to love books, to love stories and to associate the printed word with competence and pleasure.

If it feels normal and natural, books in both languages can be introduced at an early age. Developing literacy in both languages simultaneously works best when both languages are relatively well developed. Again, as in oral language, **boundaries** are helpful. If a father reads to the child in his language and the mother in her language, the child will understand the separation and compartmentalization of languages. (This hints that, to the extent that languages can be separated, learning to read in two languages at the same time is viable.) But generally, one language tends to be the initial focus of reading activity within a house and the school.

One of the exciting things about biliteracy is that children's development in **reading in the second language is greatly helped by their learning to read in the first language**. Simply stated, there is much transfer between the first and the second language when learning to read. For example, if a child learns to read in English first, and later learns to read in French, the child does not have to begin to learn to read all over again when tackling French books or writing in French. Many reading skills (and attitudes) are simply transferred from one language to the next. For example, there is transfer of: learning to recognize that letters mean sounds, decoding words as parts and wholes, making sensible guesses at words given the storyline, decoding the meaning of sentences from a string of words, and moving left to right across the page. These are not the only transfers that take place, as answers to later questions in this section will reveal.

I have tried in this book not to relate personal experiences in case they are particular or idiosyncratic. However, one of our children learned first to read in Welsh. Most books in his bedroom were Welsh language books. The policy was to establish, first of all, firm growth in minority language literacy. At the age of seven, and not an exceptional child, he picked up a book written in English at bedtime and began reading it. In sheer amazement, his mother called the family to the bedroom. With very little experience of English reading books, he moved across the page, sometimes decoding correctly, sometimes guessing and gambling. After finishing the book, we questioned him, and he revealed a fine understanding of the storyline. His learning to read words in Welsh (which has many sounds of letters different from English), plus an ability to speak English fairly fluently, prepared him to read in English. Within a year, there was almost no difference in his ability to read English or Welsh books. Many skills learned in one language had transferred to the other. This true story illustrates the idea that **learning to read in one language facilitates reading in a second language**.

Learning to read fluently, reading ever more complex books, reading independently, and learning to read critically takes **time**. Literacy skills do not occur in either language overnight but grow steadily and slowly through middle and later childhood, even into adulthood. Learning to read in one or two languages is a continuous, **gradual** development that extends to the teenage years and well beyond.

Learning to read in the second language is valuable for the development of that language. For example, reading in a second language will extend the vocabulary of that language and improve correct grammatical structuring of that language. Second language **reading develops speaking skills**, particularly when experience of that second language is not extensive. Second language reading also develops writing skills in that second language

Reading fluently has been increasingly essential this century. Reading is a way of acquiring new vocabulary and different language structures. It expands the ways of communicating within a family and in school. Reading provides a means of acquiring information and expanding horizons, manipulating and assimilating experience. It helps the development of new concepts, new ideas, encouraging empathy, enculturation and identity. Reading may also keep a language alive within an individual when there is a lack of opportunity to speak that language.

D2 Will learning to read in a second language interfere with reading in the first language?

Generally, learning to read in one language does not interfere with learning to read in a second language — rather the opposite. Learning to read in one language is preparing the ground for learning to read in a second language. However, just as in learning to speak there is some mixing of words in a sentence, so with reading. A child may read a French word with English pronunciation, say a German word as if it is spelt in English. The irregularities of the English language can so easily pose initial difficulties to those who learn to read in a language that is phonic (where the sounds of individual letters and two or three letters together have standard sounds). Just as with oral language there is a steady movement away from language mixing to language compartmentalization, so with reading. Over time, a child learns that, for example, similar spellings in two languages can have different pronunciations.

A child learns over time the irregularities of pronunciation of words in another language. As will be expressed later in this section, there are preferable ways of teaching children reading to make it pleasurable, fun and relevant. When reading merely becomes an exercise, a learning or bedtime chore, reading in both languages is discouraged. When reading is made an enjoyable experience, reading in both languages is being encouraged.

Focusing on the pleasure of reading highlights an important point. Reading is not just decoding sounds from pages of print. Learning to read is not just pronouncing letters, combinations of letters and words correctly. Such decoding skills are a means to an end, and must not be an end in themselves. The purpose of reading is to extract **meaning** from the page. Learning to read is learning to struggle to understand the message on the page. Reading is **making sense** of words, phrases, sentences, chapters and whole books.

Learning to extract meaning and sense from a page is a skill in itself. Guessing meaning, successfully struggling to understand the story is something that is learned and adults need to encourage. When a child learns such a 'making sense' strategy in reading, this **transfers** to reading in another language. The ability to understand the meaning of text, learned when reading in one language, becomes available when learning to read in a second language.

D3 If the two languages have different scripts, will learning to read and write be a problem?

A typical question is about whether two languages with totally different scripts make it harder for a child to read and write in those two languages. For example, English and Arabic have two very different scripts, similarly Chinese and French. Learning to read in a different script is still aided by learning to read in the first language. The act of character recognition, associating marks on page with sounds and meanings, the strategy of sensible guessing, still transfer. However, there is **less transfer** of skills in learning to read in two very different scripts. The child may have to learn to move in different directions, recognize totally different symbols, different constructions (as in Chinese and English), and different presentations in books.

In the less cluttered brains of children, learning two different scripts can be made enjoyable, valuable and pleasurable. If children are aware that they are learning an important competence, their motivation may be heightened and their attitude made favorable. Children do **successfully learn** to read and write in two totally different scripts. The main difference is that there will be less transfer compared with two similar scripts.

D4 When should a child begin to read in a second language?

Reading does not begin at the age of five, six or seven. Reading begins in the first year of life. If materials in both languages are available for the child to hold and glance through, and if books are read to the child in both languages, biliteracy is encouraged before a child begins to decode words on a page. The enjoyment of books begins when the child is in the first year of life. As children enter the nursery years, their enjoyment of books grows, their **curiosity** is aroused and they begin to handle books more and more. By the ages of four to seven, a child is usually beginning to read in one language, occasionally two.

During those first four or five years, there is no reason why books should not be available to a child in both languages. If parents decide to encourage reading in two languages at once, this will often occur around the ages four to six. If, on the other hand, parents decide to introduce one reading language first, the second language may be introduced around age seven or later.

This **sequential** (rather than simultaneous) **strategy** is to encourage children to read in one language first and feel a growing competence in reading. When children start to read by themselves, they seem able to begin to read in a second language or begin to write in a different script. The key factor is that reading and writing must be a pleasure to the child. It is important to induce a long-term positive attitude to books and reading from the start. It is this love of reading and love of books that is crucial in the long-term development of literacy in both languages. Skills in reading are a necessary launch pad. Having reading skills does not ensure the journey continues or the destination is reached.

D5 How should I help my child to read and write in both languages?

Reading and writing need to be fun experiences. This occurs when reading and writing involve real and natural events, not artificial stories, artificial sequences rules of grammar and spelling, or stories that are not relevant to the child's experience. Reading and writing need to be interesting, relevant to the child, belonging to the **child's experience**, allowing choice by the learner, giving children power and understanding of their world. Reading taught for its own sake is not fun. Going through a book of writing exercises following reading is not usually interesting or relevant to the child.

Children learn to read and write when there is a need to understand the **meaning** of a story, to chant a rhyme, to share the humor of a book. Writing is fun when it is **communication**. When reading and writing is contrived, when the form of words is put before their function, neither reading nor writing is encouraged. Reading and writing need to provide opportunities for shared language and shared meaning. A series of books that is based on how often words occur in a language, that tries very exactly to grade difficulty, moving from one level to another level slowly, might seem logical and sensible. Yet such books tend to have artificial stories, senseless language constructions and do not match nor cultivate the child's experience.

Children need imaginative, vivid, interesting books that both relate to, and increase their experience, which make them laugh and stir their **imagination**. They need to feel that books are interesting, unstuffy, relevant to their world and their way of thinking. Children don't just need books on the shelf. Magazines and newspapers, directories and posters, signs in the street, packages and labels are all reading material. Children writing to each other (or to their grandparents in another country) are both valuable and authentic reading and writing activities. The rules of reading and writing are latently being taught.

Some homes and classrooms are full of literacy. Not just storing neat books on tidy shelves. There are words in the kitchen, on posters inside the child's bedroom, examples of the child's writing up on the wall, pictures and writing (professional and made by the child) to demonstrate literacy and its value. Children derive considerable pleasure from writing their own simple little books with lots of pictures. Isolating skill sequences, slicing up reading and writing into ages and stages, each slice neatly following and dependent on prior ones, simplifying texts by controlling their sentence structures and vocabulary, solely concentrating on sub skills, isolating reading and writing from each other and constantly highlighting a child's difficulties or problems is not how children best learn to read. Advertisements in subways and metros, texts and inscriptions in church, street signs and billboards, teletext and sports pages in the newspaper, are all ways in which children learn to read naturally.

Children learn to read by **constructing meaning** from books. They use their prior learning and experience to make sense of texts. Readers predict, select, self-correct as they seek to make sense out of print. They guess, sometimes wrongly, sometimes correctly. They monitor their reading to make sense of the print. Learning to read means struggling to make sense, because finding meaning is the purpose of reading. There is little intrinsically enjoyable in simply making the right sounds or writing with correct spellings. Reading and writing is about communication of meaning.

A child learns to write when they are writing for somebody with a **purpose** and a message. Efficient writing means making it comprehensible for an audience. Constantly highlighting grammatical and spelling errors is soul destroying for the child. Corrections concentrate on form and not function, on the medium and not the message. Conveying meaning is important in learning to write well. Learning to read is also learning to write. A child learns to spell when learning to read. The more children read, the more their writing improves.

In **school**, particularly with average and above average children, some discussion of grammar and spelling can accelerate language development. But this should not destroy the reason for writing and reading — which is communication of meaning. At school, there is a place for correction, consideration of the form of oral and written languages. There is less place for such a formal approach at home. In the home, language is usually a means and not an end, a vehicle and not a goal.

Artificial exercises, reading single words aloud or spelling different words in a test-like situation is not real and authentic language practice. While teachers valuably provide short bursts on irregular spellings, reading difficult words, or particular grammatical constructions, and while these make efficient learning for many children, these must not become the central focus of reading and writing.

There is an analogy with a musician. It is the overall musical performance that is important. Sometimes there is a need to practice scales (octaves), arpeggios, or trills as a separate skill to improve the overall standard of musicianship. Accurately playing scales is not a musical performance. More important is the overall combination of accurate playing, interpretation of a musical score, creating an ambience with a piece of music and communicating with the listener. Similarly with reading and writing. Sometimes a teacher will concentrate on specific skills (e.g. irregular words, punctuation, spelling, grammar). Specific skills are not reading or writing. The overall activity needs to be the central focus.

Reading and writing is about enjoyable participation and risk taking. It is important to use a child's internal motivation for wanting to read and wanting to write. Giving rewards has little place in learning to read other than the natural encouragement of parent and teacher. Punishment and constant **correction** has little place. For the parent, there can be great value in discussing reading with the child. Asking the child imaginative and creative questions stimulates both reading and speaking competences. Parents can discuss a book with the child and discuss the child's writing.

Developing competence in **writing** is **slower** than learning to read. At the start, the child's composition may simply involve dictating a letter to the parent who then reads it back to the child. Where word-processors exist in the family, a child may quickly learn to use the computer to enhance the look of the finished product. In writing (as in reading), it is important to build a pupil's level of self-confidence and encourage risk taking. Expressing ideas is initially more important than perfect spelling. At the beginning, a child's writing in either language will have so many spelling errors and be so minimal that even the child may not be able to understand what they have written. Vowels will be left out and words not distinguished from each other.

However, developing writers quickly realize that **spelling** is crucial for understanding. The more pupils read and write, the less spelling mistakes tend to occur. Research suggests that, with only a few exceptions, children's misspellings are on words they write or read infrequently. With increasing reading and writing experience, spelling errors decrease — although (as with adults) rarely completely.

When children learn to read and write, they begin to develop a sense of where to **punctuate**. In reading back their writing, they often become aware of where commas and full stops are needed by self-monitoring. When children make mistakes in reading and writing, it is valuable for the child to **self-correct**. For example, ask the child to read the word again, or respell the word. If an error still occurs, the parent needs to point to the correct form where it occurs on a page. However, when there is constant correction, a child is learning the notes, but not the song. A delicate balance needs striking between reading the score and singing the song.

Parents can help their children to **enjoy writing** in two languages. Writing is essentially communication with someone else. We write to convey messages, persuade, make friends, express individuality, to question, explore, exercise the imagination, entertain, record events and for many other reasons. In writing, we reflect more deeply, learn to organize our thoughts and ideas, share our meanings and our understanding of the world with others.

Compare these aims of writing with parents and teachers who ask children to copy out a passage from a book in their best handwriting. Or when reading a child's writing, spelling errors are the main focus of feedback, alongside comments about neatness. Or the child is given a picture unrelated to their experience and asked to write one sentence underneath. In these examples, the wrong emphasis is given. While spelling and tidiness are important, neither constitute writing.

Parents can help a child learn to write in both languages, before going to school and while at elementary and secondary school. The following list presents some ideas and suggestions. Cooperating with teachers is also very important.

(1) In **Stage 1**, children initially write lots of squiggles over a page. There may be some letters, but there is much drawing that doesn't relate to adult forms of writing. Be proud, accepting and encouraging. The child has realized that writing exists, and there are varied shapes. Writing has begun.

(2) In **Stage 2**, children will write real letters from an alphabet, and increasingly words. However, children will usually be unable to read these back. Children expect the parent to be able to read and understand. Such children have become aware that writing means conveying a message with meaning. Try to make sense of the text by reading it back to the child. Discuss what was written so the act of writing is seen as a sociable, pleasurable event. Encourage by sincere and measured praise.

(3) In **Stage 3**, children move towards adult forms of writing. They reflect, write in increasingly understandable forms and convey meaning more exactly. Children learn to write in different styles and for different audiences.

(4) Initially, there are many spelling, grammatical and other structural **errors**. Try not to focus on errors at the expense of the meaning of the writing. Few adults are perfect spellers, yet unrealistically expect perfection from children at an early age. Able readers are often poor spellers. Such readers focus on the meaning of what they read rather than the form of each word. As a general rule, only focus on one or two or three errors at a time. Select what seems appropriate to the child's needs. Concentrate on what the child has almost got right and what will be used again. These corrections are more likely to be remembered.

(5) Give your children their own private notepad(s) to use as they wish. **Vary what the child writes** in the home: for example, helping to compose a shopping list, writing and rewriting a favorite family story together, writing a recipe to cook together later, keeping a diary, writing in a photo album that records family experiences, poetry, imaginative or personal stories, and writing jokes and cartoons.

(6) Ensure the child has the opportunity to read and write in the **minority or heritage language**. Parents can write with their children the important wise sayings, folk tales, family history, and funny and important incidents told by previous generations and the extended family. A self-made, treasured family book can be jointly produced. The past celebrated in the present; the contemporary recreated in the writing of the child.

D6 Which approach to teaching reading works best? The 'whole language' approach, phonics, 'look and say' or what approach?

The **look and say** approach suggests that children should learn to read and write whole words. For example, children are encouraged to focus on and remember the shape of a whole word (e.g. 'shop'). Words that are useful in everyday life are often accented (called Social Sight words, e.g. 'pay here', 'wet paint', 'subway'). Also accented are essential words that are phonically irregular (e.g. 'the', 'he', 'she', 'to', 'that'). Words that a pupil has difficulty with and constantly gets wrong are sometimes taught in this way (e.g. using home-made 'flashcards' where the word on card is 'flashed up' in front of the child). Generally, this method is not used by itself. It depends mostly on visual memory and can leave the child without the skills of 'decoding' longer and harder words and the ability to build a vocabulary of new words.

The **phonics** approach encourages children to break down the parts of the word into their separate sounds. For example, the word 'shop' has three sounds: 'sh' forms one sound; the letter 'o' another sound, and the letter 'p' a third sound. The phonics approach teaches children the sounds associated with different consonants and consonantal blends and vowels. Children then piece together each word to create its overall sound. The teaching of phonics has to avoid repetitive drills. Rather, phonics need to be taught in a fun way, through rhymes and games, for example. Some children learn to read fluently without being taught phonics. Other children rely so heavily on getting phonics correct that story meaning and enjoyment is lost. Most children are taught phonics as part of their reading repertoire. Successful, early readers tend to have phonic 'decoding' skills. The strategy of phonic analysis easily transfers from one language to another.

Both 'look and say' and 'phonics' approaches are 'skills approaches' to reading and writing. Both approaches tend to see developing reading and writing as a set sequence of hoops a child has to go through. Reading and writing are seen as constructed of independent skills that can be learnt in relative isolation.

To illustrate, a typical sequence (but not style) of teaching phonics in English is given below:

(1) Learning to recognize the **letters of the alphabet**, in upper and lower case, their names, letter sounds, initial sounds at the start of a word, their sounds at the end of a word.

(2) **Initial consonant blends** that occur at the start of words: e.g. **plod, split**

Two letters: pl fr dr pr tr sk cr br sn cl gr gl sp fl bl sw sm sc st qu sl tw

Three letters: spl squ spr str scr shr

(3) **Final consonant blends** that occur at the end of words : e.g. ra**mp**

mp st nk lt nd sp nt ng sk lp ld

(4) **Silent 'e' words** e.g. rud**e**, fat**e**, ev**e**

u_e, a_e, i_e, o_e, e_e

(5) **Vowel digraphs e.g. cow**

ow oe ar ew ou aw ue oo er ay ie ea ee ur oa au ai oy ir or oi

(6) **Consonant digraphs** e.g. **wh**ip

wh ch th sh ph tch shr thr sch

(7) **Silent letters** e.g. **g**nat , **k**not, **k**now

g k w u h b gh l t

(8) **Word endings** e.g. pict**ure**, vog**ue**, miss**ion**

ure ue ion ble cle fle ple sle y ge tion sion ed ous re

A phonic approach is often used to teach English 'decoding' skills, (although over a third of English words are phonically irregular). Different languages will use different approaches to teaching 'decoding' skills. For example, a different strategy for teaching the 'decoding' of Spanish is used (i.e. a decoding of syllables). Such 'decoding' approaches, if used exclusively, sometimes result in a child reading without understanding. A child may recognize words and pronounce them correctly without comprehension. This is highly unsatisfactory and points to the need to move beyond a 'decoding' approach.

The **whole language approach** emphasizes learning to read and write naturally, for enjoyment and purpose, for meaningful communication and for inherent pleasure. In the last question, a whole language approach was given in much of the answer to the question.

Generally, the **whole language approach** supports an holistic and integrated learning of reading, writing, spelling and oracy. The language used must have relevance and meaning to the child. The use of language for communication is stressed; the function rather than the form of language. The whole language approach is against basal readers and phonics (see above) in learning to read. Basal readers are reading books that use simplified vocabulary. There is often a set order in reading these books, moving from simple to more complex text in a gradually increasing gradient of difficulty. In a whole language approach, writing must be for real purposes. A child writes for somebody in a particular situation and for a defined reason. Writing means reflecting on one's ideas and sharing meaning with others. Writing can be in partnership with others, involving drafting and redrafting.

There are simple teaching strategies that can be used by parents (in addition to those discussed already in this section). Such strategies use important ideas from different approaches to **reading**. Three examples of strategies follow.

(1) Try to develop a 'sight' vocabulary first. For example, locate a child's favorite and often used words (e.g. fish, ice cream, teddy, granny). Using pictures alongside these whole words, encourages the child to recognize and read these words. A sense of achievement will be felt by the child. It does not matter if the words are in two languages. It matters that the words are important to the child. A phonic approach is best introduced after the child has a small but central 'sight' vocabulary. This 'start up' vocabulary is the raw material on which a child can breakdown words into their sound components. Phonic analysis of words will be more interesting to the child if they operate on personal words.

(2) Get your child to talk about an experience. One or more short sentences (or later, a story) is written down on card. A copy of the sentence is cut up and reconstructed by the child. The same activity is used later with sentences that need putting into a logical order. The activity centers on the child's own words and existing experiences to stimulate interest and motivation. Discuss the process with the child throughout the activity.

(3) Children are given a story (especially to do with their own experience or something from their parent's past) with words missing. They are asked to guess the missing words and write them in the text. This is called 'cloze procedure' or 'context cuing' and encourages comprehension and reading independence. Make the activity enjoyable.

One current line of advice for parents is to **combine** a whole language approach with a phonics approach. Making reading and writing enjoyable, varied and authentic seems the best strategy in the home — and very natural to that environment. Many teachers avoid a single approach and are eclectic in their reading and writing methods. Teachers sometimes veer away from solely concentrating on a whole language approach. Many teachers provide direct instruction on the reading and writing of particular words, sentence construction and grammar. A **combination** of a whole language, phonics and a structured element to language is an efficient and valuable way of accelerating learning. Teaching children phonically is possible in the home. Many parents naturally break down words into component parts to help a child read increasingly difficult writing. A phonic approach helps a child read the music; a whole language approach helps the notes come alive, and the sound of the music to resonate in the child.

Parents who listen to their children read are engaging in a most valuable activity. Both before the child goes to school and while in the early school years, reading with a child should be part of an evening ritual. Passive listening needs avoiding. **Parents** can do three things to make reading active. (1) Elaborate and explain the text to the child. This extends and deepens the experience of the story. (2) Relate the story to the child's own experiences. Interest in reading, understanding of the ideas and meanings of the text, and enculturation all occur if there is 'further information'. (3) Ask questions to ensure the child understands the story, thinks about the characters and plot, and extends their imagination.

One key aim for parents is to help their children become **independent readers** in both languages. Independent readers can monitor and correct themselves, search for cues and clues to make sense of unknown words and whole sentences.

D7 Should I buy books for my child to read that contain two languages or just one language?

Most books in bilingual homes will be in one language or the other. However, there are a few books on the market where one side of the page is in one language, and the other side of the page is an exact content replica, but in a different language. For example, a Spanish language story book may have Spanish on the left hand side with an English translation on the right hand side. These books may be of some value for parents who, for example, are listening to a child reading in Spanish but cannot understand Spanish themselves.

For the child however, there will be little interest in reading both pages. Having read the Spanish language version, there is no need to read the English version. Having understood the story, reading the English version is a mere exercise without much intrinsic value. The child ends up reading half the book rather than the whole book.

D8 How can I locate books for my child to read in each language?

This question is often posed by parents for whom one language used in the home is not spoken in the region. For example, how does the Finnish mother living in England acquire sufficient reading material for her children to develop literacy in Finnish as well as English? A family can build up a **resource** of reading material in a particular language. When visiting on holidays, when relatives visit, by requests to those back in the native country to send material, it is possible to build up a store of material for children of different ages.

It is valuable to try to locate other parents in a similar situation. Are there other mothers or fathers of the same language origins nearby or in neighboring areas? Is it possible to exchange books by visiting other parents or by post? This will ensure a circulating library of material in a particular language. There is much strength in developing a **community**, not necessarily geographically close, whereby **experiences, materials and resources are shared and exchanged**. Not only does this provide support for literacy development, but also psychological, emotional and educational help within a group of like-minded people.

In some minority languages, finding suitable literature for children is difficult. The literature is sometimes scarce, sometimes mostly for adults, sometimes old-fashioned. Especially in the teenage years, children in such situations may prefer to read majority language books. One partial solution can be offered. Parents can write books in the minority language for the younger child — especially containing family stories. The traditions and culture of the family can be conveyed in such home-produced books

D9 Will my child find it hard to write in two different languages?

Writing skills tend to develop later than reading skills. Given sufficient stimulation, encouragement and practice, there is little reason why children should not become literate in the written form in both languages. However writing is a harder skill to develop than listening and speaking. Whereas children often become readers in two languages, writing well in two languages tends to be a more difficult and **advanced** skill.

The development of biliteracy skills to fruition often requires **bilingual education** and not simply the education available in the home. Since reading and particularly writing develop through middle and late childhood into the teenage years, school often plays an important role in such biliteracy development. Parents of bilingual children do not always have access to such bilingual education. In such cases, literacy development in a second language takes place at home. Saturday and Sunday schools and religious instruction are alternative routes to biliteracy.

Studies of bilingual education show that it is possible for children to develop writing skills in both languages. Where primary and secondary schools encourage this, it is a natural extension of dual language listening and speaking skills. However, fewer bilinguals become fluent writers in two languages than fluent speakers.

D10 My child seems slow in learning to read. Is this due to bilingualism?

The answer is no. Not all children learn to read at the same age. Some are quicker than others in learning to read. If your child is slow learning to read, this is very unlikely to have anything to do with bilingualism. Certainly, interest in learning to read is important. The child's readiness to read, the need to decode symbols on pages is important. Having an encouraging atmosphere in the home and the school for reading to develop is also very important. Bilingualism has nothing to do with any of these situations.

The only slight possibility of bilingualism connecting with the speed of learning to read is when a child's negative **attitude** to languages, or a **lack of progress** in **either language** has occurred. This is very rare. If the child has learned to despise the minority language, learning to read in the minority language may become problematic. If the language stimulation of the home is so inadequate that a child's language skills are well behind peers, learning to read may come later rather than earlier. Where parents have developed a positive attitude to language learning and to reading and writing, bilingualism will have no relationship to the speed of learning to read.

D11 My child has problems with spelling. Is this due to bilingualism?

A frequent worry of parents is that learning to write in one language will interfere with learning to write in another language. Spellings in one language seem **imitated** when writing the second language. This is only a temporary stage that is ironed out as experience of reading and writing grows. If there are constant **spelling errors** (with dyslexia excepted), the primary cause is likely to be anxiety, a lack of reading and writing practice, a lack of stimulating reading and writing, rather than anything to do with bilingualism.

In the short term, there may be some transfer of spellings from one language to the other. From the child's point of view, this is creatively using their knowledge and experience to make headway in writing the second language. A child is making an intelligent, imaginative and thoughtful guess at spelling in the second language. This is sensible and **adaptive** behavior. As increased reading and increased writing in the second language occurs, the child learns to separate spellings in both languages. Few adults are perfect in their spelling, and bilinguals will be no different. Bilinguals are no better or worse spellers because of their bilingualism than monolinguals.

Section E
Education Questions

BASIC EDUCATION QUESTIONS

E1 How can a nursery school support children's bilingualism?

The answer to this question will only center on the language aspects of nursery schools. It will not discuss the possible benefits of nursery education in general. It is initially important to highlight situations where it may not be wise to send a child to a nursery school. If the family is attempting to raise the child in the minority language, and the nursery school runs through the medium of the majority language, parents need to make a careful decision about when to introduce the majority language. Many parents in **minority language situations** prefer to send their children to minority language nursery schools. If the minority language is in danger of extinction and in need of maintenance in the community, parents may wish their children to develop in the minority language before introducing the majority language. In such minority language situations, it is quite feasible to introduce the majority language as late as six or seven years of age with the child becoming fluent in that language within two to five years.

Most children in **minority language** situations have little difficulty in acquiring the majority language. The majority language surrounds them in the mass media, as the common denominator in the street and playground, and as the dominant cultural medium in the teenage years. In a minority language situation, it is therefore quite usual for parents to wish to send their children to nursery schools using that minority language. Such nursery schools reinforce and extend the language development of the home.

If education through the minority language is not available to language minority parents, there is a danger in sending the child to a majority language nursery school. Exposure to the majority language at an early age may decrease the chances of the minority language retaining a strong place in the child's language life. Consideration needs giving to deferring entry to such a majority language nursery school. Alternatives that will ensure the minority language is experienced fully in these formative years include: keeping the child at home, registered childminders, mother and toddler playgroups and a group of carers meeting on an *ad hoc* basis.

A different situation occurs when a **majority language** parent wants the nursery school to help a child learn a **second**, minority or majority **language**. In Wales, for example, there are preschool playgroups, mother and toddler group, and nursery schools where children from English language backgrounds attend (alongside Welsh speakers) and acquire the Welsh language. Through playing with other children, organized games and activities, simple learning experiences, playing with sand and water, words and numbers, children in a nursery school situation can easily and successfully pick up the basics of a second language. Depending on how many hours are spent in the nursery school, a child is likely to develop a good understanding of a second language. Speaking the second language fluently will come later than understanding.

Where fewer hours are spent in the nursery, speaking may blossom later in the primary (elementary) school. However, an ability to **understand** a second language achieved at nursery school is an invaluable foundation for later blossoming in the primary school. Sometimes in this situation, parents find the nursery school seems to achieving little second language development success. They expect fluent speakers too soon. If such schools enable children to understand a second language, parents will find that primary education transforms passive understanding into active speaking quite quickly.

When children spend most of their time in a nursery school, understanding and speaking may both develop well. In an effective nursery school where children spend much of the day, and where adult language stimulation is well planned and delivered, fluency in a second language is possible. Such an immersion language situation is advantageous in producing a bilingual child.

In such a situation, the **majority language** of the home is **not at risk**. There will be sufficient exposure to the majority language in the home, in the outside environment, and later in formal schooling. Acquiring a second language in a well organized and purposeful nursery school is usually straightforward and enjoyable. An early and valuable foundation is laid for bilingualism. Preschool playgroups and nursery schools that are relaxed yet purposeful provide a context where children acquire a second language in a hidden and thorough manner.

E2 Should my child go to a bilingual school?

Where parents have a **choice** of schooling, and this is not always the case, a **variety of factors need considering** when choosing an appropriate school for a child. The language (or languages) used in the school is an important part of that decision. Language should not be the only factor. Schools which support children's bilingualism range from the excellent, to the good, to the tolerable, and include the bad. A bilingual school is no guarantee of an effective or successful school. The ethos of the school, the commitment of the teachers, the success of the school in achieving literacy and numeracy, creativity in the expressive arts, a sound scientific foundation, moral and religious development, a well integrated and harmonious relationship between pupils, good cooperation with parents are just some of the factors that parents need to consider in deciding upon a suitable school.

In inquiring about the **language policy of the school**, it is important to hunt down the real language goals of the school. Schools are increasingly good at self-publicity, broadcasting missionary aims with regard to language and other policies. **Visits to classrooms**, careful questioning of the Headteacher, Principal, School Administrator, and/or other teachers will reveal the language economy of the school, the language reality and what a school actually achieves rather than what it says it hopes to achieve.

Some schools have a **language policy** that encourages bilingualism. Yet close inspection reveals only a token use of the second language in the classroom. There are schools which broadcast themselves as having bilingualism as an aim yet only provide a shallow diet of half an hour language lessons per day. Other schools create linguistic and cultural diversity with ease and success, at no cost to their other aims and objectives.

Another situation is when there is **temporary bilingual support** given by the teacher or bilingual teacher helpers (sometimes called bilingual aides, auxiliaries or assistants). For example, in some schools in England, children from Asian language backgrounds use their home language for one or two years with the help of a bilingual aide in the classroom. A similar pattern occurs with some Spanish speakers in particular schools in the United States. Such schools may have a bilingual policy and may support bilingualism. However, the reality is that such schools aim for a quick transition from the Asian or Spanish language to working solely in the school language of English. Bilingualism is only temporarily supported for the child to feel 'at home' in the school. Children are soon encouraged not only in their development of English, but to operate solely in the curriculum in the English language. This is called transitional bilingual education and is considered in a separate question later.

In a **language minority situation**, the parent is likely to be interested in the minority language being present in the primary and the secondary school where possible. Sometimes called heritage language education, the aim of the school will be to support language development in the minority language. Literacy is encouraged in the minority language first. Around seven years of age, the majority language is likely to be introduced in the classroom. Once literacy in the minority language is well established, literacy in the second language — a majority language — soon develops. Generally, education through the minority language for a language minority child is the best option. A language minority child tends to be more successful in the curriculum than a similar child going to the majority language school. This will now be explained.

If the school supports the child's minority language, it is supporting the child itself, the child's home, the child's family and the child's heritage. Thereby, the school is maintaining the child's self-esteem and sense of self-confidence. If a child in a language minority situation is suddenly forced into using the majority language in school, their home, their parents and their self-image may be rejected. International research tends to show, in a variety of minority language situations, that **minority language children succeed better when educated through their minority language**. Such children still become fully bilingual and biliterate. A good heritage language bilingual school will ensure children can operate fluently and effectively in either language and become fully literate in both languages. Unless schools do this, they are not giving their children an equal chance of employment, economic advance and affluence in majority language dominated economies.

When children are raised in the **majority language at home**, a different policy can be adopted about bilingual education. One example is Canada. In many parts of Canada children who speak English in the home attend (from kindergarten onwards) schools that teach through the medium of French. Such schools are considered in more detail under a later question about **immersion bilingual education**. For the moment, children from majority language homes appear to be successful when **taught initially through a different majority language**. Eventually, such children are taught through both languages in the primary school. Through a gentle immersion at an early age in a second majority language, children become bilingual and biliterate with no loss to their academic performance. The essential point about such schools is that a child's home majority language is not replaced but added to (i.e. another majority language is gained). Children in such schools tend to start from the same basis — all are beginners in French.

A similar pattern is found with **majority language children taught through a minority language**. One example is Wales where increasing numbers of English-speaking parents opt to send their children to Welsh-medium primary and secondary schools. Particularly when such children start their education in Welsh at age four or five, their English language competence and curriculum performance does not suffer. Instead, they add a language and culture without cost to their home language and achievement in different school subjects.

The answer to this question has highlighted that a school may say it has a **policy of bilingualism**. Its real intentions, its effectiveness in producing bilingual and biliterate children, and typical outcomes in both languages need to be carefully assessed by parents. Some bilingual schools are really routes into majority language monolingualism. Schools which teach through the medium of the minority language and those that introduce majority language children to a second majority or a minority language are the ones where bilingualism and biliteracy is most cultivated. Some bilingual schools are usually effective because they have this extra commitment to children's language development. There is a mission and an extra *raison d'être* that permeates the school.

E3 What should I look out for in choosing a school for my bilingual child?

The answer to the previous question highlighted that it is important to seek out a school's bilingual policy and actual **use of languages throughout the curriculum**. Is one language only taught as a language for half an hour per day? Is one language only used to teach one subject such as Religious Education? How are two languages divided in teaching the curriculum? How are languages separated in the school? A good bilingual school will have a detailed and thorough policy regarding the development of two languages in the school and a policy about biliteracy. The school should have considered in detail the separation of the two languages inside the school curriculum and in the playground. Do teachers support the development of both languages — or is one language in reality given little status?

Another issue that needs considering is the **language balance amongst children** in the school. Part of language learning in the classroom and in the playground is the language interaction between children themselves. In primary school, when group work, project work, co-operation and discussion are particularly evident, and formal teaching by the teacher is much less evident than in the secondary schools, the **informal language of the classroom** needs to be considered. Do children constantly switch to a common denominator language such that the other language is insufficiently experienced in interaction between children?

Have a look at **displays of children's work** in different classrooms. Are both languages adequately represented on wall displays? Are the displays of children's work, posters, signs and information in the school monolingual, bilingual or multilingual? Have a look at the books and other language materials used in the classrooms. Is there an adequate supply of reading books, stimulating language materials, cassettes and work books to ensure that, by the latter stages of primary education, both languages will be well developed in terms of oracy and literacy?

Ask about the **examination** and **test results** of the school. There is a great danger of too narrowly focusing on exam results, test scores and school rankings in league tables. Such results are only one dipstick to measure a school. Many valuable aspects of a school evade simple exams and tests. Nevertheless, it is important to enquire about the language performance of the school in area-wide tests and exams. Can children follow both their languages to achieve 'passes' or graduation? Does the school encourage or allow children to take external exams for non-school languages (e.g. in Britain, Institute of Linguists exams for non-school languages such as Finnish)?

Ask about the **extra curricular activities** of the school. Will such activities support the child's bilingual development or lead to one language increasingly becoming dominant and preferred? In a minority language situation, is there provision for extra curricular activity through the minority language (e.g. competitions, dancing and singing festivals, discos that operate through the minority language)?

Try to determine the **partnerships that exist between teachers and parents**. In an effective school, there is a close working relationship between parents and teachers, times for discussion with parents about how to extend the child's education in the home. Effective schools aim for an integration of activity and purpose between home and school. This is important for an intercultural marriage (e.g. English–Finnish family). If a school understands the nature of an **intercultural family**, a child's self-esteem can be raised and dual cultural identity confirmed, even celebrated. Schools that are unable to support the child's home language (e.g. because only one child in the school speaks that language), should nevertheless have a positive attitude to the child's 'different' language. The bilingual nature of the child will be accepted, encouraged even celebrated in an effective school.

Bilingual schools will not have a bilingual policy just to support bilingualism or the maintenance of a minority language. They **support bilingualism because they support children**. Such schools are interested in the best interests of bilingual children. The ultimate language aims of the school must be the language interests of the child and not the fate of languages in society. A teacher once told me that she didn't teach through the medium of Welsh in the interests of the Welsh language and its future, but in the best interests of children. In bilingual education, such child centered aims must be paramount.

Language and education can pull in different directions. Every parent wants the standard of education for their children to be as high as possible. Among bilingual schools, monolingual schools and multilingual-speaking schools, there will be effective and less effective schools. Language is only one factor among many that makes a school valuable and effective.

The overall reputation and child-centered effectiveness of the school must be considered in a choice of school. The all-round accomplishment of the school is paramount over language (although language is a part of such success). Almost all parents would rather their child go to a stimulating and happy school than a school which is poorer in this respect but has a preferable language environment. A personal visit to the school and some 'intelligence gathering' is needed to make a sensible choice of schooling.

E4 Should my child be taught bilingually in the primary school but not in the secondary school?

Primary education often teaches children; secondary education often teaches subjects. While this is an exaggeration and an over-generalization, there is a grain of truth that has implications for the way parents view bilingual education. Some parents find it quite natural for their children to be educated bilingually in the **primary school** because such schools are often **child-centered**. There is curriculum time and an informal, pleasant atmosphere for language acquisition to occur in the primary school. The primary years seem a time when language acquisition is a higher priority compared with the demands of later secondary school examination success. Some parents therefore see the primary school as the ideal arena where a child's bilingualism flourishes.

Sometimes, the same parents have different ideas for **secondary education**. Secondary education is viewed as a time to become serious about **subject learning**, examination success and readiness for the employment market. During secondary education, both teachers and parents become increasingly interested in the child's achievement in Mathematics and Science, the majority language and Humanities. A second language becomes an examination subject. Bilingual development for some parents does not become so important during the secondary years. The goal is examination success, graduation, movement into college or university, opening up employment prospects and securing a school performance that places the child on the fast track to a relatively high quality of life.

In countries where bilingual education flourishes successfully at the primary level, too often educational administrators, politicians and parents find bilingualism and bilingual education a lower priority in secondary schooling. Nevertheless, in Spain, Wales and Canada, for example, there are research evaluations that show that bilingual secondary education can be effective in examination success and subject achievement for older children. One reason for bilingual secondary education is that it provides educational **language continuity** for the child. Having been taught through two languages to the end of primary education, it is quite sensible for the child to continue the primary school language pattern in the secondary school curriculum. Research tends to suggest that dual use of language in the secondary school curriculum will not have a negative effect on children's progress and later success. Indeed, there may be a slight gain to be made in achievement across the curriculum and, at the least, in securing a high standard in a second language.

Bilingual secondary schools often produce children whose bilingualism and biliteracy are both well developed. One requirement is that children enter secondary education with sufficient language competence to cope with the language level used by teachers and found in curriculum materials.

Another requirement in **language minority** situations is that schools have appropriate curriculum materials in the minority language. Quick translations from the majority language, poorly produced, photocopied worksheets and handouts are no substitute for professional, well thought out, high quality presentation, and modern curriculum materials in the minority language. This is expensive but fairly essential. Such language minority secondary schools sometimes resort out of apparent necessity to glossy, majority language curriculum resources. In this circumstance, the majority language is not only promoted at the expense of the minority language, the relative status of the two languages is also projected. The minority language is shown to be deprived and inferior. This is an international problem found in many minority language schools.

One barrier for parents in sending their children to bilingual secondary schools is that they may be unable to help children with their **homework**. Children whose two languages are both well developed often have little difficulty in translating to help parents understand the problem. The act of translating sometimes seems to help understanding. While it may take a little extra time to translate, the secondary school child and monolingual parent can interact and think through a homework problem together.

In addition, when both languages are well developed, there seems little problem in the secondary years of a child having **books** in both languages. Children in secondary education can have their textbooks in one language with parallel or similar textbooks in a second language also available. Therefore, in Mathematics and the Sciences, children can have access to explanations and illustrations in both languages. This seems to increase their probability of understanding and their depth of understanding.

Another objection by some bilingual parents to bilingual secondary schooling is that the language of universities and colleges is often a majority language. By the age of sixteen, seventeen and eighteen, bilingual children seem so fluent at switching between languages that they can relatively easily adapt to working at university or college in either language. So long as the language to be used at university has been well developed and there is the depth of vocabulary and complexity of linguistic structure required in **higher or tertiary education**, there is little reason a child cannot switch languages from school to college. The diversity of experience that bilingual students bring to tutorials and seminars only adds to the education experience for all.

E5 Should older children not be placed in bilingual education?

As children and parents move from one area to another, one region to another, so difficulties may arise in the language medium of the school. For example, when children are between the ages of seven and sixteen, and their language has not developed sufficiently to allow them easy entry into the language used in the curriculum of the school, what alternatives exist?

For **language minority children**, when there is a choice between attending a minority language or majority language school, wise parents will usually opt for the minority language school. For a language minority child to switch suddenly to working in the majority language in the curriculum, is like pushing that child into the deep end of a swimming pool, expecting the child to sink or swim. Some children do initially splash around and quickly learn to swim. Others become isolated or aggressive, lose self-confidence and status within the peer group and with teachers.

If a **minority language child** has to move into majority language medium education (e.g. due to moving to live in another country), the parent may wish to ensure a foundation for that child by increased exposure to the majority language before the child moves school. This may involve language lessons before moving, and using specific times and places in the home for increased exposure to the majority language. Such a switch from minority language to majority language education requires friendly discussions between parent and child about anxieties so as to ease the transition. In this situation, parents also need to visit the new school. Discussions with teachers to explain the language situation of the family will make teachers more sensitive to the language needs of the child, aid the transition of the child into a new language environment, and may give the extra language support required by the child in the initial stages. Also, parents may be able to encourage friendships for their child with similarly placed families in the new locality.

If a **majority language** parent moves to a different majority language environment or a minority language environment, the same advice applies. There may be supplementary language courses before, or as soon as the child enters the new school. For example, in Wales, there are sometimes language centers for majority language in-migrants into the area. The children spend fifteen or more weeks in such minority language centers before entering primary school. The children are taught the new language in a lively and attractive way, and simultaneously, efforts are made to ensure that their work throughout the core curriculum is kept up to age expectations. When children are sufficiently fluent to understand that language in the classroom, they are transferred to a mainstream primary school.

In other cases, there are classes (e.g. withdrawal classes) within a school specially set aside for children who are late entrants (and when there are language differences). While long-term use of separate classes tends to stigmatize children, in the short term there may be a language necessity for extra provision to be given.

Older children experience a more advanced curriculum and therefore a more advanced language is required to cope in the curriculum. Hence, movement from one language medium to another tends to become more difficult as children progress through their school years. If sympathetically, sensitively and carefully handled, language transition is possible. After initial worries and concerns by children and their parents, children are amazingly resilient and adaptable to new situations, including new language situations. It is important that children are accepted, their self-esteem is preserved, their confidence in their academic ability is maintained and their first language is not the subject of derision and disparagement.

There are some situations when parents have the choice of moving their relatively older child to a bilingual school and away from a monolingual school. In parts of **Canada** there has been this choice. Children entering middle or late immersion programs (see later) learn through the medium of French and English. However, there are large numbers of children in the same boat in such situations. Children are not oddities or regarded as idiosyncratic.

There are usually **few problems** in moving to a school which uses a different language **up to the age of seven** at least. After the age of seven, there is often a need for a child to acquire quickly a **language competence sufficient for working in the curriculum**. If such language competence can be relatively speedily acquired, a switch to a different language medium is possible throughout the primary school years.

When a child will struggle in the long term (and not just short term) to catch up with the language competence required to cope in the curriculum, parents may need to consider carefully the alternatives. Whether or not bilingual education is the appropriate alternative needs careful consideration. Parents relative priorities in schooling (e.g. exam success, moral and social development) need weighing against language priorities. Maintaining a child's positive academic self-concept and positive achievement in the curriculum is essential to ensure that success breeds success.

E6 Is there a 'critical age' when children shouldn't be moved to a school with a different language pattern in the curriculum?

There are **no critical ages** in language development. A critical age is when an aspect of development can *only* occur at one (usually very early) time in a person's life. In language development, advances are possible later in life if they have not occurred earlier. A second language can be successfully acquired from birth or in retirement years.

In the 1960s, a debate existed about the plasticity of the brain. One viewpoint suggested that there was a particular critical period in young children for language to develop easily. Research has suggested that there are no critical periods within a child's language development. Seventy- and eighty-year-old adults have been known to learn a new language with great success, making the idea of critical periods absurd.

However, there are often **advantageous periods**. Acquiring a second language very early in life has advantages for pronunciation. Developing a second language in the primary school is advantageous, giving an early foundation and many more years ahead for that language to mature. In the nursery, kindergarten and primary school years, a second language is acquired rather than learnt. So while there are no critical periods, there are advantageous periods. Such periods occur when there is a higher probability of language acquisition due to circumstances, time available, teaching resources and motivation.

The question points to an important decision for parents who move to a different geographical area. Children vary considerably in their ability to adapt to a new language environment, and their attitude and motivation to picking up a new language quickly. The quality and quantity of practice in the new language available in the school and outside school also varies. However, as a rough guide, and with many children being exceptions to this guide, here is a suggestion. Up to the **age of seven**, there seems little problem with children quickly adapting to the new language environment of a school. The language used in the classroom in the infant years tends to be relatively simple and straightforward, and fairly quickly acquired by children. The infant classroom involves project work, plenty of actions and role playing, plenty of interaction with other children that enables children to acquire a new language relatively quickly.

In the remaining years of primary education, **between the ages of seven and eleven or twelve**, children need support within and outside the classroom to enable them to acquire sufficient competence in a language to cope in the classroom. As age increases in these primary years, so does the need for extra help and for the quantity and depth of language support. As curriculum areas become more complex, as present learning is built on prior learning, as ideas and concepts become more complex, a child's level of language needs to be more advanced to cope in the curriculum. Such children will probably need extra language support in the classroom for a year or more, extra tuition in language inside the classroom or in Withdrawal classes, and where possible, language support and encouragement outside the classroom.

In secondary education, **after the ages of twelve and thirteen**, it becomes difficult for a child to face a completely new and different language pattern in the curriculum. During the secondary years of schooling, the subject-based curriculum, the move to assessments and examinations, the increasing complexity of Science and Mathematics, Geography, History, Social Sciences and Expressive Arts all make coping in a different language difficult.

In late immersion bilingual education (see a later question), the Canadians have shown that it is possible for children to learn through a different language in secondary education. The difference here is that children in late Immersion Bilingual education will all start from the same language point. There is homogeneity within children in the class, and children will have had French lessons in the primary/elementary school before moving into late Immersion.

In the very **early years of secondary schooling**, if sufficient language support is given inside the curriculum, in extra language classes outside the usual subject curriculum, if the child is relatively optimistic, has a positive attitude and motivation to learning in the new language, and if there is parental support and encouragement, it is possible that a child may adapt. However, in reality, after one or two years of secondary schooling, using a new language in the curriculum will be quite difficult. At this stage, parents need to consider alternative options — such as the child remaining in their current school, living with the extended family or friends, thereby retaining continuity in schooling.

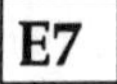

E7 My children can hold a conversation in a second language. Is that sufficient for them to be taught in that language at school?

Experts in bilingualism tend to agree that there is an important distinction between **conversational language and classroom language**. There is a level of language skills required to hold a conversation in the shop, on the street, and in the home. A different level of language competence is required to operate successfully in the classroom. Classrooms are more tacit, more complex and more abstract in their language transactions. While this distinction is useful when discussing bilingualism, the reality is closer to dimensions along which people differ in their language competences.

In the street, in the shop, on the television screen and sitting on the sofa at home, language is relatively simple. There are plenty of cues and clues in the environment, plenty of body language, pointing and gesticulating to convey messages and information. There is a level of simple communication that does not require complex language skills. In the **classroom**, as children grow older, there are fewer contextual cues and clues. The jargon of Science and Geography, Literature and Technology enter. The language of mathematical and historical concepts becomes more complex, requiring a higher level of language competence to decode the messages of the classroom.

Scholars are agreed that one danger with bilingual children is that their level of conversational skills is not sufficient to cope in the more difficult language environment of the classroom. Children who have recently learned a language may not have the level of **language competence to enable them to understand the teacher's instruction**, the curriculum content of textbooks, and discussions among peers. Thus, a bilingual whose second language is not so well developed as their first language needs monitoring to ensure that their second language skills are sufficiently advanced to cope in the more complex, abstract and contrived classroom language situation.

Not all teachers recognize this distinction in language learning and language performance. It is easy to **confuse conversational competence with academic competence in a language**. In between, there are many shades of gray, many rungs on the ladder. The thresholds of language development for classroom use may be impossible to define. Nevertheless, the distinction is important because it highlights a trap for teachers and parents. The trap is expecting children to work in the curriculum with insufficient language development in their second language. Recognition of this distinction allows a parent and teacher to attempt to establish such language competence as is needed for a child to cope in the curriculum, before presenting that child with overly complex curriculum material.

E8 My child is learning through a second language at school. Should we change our language pattern at home?

If a child is coping well at school, including learning through a language that is not used in the home, a different language may be used at home. Only if the child is having real longer-term difficulties in understanding the language of the classroom should parents consider switching the home language to help the child's educational development. Language is not like a switch with an 'on and off' button. Language patterns in a home tend to be well established. There is difficulty in changing. So generally, it is important to be **natural** in the language of the home, to establish continuity and a stimulating language environment.

If the **school** language is a majority language, there is usually no need to change the home language. There are sufficient hours in school and when doing homework to ensure development in that language. When a child from a minority language is studying through a majority language at school, wherever possible, parents should continue to support the minority language to support the child's psychological development.

A **language minority** child in a majority language mainstream classroom may sometimes be the one that has educational difficulties in educational adjustment. This situation places minority parents in a difficult and paradoxical situation. To switch to the majority language in the home means denying heritage and home, part of family and personal identity and a possible rejection of roots. Such a child in the majority language school may be failing due to being submerged among children who can speak that majority language fluently. If minority language education is available, parents may feel it appropriate to educate their children through that minority language, while ensuring that they become fully bilingual.

What **if the only available schooling for the language minority child is through the majority language**? The temptation is sometimes to change to the majority language at home. The advice from well meaning professionals is often to switch to the majority language. The preference of politicians and public is often that language minority in-migrants, in particular, integrate and assimilate through dropping their minority language. This is a real dilemma that involves a careful calculation of priorities in family and educational life. Continuity of language and culture must be weighed against attempted language enablement and empowerment of the child to suit a monolingual school and a monolingual society.

If parents decide to retain the minority language in the home, it may be worthwhile to provide majority language resources, majority language encouragement and opportunities for practicing the majority language in the community for that child. Parents can provide out-of-school support for the child's learning, particularly when there is slow development. Such support can be given by extra lessons, by using friends and neighbors, by parents involving themselves in their child's learning. The child needs to be thoroughly supported and thoroughly encouraged in majority language school work. The attitude of the parents, a positive and facilitative environment in the home may support the child through difficult acclimatization periods.

If parents decide to use of the majority language in the home (to develop the child's majority language skills for intended more effective school performance), parents need to consider carefully how the family identity, heritage, and culture can still be maintained so that there is a bedrock and strength to establish family continuity.

E9 How easy or difficult will it be for my children to find a job if they are bilingual?

Bilingualism and bilingual education provide no guarantee that a child obtains a job. However, bilinguals seem increasingly required as international trade barriers fall and a more global economy grows. The danger of this statement is that it alludes to many high status jobs — airline hosts, workers in transnational companies, international market operators, diplomats, politicians, United Nations and European civil servants. However, among other sectors of the market, there is also a movement across language and national borders. Moving country to find work or better employment has increased in the last decade. Just as students in Europe have increasingly opted for programs that allow them to take part of their higher education at one or more European universities as well as their 'home' university, so people of different nations tend to be looking to an alternative employment market in other countries. Around half of the Irish population since 1820 has emigrated to find work. Germany and the Benelux (Belgium, Netherlands, Luxembourg) countries are particularly good examples of where movement among workers has occurred.

As the economic expansion of the Pacific Rim grows, the value of those who speak particular Asian languages will grow considerably.

There is another variety of bilingual who may find their bilingualism an advantage in the employment market. As central international trade increases, there is also increasing concern about peripheral areas of countries. Where rural areas with scattered populations are in need of economic development, there is a growing European interest in assuring that economic advantage and affluence is shared as widely as possible. Therefore, in places such as rural Ireland and Wales, the highlands and islands of Scotland, there have been major attempts at economic regeneration where the minority language is strong. Among such marginalized language minority communities, there is an awareness that **language maintenance requires economic regeneration**. Unless there are jobs for minority language speakers in the area, they will migrate and lose their language.

Therefore, many **new rural industries** have grown. There is more economic aid to areas where minority languages co-exist with less economic growth, attempting simultaneously to support economic regeneration and language preservation. In other minority language communities, there are self-help, language minority group generated industries and activities.

The Asians in England are a particularly good example of a language minority creating and supporting their **own industries** (e.g. the clothing industry). The Chinese throughout the world also seem able to establish their own businesses and simultaneously engage in language preservation in a local Chinese community. Yiddish- and Hebrew-speaking peoples have also taken part in the strong Jewish tradition of economic vitality alongside religious and language vigor.

Bilingualism is no guarantee of a job, of financial fortune or a high quality of life. There is a current indication that it may give the edge, an extra qualification in the race for employment and affluence in a rapidly changing economy.

TYPES OF BILINGUAL EDUCATION

E10 What types of bilingual education exist?

There are many different types of bilingual school. The main types of bilingual schools will now be briefly introduced and then considered in detail in different questions in this section. In Canada, there are **Immersion schools** where English speakers are taught mostly or partly through the medium of French. Such schools also subsequently appeared in Europe and Asia using two majority languages. The 'immersion' child already owns one prestigious language, and acquires another high status language in school. Immersion children usually become bilingual and biliterate.

For language minority children, there are **Heritage Language schools** (with a variety of different names). Such schools are found in many areas of the world: for example, Australia, New Zealand, Catalonia, the Basque country, Africa, India, the Middle and Far East, Wales, Ireland, Canada and the United States. A Heritage Language school seeks to deliver much of the curriculum in the child's minority language. The Heritage Language may be an indigenous language (e.g. Navajo in the United States) or an 'immigrant' language (e.g. Spanish in the United States). What constitutes a heritage language is thus wide and not exclusive. By the age of leaving an elementary Heritage Language school, children are usually bilingual in the heritage and a majority language as well as being biliterate.

There are more than 850 International schools in over eighty countries. Such schools teach through a majority language (often English) and may incorporate a local language(s) into the curriculum. For example, in Kuwait, such International schools teach through English and Arabic. The European Schools Movement is one particular example of such International schools, and is considered later. The aim of International schools is often, but not always, bilingualism and biculturalism. English is usually the dominant language of the school.

Dual Language schools are increasingly found in the United States. There are a variety of **terms** used to describe such United States schools: Two-Way Schools, Two-Way Immersion, Two-Way Bilingual Education, Developmental Bilingual Education and Dual Language Education. Dual Language schools contain an approximate balance of language majority and language minority children. Such schools use two languages approximately equally in the curriculum so that children become bilingual and biliterate.

Immersion schools, Heritage Language schools, International schools and Dual Language schools are usually **'strong' forms of bilingual education**. The promotion of two or more languages is attempted, as is biliteracy and biculturalism or multiculturalism. Each 'strong' type of bilingual school aims to enrich the child, particularly linguistically. There are also **'weak' forms of bilingual education**. These 'weak' forms of bilingual education include: Submersion, Submersion with Withdrawal Classes, Structured Immersion, Sheltered English and Transitional Bilingual Education. They are found in countries such as the United States and England where the aim is to enable the language minority child to operate in the majority language of the country. If the child's minority language is supported, it is only for a temporary period. The intended outcomes of 'weak' forms of bilingual education often include monolingualism in the majority language of the country (or limited bilingualism) and **assimilation** into mainstream culture, values and attitudes.

In England, the aim of the education system is to ensure that speakers of different Asian languages (and Greeks and Turks) are taught through the medium of English, to speak standard English and become patriotic citizens of Britain. In the United States, 'weak' forms of bilingual education attempt to submerse Spanish speakers, for example, in the English language, or provide a fast transition from dominance in Spanish to dominance in English. The justifications, politics and problems of 'weak' forms of bilingual education are discussed below in succeeding questions.

E11 What are Dual Language schools?

Dual Language schools contain a balance of language majority and language minority children. Such schools use two languages approximately equally in the curriculum so that children become bilingual and biliterate. Mostly found among United States elementary schools, such institutions have bilingual teachers who aim to keep the two languages separate in their classrooms.

Dual Language classrooms embrace a mixture of language majority and language minority **students**. For example, half the children may come from Spanish-speaking homes; the other half from English language backgrounds. A **language balance** close to 50%–50% is attempted. If one language becomes dominant (e.g. due to much larger numbers of one language group), the aim of bilingualism and biliteracy may be at risk.

An **imbalance** in the two languages among students may result in one language being used to the exclusion of the other (e.g. Spanish-speaking children having to switch to English to work cooperatively). Alternatively, one language group may become sidelined (e.g. Spanish speakers become excluded from English-speaking groups). Segregation rather than integration may occur. In the creation of a dual language school or classroom, careful student selection decisions have to be made to ensure a **language balance**.

If an **imbalance** does exist, it may be preferable to have slightly more language minority children. Where there is a preponderance of language majority children, the tendency is for language minority children to switch to the higher status, majority language. In most (but not all) language contexts, the majority language is well represented outside of the school (e.g. in the media and for employment). Therefore, the balance towards the majority language outside the school can be complemented by a slight balance towards the minority language in school (among student in-take and in curriculum delivery). However, if the school contains a particularly high number of language minority children, the prestige of the school may sometimes suffer (both among language majority and language minority parents).

There are situations where **attracting language majority students** to a Dual Language school is difficult. Where the monolingual mainstream school is as (or more) attractive to prospective parents, recruitment to Dual Language schools may be a challenge. For parents, allocation of their children to such Dual Language Bilingual Programs will be voluntary and not enforced. Hence, the good **reputation**, perceived effectiveness and curriculum success of such Dual Language schools becomes crucial to their continuation. Evidence from the United States suggests that language minority parents may be supportive of such a program. Majority language parents may need more persuading. Community backing and involvement in the school may also be important in long-term success.

The **development** of Dual Language schools often starts with the creation of a dual language kindergarten class rather than an implementation throughout a school. As the kindergarten students move through the grades, a new dual language class is created each year. Apart from Elementary Dual Language schools, there is also Dual Language secondary education in the United States and, with different names, in many other countries of the world (e.g. Wales, Spain, India). A Dual Language school may be a whole school in itself. Also, there may be dual language classrooms within a 'mainstream' school. For example, there may be one dual language classroom in each grade.

The **aim** of a Dual Language schools is not just to produce bilingual and biliterate children. To gain status and to flourish, such a school needs to show success throughout the curriculum. On standardized tests, on attainment compared with other schools in the locality, and in specialisms (e.g. music, sport, science), a Dual Language school will strive to show relative success. A narrow focus on proficiency in two languages will be an insufficient aim.

The **aims** of Dual Language schools may be couched in terms such as 'equality of educational opportunity for children from different language backgrounds', 'child-centered education building on the child's existing language competence', 'a community dedicated to the integration of all its children', 'enrichment not compensatory education', 'a family-like experience to produce multicultural children', and 'supporting Bilingual Proficiency not Limited English Proficiency'. Such Dual Language schools thus have a diversity of aims. These essentially include achievement throughout the curriculum, social integration of children in the school and community, a positive self-image in each child, and attempting equality of access to opportunity among all students. Such equality of opportunity is offered to recent or established in-migrants, and to those living in language minority or language majority homes.

One of the special aims of Dual Language schools (e.g. compared with mainstream schools) is to produce thoroughly **bilingual, biliterate and multicultural children**. Language minority students are expected to become literate in their native language as well as in the majority language. Language majority students are expected to develop language and literacy skills in a second language. At the same time, majority language students must make normal progress in their first language. To achieve these aims, a variety of practices are implemented in Dual Language schools.

(1) The two **languages** of the school (e.g. Spanish and English, Chinese and English, Haitian Creole and English) have **equal status**. Both languages will be used as a medium of instruction. Math, Science and Social Studies, for example, may be taught in both languages.

(2) The **school ethos** will be bilingual. Such an ethos is created by classroom and corridor displays, notice boards, curriculum resources, cultural events, dinner-time and extra curricula activity using both languages in a relatively balanced way. Announcements across the school address system will be bilingual. Letters to parents will also be in two languages. While playground conversations and student-to-student talk in the classroom is difficult to influence or manipulate, the school environment aims to be transparently bilingual.

(3) In some Dual Language schools, the two **languages** are **taught** as languages (sometimes called Language Arts instruction). Here, aspects of spelling, grammar, metaphors and communicative skills may be directly taught. In other Dual Language schools, use of both languages as a medium of instruction is regarded as sufficient to ensure bilingual development. In such schools, children are expected to **acquire proficiency** in language informally throughout the curriculum. In both cases, reading and writing in both languages are likely to receive direct attention in the curriculum. Biliteracy is as

much an aim as full bilingualism. Literacy will be acquired in both languages either simultaneously or with an initial emphasis on native language literacy.

(4) **Staff** in the dual language classrooms are often bilingual. Such **teachers** use both languages on different occasions with their students. Where this is difficult (e.g. due to teacher supply or selection), teachers may be paired and work together closely as a team. A teacher's aide, paraprofessionals, secretaries, custodial staff, parents offering or invited to help the teacher may also be bilingual. Language minority **parents** can be valuable 'teacher auxiliaries' in the classroom. For example, when a wide variety of Spanish cultures from many regions is brought to the classroom, parents and grandparents may describe and provide the most authentic stories, dances, recipes, folklore and festivals. This underlines the importance of the cultural heritage of language minorities being shared in the classroom to create an **additive** bilingual and multicultural environment.

(5) The **length of the Dual Language program** needs to be longer rather than shorter. Such a program for two or three grades is insufficient. A minimum of four years extending through the grades as far as possible is more defensible. Length of experience of a Dual Language program is important to ensure a fuller and deeper development of language skills and biliteracy, in particular. Where a United States Dual Language program exists across more years, there is a tendency for the curriculum to be increasingly taught in the majority language — English.

A central idea in Dual Language schools is **language separation and compartmentalization**. In each period of instruction, only one language is used. **Language boundaries** are established in terms of time, curriculum content and teaching. These will each be considered.

First, a decision is made about **when** to teach through each language. One frequent preference is for each language to be used on **alternate days**. On the door of the classroom may be a message about which language is to be used that day. For example, Spanish is used one day, English the next, in a strict sequence. Alternately, **different lessons** may use **different languages** with a regular change-over to ensure both languages are used in all curricula areas. For example, Spanish may be used to teach Mathematics on Monday and Wednesday and Friday; English to teach Mathematics on Tuesday and Thursday. During the next week, the languages are reversed, with Mathematics taught in Spanish on Tuesday and Thursday.

There are other possibilities. The division of time may be in half-days, alternate weeks, alternate half-semesters. The essential element is the distribution of time to achieve bilingual and biliterate students.

The amount of time spent learning through each language varies from school to school. Often, a 50%–50% balance in use of languages is attempted in early and later grades. In other classrooms, the minority language will be given more time (60%, 75% and 80% is not uncommon), especially in the first two or three years. In the middle and secondary years of schooling, there is sometimes a preference for a 50%–50% balance, or more accent on the majority language (e.g. 70% through English–30% through Spanish).

Whatever the division of time, instruction in a Dual Language school will keep **boundaries** between the languages. Switching languages within a lesson is not preferred. If language mixing by the teacher occurs, students may wait until there is delivery in their stronger language, and become uninvolved at other times. When there is clear separation, the Spanish speakers, for example, may help the English-speakers on Spanish days, and the English-speakers help the Spanish-speakers on English days. Inter-dependence may stimulate cooperation and friendship, as well as learning and achievement. The potential problems of segregation and racial hostility may thus be considerably reduced.

However, the two languages will sometimes be switched or mixed in the classroom (e.g. in private conversations, in further explanations by a teacher, and internal use of the dominant language). Use of languages by children, especially when young, is not usually consciously controlled. Switching language can be as natural as smiling.

There is an important **paradox** in Dual Language schools. Boundaries are kept between languages so that separation does not occur between children. English and non-English speakers are integrated in all lessons through language segregation.

Second, bilingual **teachers** ensure they do not switch languages. Children hear them using one language (during a lesson period or during a whole day) and are expected to respond in that same language. When, as in many forms of 'strong' bilingual education, there is a shortage of bilingual teachers, a pairing of teachers may ensure language separation. A teacher using Spanish only will work in close association with a teacher who only uses English with the same class. Such teamwork requires teachers to be committed to bilingualism and multiculturalism as important educational aims.

Third, language boundaries may be established in the **curriculum**. This may occur according to which 'language day' it is. Alternatively, in some schools, different parts of the curriculum are taught in different languages. For example, Social Studies and Environmental Studies may be taught in Spanish, Science and Math in English. Such a policy establishes separate occasions where each language is to be used, and keeps the two languages apart. However, one danger is that the majority language becomes aligned with modern technology and science, while the minority language becomes associated with tradition and culture. This may affect the status of the language in the eyes of the child, parents and society. The relationship of languages to employment prospects, economic advantage and power thus need considering.

Such Dual Language schools differ from **Transitional Bilingual Education** (see later) and **Submersion/Mainstream/English Second Language** approaches by teaching through the medium of two languages over four or more grades. United States Transitional Bilingual education essentially aims to move children into English-only instruction within two or three years. In contrast, Dual Language schools aim to enable the child to achieve increasing proficiency in two languages (e.g. Spanish and English in the United States). Dual language schools differ from **Immersion Bilingual Education** (see later) in the language backgrounds of the students. Immersion schools normally contain only language majority children learning much or part of the curriculum through a second language (e.g. English-speaking children learning through the medium of French in Canadian schools). Dual Language schools contain a balanced mixture of children from two (or more) different language backgrounds (e.g. from Spanish-speaking and English-speaking homes in the United States).

E12 What are International schools?

International schools are a diverse collection of schools throughout the world. Numbering over 850 schools, they are found in more than 80 countries, mostly in large cities. Mainly for the affluent, parents pay fees for mostly **private, selective, independent education**. Children in these schools often have parents in the diplomatic service, multinational organizations, in international businesses and who are geographically and vocationally mobile. Other children in an International school come from the locality, whose parents want their children to have an internationally flavored education.

One **language** (sometimes *the* language) of the school is ordinarily English. Such schools become bilingual when a local or another international language is incorporated in the curriculum. Sometimes the second language taught for up to twelve years is only taught as a language. In other schools, the second language is used as a medium to teach part of the curriculum. Some schools enable their students to acquire third and fourth languages. Generally, the languages of International schools are majority languages with international prestige. Minority languages are rarely found in such schools.

The primary and secondary **curriculum** tends to reflect United States, British, as well as the local curriculum, tradition. The teachers are from varying countries, usually with a plentiful supply of British and American trained staff. Sometimes preparing children for the International Baccalaureate, United States tests or British examinations, most prepare their clientele for universities in Europe and North America.

A flavor of the varied nature of such schools is portrayed in ten **brief examples** of International schools given below. A book listing and describing such schools in every part of the world is: *The ECIS International Schools Directory*. It is published by the European Council of International Schools (ISBN 0-9524052-1-0). The book is updated every year.

(1) **Ecole Active Bilingue Jeannine Manuel**. Situated in Paris. Age range: 3 to 19. 150 students. The teachers come from ten nationalities. The school aims to 'develop bilingualism and biculturalism' in French and English. Japanese is begun at primary level and continued through the secondary school. Science and Humanities are available in French or English. United States university and college exams and tests (e.g. SAT, Achievement Tests, PSAT), the French Baccalauréat, and the International Baccalaureate can be taken.

(2) **John F. Kennedy School**. Situated in Berlin. Age range: 5 to 19. 1280 students from 23 nationalities. Fifty per cent of teachers are from the United States; 50% from Germany. The school is bilingual, binational and bicultural in German and English. Instruction is 'conducted in both languages continuously'. Tuition is free.

(3) **International School of London**. Situated in London. Age range: 4 to 18. 170 students from 36 nationalities. Teachers come from twelve nationalities. Mother tongue education 'can be made available in most languages. Currently the school offers: Arabic, French, Italian, Japanese, German, Portuguese and Spanish native language instruction. Language instruction in 20 languages can be arranged.

(4) **Chinese International School**. Situated in Hong Kong. Age range: 4 to 18. 1045 students from 23 nationalities. Teachers come from eight nationalities. The school is 'dedicated to providing an education in the language and culture of both the Chinese and Western worlds'. Chinese (Mandarin) and English is taught. Children come from

diverse ethnic, religious and linguistic backgrounds, mostly being United States, British and Chinese students, but also from seven other countries.

(5) **Nishimachi International School**. Situated in Tokyo. Age range: 5 to 15. 429 students from 360 nationalities. Teachers come from twelve nationalities. The school is a 'dedicated center for dual language (English–Japanese), multicultural studies'. The student composition is 20% Japanese; 35% United States; 20% one parent Japanese–the other parent from another nationality; 25% other nationalities.

(6) **Bayan Bilingual School**. Situated in Kuwait. Age range: 3 to 17. 880 students from 14 nationalities. Teachers come from 15 nationalities. It is a 'bilingual school for Arab children which stresses Arab culture, traditions, heritage and identity while preparing its graduates for college and university placement throughout the world'. The languages of instruction are Arabic and English.

(7) **Aloha College**. Situated in Marbella, Spain. Age range: 3 to 18. 440 students from 33 nationalities. Teachers come from two nationalities. Up to 40% of the curriculum is taught in Spanish; the remainder in English. French, German, Swedish and Arabic are also available. The students are 45% Spanish, 25% British and 10% Scandinavian and go on to college or university in Europe or North America.

(8) **International School of Berne**. Situated in Switzerland. Age range: 4 to 19. 174 students from 33 nationalities. Teachers come from ten nationalities. 'Tolerance of racial, religious, cultural and political differences is stressed. The school aims to foster an appreciation and understanding of diverse cultures and to promote open communication, open-mindedness, fairness, and respect for the particular backgrounds of its students.' The languages of instruction are English, French and German.

(9) **Al Mawakeb School**. Situated in Dubai, United Arab Emirates. Age range: 3 to 18. 1846 students from 40 nationalities. Teachers come from 16 nationalities. Trilingual education is provided in Arabic, French and English which are regarded as core subjects in the curriculum. Science, Mathematics and Economics are taught in English.

(10) **United Nations International School**. Situated in New York. Age range: 5 to 18. 1442 students from 102 nationalities. Teachers come from 46 nationalities. There are two campuses: one in Manhattan, the other in Queens. Languages include: English, French, Spanish, Arabic, Chinese, Dutch, German, Italian, Japanese, Russian and Swedish.

E13 What is Heritage Language Bilingual Education?

Heritage Language Bilingual Education is where **language minority children** use their native, ethnic, home or heritage language in the school as a medium of instruction and the goal is full bilingualism. Examples include education through the (minority language) medium of Navajo and Spanish in the US, Catalan in Spain, Ukrainian in Canada, Gaelic in Scotland, Finnish in Sweden and Welsh in Wales. The child's native language is protected and developed alongside development in the majority language. In New Zealand, the Maori language has increasingly been promoted in schools. In Ireland, Irish-medium education is often available for children from Irish language backgrounds. The students will learn English and Irish, and possibly other European languages. The language **aim** is **to protect the indigenous** Irish **language** in school lest it wither and die amongst the all-pervading growth of English, and lately of other European majority languages.

In the United States, there are schools which are termed **'ethnic community, mother tongue schools'**. Numbering over 5,000 and located in every State of the United States, the list includes schools using the mother tongue of the following varied communities: Arabs, Africans, Asians, Jewish, Russian, Polish, Latin American, Dutch, Bulgarian, Irish, Rumanian, Serbian and Turkish. Maintained by communities who have lost, or are losing, their 'native' language, the schools mostly teach that native language and use it as a medium of instruction.

The 'public school' United States instance of Heritage Language Bilingual Education is often called **Maintenance Bilingual Education** or **Developmental Maintenance Bilingual Education**. These are few in number. In Canada, the term used to describe such education is **Heritage Language Education**. However, in Canada, there is a distinction between Heritage Language lessons and Heritage Language Bilingual Education:

(1) Heritage Language Programs give around two and a half hours per week **language teaching lessons**, currently in more than 60 languages to about 100,000 students. These lessons often occur during dinner-hours, after school and at weekends.

(2) In provinces such as Manitoba, British Columbia, Saskatchewan and Alberta, there are Heritage Language Bilingual Education Programs. The heritage language is the **medium of instruction** for about 50% of the day (e.g. Ukrainian, Italian, German, Hebrew, Yiddish, Mandarin Chinese, Arabic and Polish).

In essence, heritage or maintenance language education refers to the education of **language minority** children through their minority language in a majority language society. In most countries, the majority language will also be present in the curriculum, ranging from second language lessons to a varying proportion of the curriculum being taught through the majority language.

The **term** 'heritage language' may also be called 'native language', 'ethnic language', 'minority language', 'ancestral language', or, in French, '*langues d'origine*'. The **danger** of the term 'heritage' is that it points to the past and not the future, to traditions rather than the contemporary. Partly for this reason, one modern term tends to be 'community language'. The heritage language may, or may not, be an indigenous language. Both Navajo and Spanish can be perceived as heritage languages in the United States depending on an individual's perception of what constitutes their heritage language. Developmental Maintenance programs in the United States (also Heritage language programs in Canada and other countries) vary in structure and content. Some of the likely features are as follows:

(a) Many, but not all of the children will come from language minority homes. Many classrooms will tend to contain a varying **mixture of language majority and language minority children**. At the same time, the minority language may be the majority language of a local community. In certain areas of the US, Spanish speakers are in a majority in their neighborhood or community. In Gwynedd, North Wales, where the minority language (Welsh) is often the majority language of the community, heritage language programs are prevalent.

(b) **Parents** will often have the **choice** of sending their children to mainstream schools or to heritage language education. Ukrainian, Jewish and Mohawkian heritage language programs in Canada, for example, gave parents freedom of choice in selecting schools.

(c) The language minority pupil's home language will often be used for approximately half of **curriculum time**. The Ukrainian programs in Alberta and Manitoba allotted half the time to Ukrainian, half to English. Mathematics and Science, for example, were taught in English; Music, Art and Social Studies in Ukrainian. There is a tendency to teach technological, scientific studies through the majority language.

(d) Where a minority language is used for a majority of classroom time (e.g. 80% to almost 100% in Wales), the justification is usually that **children easily transfer ideas, concepts, skills and knowledge into the majority language**. Having taught a child multiplication in Spanish for example, this mathematical concept does not have to be re-taught in English. Classroom teaching transfers relatively easily between languages when such languages are sufficiently developed to cope with concepts, content and curriculum materials.

(e) The **justification** given for heritage language education is also that a minority language is easily lost, a majority language is easily gained. Children tend to be surrounded by the majority language. Television and train adverts, shops and signs, videos and visits often provide or induce bilingual proficiency in an incidental way by accenting a majority language. Thus bilingualism is achieved by a concentration on the minority language at school.

(f) Heritage language schools are mostly **elementary schools**. This need not be the case. In Wales, for example, such schools are available to the end of secondary education and the heritage language can be used as a medium of study at college and university.

E14 My child is in a Transitional Bilingual Education class. What are the implications for achievement in school?

In the United States and England, for example, children from Spanish-speaking backgrounds and Asian backgrounds respectively are often placed in what educationists call Transitional Bilingual Education. Rather than immediately submerging language minority children in an English language monolingual class, they are allowed to splash around in their home language for one or two years. The idea is to make a **relatively quick transition from the home language to the language of the school** — English. The value of such classes is that they provide a year or two's language buffer to militate against the effects of the 'sink or swim' Submersion approach. Children are allowed a transition period that provides temporary support for their home language, temporary acceptance of their home, heritage and history. In many areas of England and the United States, such transitional classes are preferred to Submersion (see Glossary). A temporary period of using the home language in Transitional Bilingual Education is better than none at all (Submersion).

The **problem** with such transitional classes is that they deny, after one or two years, the learning experiences and minority language linguistic resources of that child. After one or two years, the minority language and culture is forgotten in the school. Children are mainstreamed and expected to behave linguistically, culturally and educationally as their monolingual, monocultural peers. Research in the United States has suggested that the longer a child is left in a Transitional Bilingual Education classes (e.g. for up to four or five years), the more success the child will have at school. **The more children are allowed to use their home language in a school, the better will be their language and curriculum achievement**. Children who are allowed to use their home language for more rather than fewer years still become fluent in the English language. There is sufficient support in school and in the community for them to become bilingual. In Transitional Bilingual Education the chance is lost of full development in the minority language, cultural pluralism, and a full immersion in the language diversity of society.

One paradoxical education situation in England and the United States is that such minority language children's home language is slowly eradicated. Yet in the secondary years, they are encouraged to begin to learn a new European language. Second language learning is increasingly viewed in these countries as an essential resource to promote foreign trade and world influence. Thus, the **paradox** is that while bilingual education to support minority languages has tended to be depreciated in the United States and England, the current trend is to appreciate English speakers who learn a second language. There is a tendency to value the acquisition of languages while devaluing the language minorities who have them. On the one hand, we encourage and promote the study of foreign languages for English monolinguals at great cost and with great inefficiency. At the same time, we destroy the linguistic gifts that children from non-English language backgrounds bring to school.

E15 What is the European Schools Movement?

The European Schools Movement **aims** to produce children who are bilingual and biliterate in at least two languages of the European Union. The schools are located in various countries in Europe. Children learn through their home language and a second language. They are also taught a third language. Classroom time is allocated for activities to integrate children of diverse language backgrounds.

The **European Schools Movement** started in 1958 in Brussels. Its schools are found in Belgium, Italy, Germany, the Netherlands and England. The schools were originally designed to provide education for the children of European Union workers. Sons and daughters of diplomats, civil servants, translators, technicians and domestic workers have priority of access. Spare places are made available to other children within the locality, to balance the language mix of the school.

Education is free, although non-European Union parents pay a small contribution to the costs of running the school. The schools are multilingual in character and cater for some 12,000 children from a wide variety of different European Union nations.

Eight of the official languages of the European Union have **equal status** within the schools. Therefore, each school may have up to eight sub-sections reflecting the **first language** of the children. One central aim of the school is to support and extend the child's first language. Thus, in the primary years, much of a child's instruction is through their native language. Children become thoroughly literate in their native language and are taught its attendant culture.

Such schools promote **bilingualism** for all. **Biliteracy** is also thoroughly developed. The schools deliberately engineer the integration between children from different regions. In the primary school years, all children begin to learn a second language (either English, French or German). As the second language develops, older children take part of their curriculum through the medium of that second language. The European Schools Movement calls this second language a **vehicular language**.

The **vehicular language** is taught by native speakers. Native student speakers of that language will also be present in the school. Such students valuably act as language models for second language learners. The vehicular language will be used to teach subjects (e.g. History, Geography and Economics) to a group of pupils from a variety of language backgrounds. Second language medium teaching in these subjects starts in the third year of secondary education. In addition, pupils are taught a third language for a minimum of 360 hours. Some children opt to learn a fourth language.

The **second language** is taught from the beginning of the primary school. The language is taught by native speakers and not the class teacher to ensure excellent role models. For children coming into the school late, there are 'catching-up classes' and 'support classes' to increase proficiency in the second language. By the end of primary education, approximately 25% of the curriculum is taught through the second language. This proportion increases as the child goes through secondary education.

In the first and second grades, the **second language** will only be taught as a subject. In these grades, no curriculum subjects will be taught through the second language. In the third, fourth and fifth grades, such language teaching continues. Physical Education and 'European Hours' will be taught through the second language. In Grades 6 through 8 in the secondary school program, the second language will be taught as a subject and the following subjects can be taught through that second language:

Design Technology, Music, Physical Education and complementary activities. In Grades 9 through 12, History, Geography and options such as Economics and Social Sciences and Music will be taught through the second language.

European Schools ensure the development of the child's first language and cultural identity. They also aim to promote a sense of **European identity**. Many centuries of rivalry and conflict in Europe have meant that national differences rather than a shared European identity are still common. An English, French or German person tends to take great pride in their national identity with the concept of European identity being new and sometimes strange. With a considerable mix of different nationalities within a European School, teachers are on guard against prejudice and rivalry. European Schools have become laboratories for testing whether integration and harmony can be engineered within an educational setting.

One form of integration is through **communal lessons**. The more the child progresses through the grades, the more lessons are taught to mixed language groups. In the primary school, these communal lessons are known as **European Hours**. Starting in the third year of primary education, there are three such lessons a week lasting two hours and fifteen minutes.

The primary aim is for children from different language sections to work and play together. As the lessons develop, children should become more aware of their similarities rather than differences, of their **common European heritage**, and of the importance of living peacefully and harmoniously together. In classes of 20 to 25 students, co-operative activities such as cooking, constructing objects (e.g. making puppets) are used to integrate children. Teachers are given freedom of choice of activity so long as such activity engages cooperation between children. All elementary school teachers are involved in the European Hours. However, teachers change classes during the school year to ensure the multicultural and multilingual aspects of European Hours are reinforced through changes in teacher.

The classroom atmosphere and **ethos** of European Hours is regarded as essential. Enjoyable, motivating projects are used, with satisfying and attainable goals. Small multilingual groups work together to attain a goal. Cooperation is essential for a successful outcome. The results of the project are valued by the students. The work may be exhibited in classrooms and corridors. Dances and songs may be performed in front of the whole school.

Given that five or six different languages may co-exist among students within the European Hours classroom, children act as translators for the teacher. If the instruction is given in French and that teacher cannot speak German, children who can speak in French and German act as informal interpreters.

Two **European Hours** lessons per week are conducted in the classroom. The third European Hours lesson is a games activity with the same aims and processes. No child is forced to use a particular language in European Hours. Valuably, the circumstances create a hidden curriculum. The hidden message to the child is of the importance of cooperation between languages, of accepting multilingualism as natural and workable.

The demands of using a second or a third language are lessened for the child. The nature of the **European Hours project** makes is cognitively less demanding than other subjects. The project also tends to be **'context embedded'** (see Glossary). That is, the activity does not depend on language alone, but actions (non-verbal communication) can relay a lot of information between children. This teaches the child that harmony and cooperation can occur with relative ease and that languages are not barriers to cooperation. Does it work? In one research study, it was found that in the latter stages of secondary schooling, the majority of students had best friends in a language section *other* than their own.

Teachers are recruited from different European education systems. All teachers are **native speakers** of a school language. They must also be **bilingual** or multilingual. No special teacher training or certification is required to work in a European School. Only a National Teachers Certificate is needed from that person's native country. There is currently almost no training in Europe for working in a multilingual or multicultural school such as a European School. Therefore, teachers learn 'on the job'. New teachers usually spend two or three weeks observation before starting teaching. New teachers are placed in the care of an experienced 'mentor' teacher.

Within the European Schools Movement, there are **in-service training** sessions for its teachers. This covers both refreshing and updating on language and subject content. Other professionals in the school look after the library, science and technology laboratories, and have responsibility for particular grades.

Communication with parents is multilingual. Meetings with parents are usually for that parent's language group only. When a large meeting of parents needs to take place, interpretation facilities will often be available. Parents who send their children to such European Schools tend to be bilingual or multilingual themselves. Therefore, their children start with an extra interest and accustomization to bilingual or multilingual settings. Many students come from literacy-oriented, middle class homes, with a positive view of bilingualism.

Research on the effectiveness of European Schools suggests that there are usually no detrimental effects on academic achievement stemming from the bilingual and multilingual policies. Students tend to succeed in the European Baccalaureate Examination and many go to university. While the school provides a fine example of the production of bilingual and biliterate children, it produces relatively privileged European School children. European Schools produce children secure in their own national culture and having a supranational European identity. However, there is the issue of whether it produces an educational and cultural **elite**. The Schools may be reproducing families who already have a considerable bilingual advantage.

European Schools differ from **Heritage Language Schools**. A Heritage Language School is mostly populated by language minority students. The minority language is the main medium of instruction (e.g. Irish-medium schools in Ireland, Welsh-speaking schools in Wales). In contrast, European Schools tend to recruit children from majority language backgrounds who are taught through two majority languages.

European Schools have many similarities with **immersion bilingual education**. Both forms of bilingual education tend to recruit from the middle classes and offer education through two majority languages.

A major **difference** between the European Schools Movement and the Canadian Immersion program (see below) is that the second language is taught as a subject in the European Schools *before* being used as a medium of instruction. In Canadian immersion programs, the second language is used as a medium of instruction from the beginning. In the European Schools Movement, there is also relatively more emphasis on the second language being taught as a subject in itself.

E16 What is meant by the term 'immersion bilingual education'?

Immersion bilingual education derives from a Canadian educational 'experiment'. The immersion movement started in St Lambert, Montreal, in 1965. Some disgruntled **English-speaking**, middle class parents persuaded school district administrators to set up an experimental kindergarten class of 26 children. The aims were for pupils: (1) to become competent speakers, readers and writers in **French**; (2) to reach normal achievement levels throughout the curriculum including the English language; (3) to appreciate the traditions and culture of French-speaking Canadians as well as English-speaking Canadians. In short, the aims were for children to become bilingual and bicultural without loss of achievement. The latent agenda was possibly that such children would be very marketable. Bilinguals who could switch between the French- and English-speaking communities in Canada would be able to find good employment, have varied job opportunities, and have an edge in the promotion and advancement market.

Immersion education is an umbrella term with variations in:

(1) **Age** at which a child commences the experience. This may be at the kindergarten or infant stage (**early** immersion); at nine to ten years old (delayed or **middle** immersion), or at secondary level (**late** immersion).

(2) The amount of **time** spent in immersion in a day. **Total** immersion usually commences with 100% immersion in the second language, after two or three years reducing to 80% for the next three or four years, finishing junior schooling with approximately 50% immersion. **Partial** immersion provides close to 50% immersion in the second language throughout infant and junior schooling. **Early total immersion** is the most popular program, followed by late and middle immersion. The following histogram illustrates **early total immersion**.

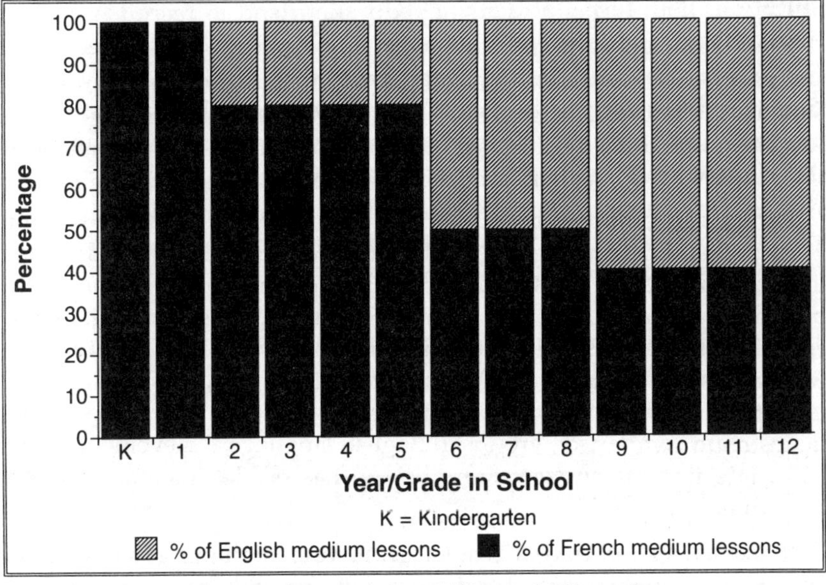

Early Total Immersion Bilingual Education

The St Lambert experiment suggested that the aims were met. Early immersion pupils are eventually able to read, write, speak and understand **English** as well as youngsters instructed in English in the mainstream English schools. For the first four years of **early total immersion**, pupils tend not to progress in English as do monolingual English pupils in mainstream classes. Reading, spelling and punctuation, for example, are not so developed. Since such children are usually not given English language instruction for one or two or three years after starting school, these results are to be expected. However, the initial pattern does not last. After approximately six years of schooling, early total immersion children have caught up with their monolingual peers in English language skills. By the **end of elementary schooling,** the early total immersion experience has generally not affected first language speaking and writing development. Parents of these children believe the same as the attainment tests reveal.

Indeed, when differences in English language achievement between immersion and mainstream children have been located by research, it is often in favor of immersion pupils. This finding links with the possible thinking (cognitive) advantages consequential from bilingualism. If bilingualism permits increased linguistic awareness, more flexibility in thought, more internal inspection of language, such cognitive advantages may help to explain **the favorable English progress of early immersion pupils**.

In addition, and at no cost, immersion pupils can also read, write, speak and understand **French** in a far superior way than English pupils who are taught French as a second language. Most students in **early total immersion programs** approach native-like performance in French in receptive language skills (listening and reading) at around eleven years old

Partial early immersion pupils tend to lag behind for three or four years in their English language skills. Their performance is little different from that of total early immersion pupils, which is surprising since early partial immersion education has more English language content. By the end of elementary schooling, partial early immersion children catch up with mainstream peers in English language attainment. Unlike early total immersion pupils, partial immersion children do not tend to surpass mainstream comparison groups in English language achievement. Similarly, **late immersion** (see figure below) has no detrimental effect on English language skills.

If immersion education results in children becoming bilingual in French and English, the question is whether this is at the cost of **achievement in other curriculum areas**. Compared with children in

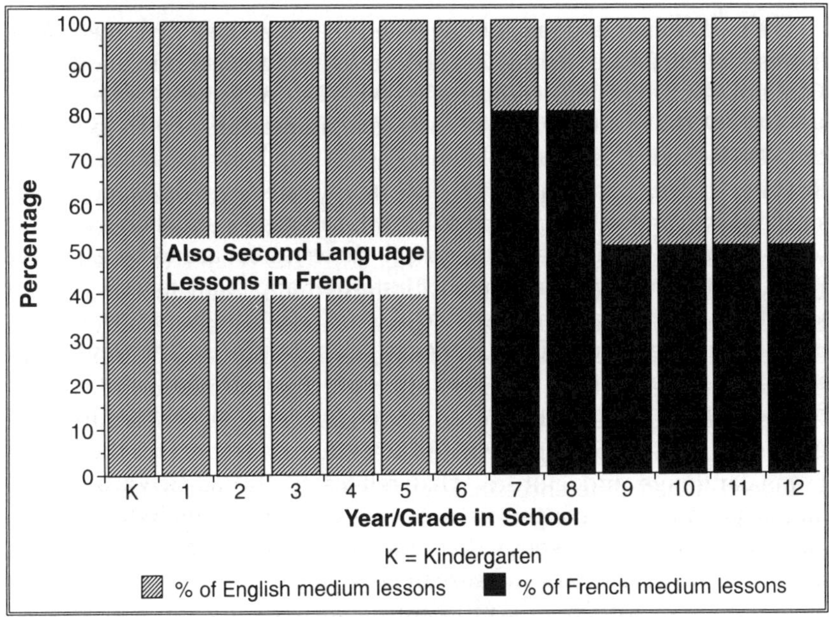

Late Immersion Bilingual Education

mainstream education how do immersion children progress in curriculum areas such as Mathematics and Science, History and Geography? The reviews of research suggest that **early total immersion** pupils generally perform as well in these subjects as do mainstream children.

The evaluations of **early partial immersion education** are not quite so positive. When children in early partial immersion learn Mathematics and Science through the medium of French, they tend to lag behind comparable mainstream children, at least initially. This may be because their French skills are insufficiently developed to be able to think mathematically and scientifically in their second language. The results for **late immersion** are similar. The important factor appears to be whether second language skills (French) are sufficiently developed to cope with fairly complex curriculum material.

The results overall suggest that bilingual education by an immersion experience need not have negative effects on curriculum performance, particularly in early total immersion programs. Indeed, most children gain a second language without cost to their performance in the curriculum. However, the **key factor seems to be whether their language skills have evolved sufficiently in order to work in the curriculum in their second language.**

Since 1965, immersion bilingual education has **spread rapidly** in Canada and in parts of Europe and Asia. There are currently over a quarter of a million English-speaking Canadian children in some 1600 French immersion schools. This represents some 6% of the total school population in Canada.

What are the essential features of this speedy educational growth? *First,* immersion in Canada aims at bilingualism in **two prestigious, majority languages** (French and English). This relates to an **additive bilingualism**. *Second,* immersion bilingual education in Canada has been **optional not compulsory**. Parents choose to send their children to such schools. The convictions of parents, capabilities of children plus the commitment of the teachers may aid the motivation of pupils. Immersion appears to thrive on conviction not on conformity. The Canadian immersion experience ensures there is respect for the child's home language and culture. This relates to the **additive** bilingual situation. Parents have generally been seen as partners in the immersion movement and some dialogue has existed between parents, administrators, teachers and researchers.

Third, children in early immersion are often **allowed to use their home language for up to one and a half years for classroom communication.** There is no compulsion to speak French in the playground or dining hall. The child's home language is appreciated and not belittled. *Fourth,* immersion teachers are competent bilinguals. However, they initially appear to the children as able to speak French but only understand (and not speak) English.

Fifth, the **content** of the curriculum becomes the focus for the language. Perpetual insistence on correct communication is avoided. Learning second language French in early immersion becomes incidental and unconscious, similar to the way a first language is acquired. Emphasis is placed on understanding French before speaking French.

Sixth, the pupils **start immersion** education with a similar lack of experience of the second language. Most are monolingual. Starting with relatively homogeneous language skills not only simplifies the teacher's task. It also means that pupils' self-esteem and classroom motivation is not at risk due to some pupils being linguistically more expert. *Seventh,* pupils in immersion education experience the same curriculum as mainstream 'core' pupils.

One of the **limitations of immersion** bilingual education is that for many students, French can become a school-only phenomenon. Outside the school walls, immersion students tend not to use French any more than 'drip feed, 30 minutes a day' second language students. Immersion students are competent in French, but tend not to communicate in French in the community. Potential does not necessarily lead to production; skill does not ensure street speech. Lack of spontaneous or contrived French language opportunity and a dearth of French cultural occasions to actively and purposefully use the second language may partly be the explanation. Immersion programs have been criticized for being strong on language, but weak on widening immersion students' cultural horizons.

Various other possible **limitations** in immersion education need sharing. *First,* immersion students do not always become grammatically accurate in their French. Immersion students also tend to lack the social and stylistic sense of appropriate language use which the native speaker possesses.

Second, there is difficulty in pinpointing the crucial factors that create an effective immersion experience. There are, for example, factors such as teaching techniques that may change the success of the immersion experience for pupils. Is it immersion as a system that leads to relatively successful outcomes or, (or as well as), factors such as student motivation, teachers' preparation, home culture, parental attitude, community vitality, and amount of time studying different curricula? Individualized, **activity-based teaching** techniques may be more effective than traditional 'whole class' techniques. **Intensity of language learning**, for example, how many hours per day, is likely to be more important than the length of language learning (e.g. the number of years of second language learning).

Third, immersion programs can have **effects on mainstream schools**. For example, effects may include: a redistribution of classroom teachers and leaders, a change in the language and ability profile of mainstream classes, and discrepancies in class size with increasing numbers of mixed-age classes.

Fourth, it is important not to view immersion education in Canada in purely educational terms. Behind immersion education are political, social and cultural beliefs and values. Immersion education is not just immersion in a second language (French). It is important to see immersion education not just as a means to promote bilingualism, but also as a move to a different kind of society. By promoting bilingualism in English speakers, immersion education in Canada may support French language communities, increase the opportunities for Francophones outside Quebec and help promote bilingualism in the public sector (and debatably in the private sector).

Immersion education is seen as a Trojan horse of further English assimilation by some Francophones. Some Francophones question whether an increase in bilingual Anglophones will simply deprive them of their historical advantage in occupying bilingual jobs. This is linked to the finding that children from higher socioeconomic backgrounds tend to be over-represented in immersion programs. Thus immersion education may act to reproduce elite groups, giving Anglophone children with bilingual abilities an advantage in the jobs market.

Fifth, there is danger of generalizing from the Canadian experience to elsewhere in the world. In Canada, immersion concerns **two major high status international languages**: French and English. In many countries where bilingualism is present or fostered, the situation is different. Often the context is one of a majority and a minority language (or languages) co-existing. This links with additive and subtractive bilingual situations. Canada is regarded as an additive bilingual context. Immersion bilingual education is an example of additive bilingual education. Many countries across the five continents contain subtractive bilingual contexts. For example, in the United States, one aim of Transitional Bilingual Education (see a separate question) is to replace (or 'subtract') the home, minority language (e.g. Spanish, Italian, Greek) with English.

Canadian immersion bilingual education has been an educational experiment of unusual success and growth. It has influenced bilingual education in Europe and beyond. For example, with variations to suit regional and national contexts, the **Catalans and Basques** and the **Welsh and Irish** have emulated the experiment with similar success. In Catalonia, research indicates that Spanish-speaking children who follow an immersion program not only become fluent in Catalan, but also their Spanish does not suffer. Throughout the curriculum, such Catalan immersion children perform as well and sometimes better than their peers who do not follow an immersion program.

E17 What are the main classroom features of successful immersion programs?

First, the **minimum time** the second language needs to be used as a medium to ensure 'receptive' (listening and reading) second language proficiency is four to six years. Around the end of elementary schooling, immersion students show equal or higher performance in the curriculum compared with their mainstream peers.

Second, the **curriculum** tends to be the same for immersion children as for their mainstream peers. Thus, immersion children can easily be compared with mainstream children for levels of achievement. Immersion students compared with mainstream students are neither more advantaged nor more disadvantaged by studying a **common curriculum**.

Immersion needs to attempt to cultivate empathy for the new language **culture** (e.g. French culture in Canada). The immersion curriculum needs to have distinct components in it that develop **participation** in that language's distinctive culture. The danger is then that French becomes the language of school, and English the language of the playground, street and vocational success. The English language cultural influence is often so strong and persuasive that French immersion children are in danger of becoming passive rather than active bilinguals outside the school gates.

Third, studies of bilingual education indicate that it may be preferable to **separate languages in instruction** rather than to mix them during a single lesson. It tends to be regarded as preferable that one language is used for one set of subjects; the other language for a separate set. When there is language mixing inside a lesson, students may wait for the explanation in their stronger language. Such students may simply switch off when transmission is in their weaker language. Sustained periods of monolingual instruction will require students to attend to the language of instruction, both improving their language competences and acquiring subject matter simultaneously.

The **fourth** issue is how much **time** should be devoted to the two languages within the curriculum? The typical recommendation is that a minimum of 50% of instruction should be in the second language. Thus, in French immersion, French-medium teaching and learning may occur from 50% to 100% of the school week. In French immersion in Canada, the amount of instruction in the English language increases as children become older. One factor in such a decision can be the amount of exposure a child receives to English outside school. Where a child's environment, home and street, media and community are English medium, such saturation may imply that a smaller proportion of time needs to be spent on English in the school. At the same time, the public will usually require bilingual schools to show that children's majority language skills, particularly literacy, are not affected by bilingual education. Bilingual schools need to ensure that, through school instruction and school learning experiences, majority language proficiency and literacy is monitored and promoted. Such majority language instruction may range from a minimum of 10% for seven-year-olds and older, to 70% or more for those in examination classes at secondary level schooling.

Fifth, immersion education has been built around the twin towers of teacher enthusiasm and parental commitment. French immersion **parents** in Canada tend to be middle class, involved in school teacher–parent committees, and take a sustained interest in their children's progress. Immersion education in Canada has, from its beginnings in Montreal in 1965 to the present, been powerfully promoted by parents. The first immersion classroom in 1965 owed much to parent initiation. Since then, the Canadian Parents for French organization has been a powerful pressure group for the recognition and dissemination, evolution and dispersal of immersion education. Parents in other countries have also been powerful advocates at the grass roots level for other 'strong' forms of bilingual education (e.g. Wales). Through localized pressure groups, schools which give native language medium teaching have successfully developed.

Teachers in Canadian immersion classrooms tend to have native or native-like proficiency in both French and English. Such teachers are able to understand children speaking in their home language but speak to the children almost entirely in French. Teachers are thus important language models through their status and power role, identifying French with something of value. Immersion teachers also provide the child with a model of acceptable French pronunciation and style. The teacher is a language model for the child, providing a variety of language experiences and models of different language usage.

Most **immersion teachers** are particularly committed to bilingual education, enthusiastic about bilingualism in society, acting as language missionaries. Research in Wales suggests the **importance of teacher commitment** in immersion bilingual education. This commitment exists beyond teachers' interest in the education of children. In the equation of a successful bilingual school, such enthusiasm and commitment by Headteachers and Principals, teachers and auxiliary workers, may be an important and often underestimated factor in success. There is a danger of seeing success in bilingual education as due to the system (e.g. immersion) and use of two languages in school. The commitment of bilingual teachers, and the special skills that a bilingual teacher uses beyond those required of a monolingual teacher, may be underestimated in the equation of successful bilingual schooling.

Sixth, the French immersion approach allows a relatively **homogeneous language classroom**. For example, in Canadian early total immersion, children will start from the same point. All are beginners without French proficiency. This makes the task of the teacher relatively easy. Children can grow in the French language under a shared teaching and learning approach. Initially, there will be no disparity of status due to some children being more proficient than others in French.

On a comparative education note, the term 'immersion' is used in Wales and Ireland. In these Celtic situations, there is often a **classroom mixture** of those who are fluent and those who are less fluent in the classroom language. For example, in an Irish immersion school, the classroom may be composed both of children whose home language is Irish and those whose home language is English but whose parents are keen for their children to be taught through the medium of Irish.

The Irish and Welsh experience tend to suggest that most children whose home language is English will cope successfully in **minority language immersion** classrooms. For such children, the language context is additive rather than subtractive. The danger is that the majority language of English, being the common denominator, will be the language used between pupils in the classroom, in the playground and certainly out of school. A balance towards a greater proportion of language minority speakers may help to ensure that the 'common denominator' majority language does not always dominate in informal classroom and playground talk.

Seventh, immersion provides an **additive bilingual environment**. Students acquire French at no cost to their home language and culture. Such enrichment may be contrasted to subtractive bilingual environments where the home language is replaced by the second language. For example, where the home language is Spanish and the submersion approach is to replace Spanish by English, negative rather than positive effects may occur in school performance and self-esteem. This underlines that the term immersion education is best reserved for additive rather than subtractive environments. The term 'immersion education' is appropriate only when the home language is a majority language and the school is adding a second minority or majority language.

E18 What language strategies are used in immersion classrooms?

Immersion education is based on the idea that a first language is acquired relatively unconsciously. Children are unaware that they are acquiring a language in the home. Immersion attempts to copy this process in the early years of schooling. The **focus is on the content and not the form of the language.** It is the task at hand that is central, not conscious language learning. In the early stages, there are no formal language learning classes, although simple elements of grammar such as verb endings may be taught informally. In the latter years of elementary schooling, formal consideration may be given to the rules of the language (e.g. grammar and syntax). The **early stages of immersion tend to mirror the unconscious acquisition of learning of the first language**. Only later will a child be made conscious of language as a system, to reinforce and promote communication.

Immersion also tends to assume that the **earlier a language is taught the better**. While teenagers and adults may learn a second language fluently and proficiently, research evidence tends to suggest that young children acquire authentic pronunciation better than adults. A young child is more plastic and malleable. The argument for immersion schooling tends to be, 'the earlier the better'.

In the early stages in Early French immersion classrooms, the teacher concentrates on **listening comprehension skills**. Oral skills are given more importance in kindergarten to Grade 3; reading and writing skills, even though started as early as Grade 1 (age 6), are stressed in Grades 4 to 6. Students are not made to speak French with their teacher or with their peers in the initial stages. Children will initially speak English to each other and to their teacher, without any penalty. Immersion teachers do not force children to use French until they are naturally willing to do so. Early insistence on French may inhibit children and develop negative attitudes to the French language and to education in general. Over the first two years, immersion children develop an understanding of French and then begin to speak French, particularly to the teacher.

The most frequent grade in which **English** becomes part of the formal curriculum in Early Total French Immersion is Grade 3. Other practices include introducing English at an earlier grade or kindergarten and at Grade 4.

In the early stages of immersion, it is crucial that the **teacher is comprehensible** to the children. The teacher needs to be sympathetically aware of the level of a child's vocabulary and grammar, to deliver in French at a level the child can understand, and simultaneously, be constantly pushing forward a child's competence in French. The teacher will be aiming to push back the frontiers of a child's French by ensuring that messages are both comprehensible and are slightly ahead of the learner's current level of mastery of the language.

The language used to communicate with the child at these early stages is often called **caretaker speech**. For the first year or two in immersion, the vocabulary will be deliberately limited. There will be a simplified presentation of grammar and syntax. The teacher may be repetitive in the words used and the ideas presented, with the same idea presented in two or more ways. The teacher will deliberately speak slowly, giving the child more time to process the language input and understand the meaning. This tends to parallel the simplified talk of mother to child (**motherese**) and **foreigner talk** (a person deliberately simplifying and slowing the language so a foreigner can understand). During this caretaker stage, the teacher may be constantly questioning the child to ensure that understanding has occurred.

A teacher may also present the language to be used before a lesson topic is presented. When new words and new concepts are being introduced into a lesson, the teacher may spend some time in introducing the words and clarifying the concepts so that the language learner is prepared. Such teachers may also be sensitive to **non-verbal feedback** from students: questioning glances, losing concentration and a glazed look. A student may be encouraged to question the teacher for clarification and simplification when understanding has not occurred.

These strategies cover two different areas: the importance of **understandable instruction** and the importance of **negotiating meaning**. The worst case is when neither the teacher nor the pupil is aware that misunderstanding (or no understanding) has taken place. A more effective classroom is when pupils and teachers are negotiating meaning, ensuring that mutual understanding has occurred. Not only is the negotiation of meaning important in language development and in maximizing achievement throughout the curriculum, it is also important in aiding motivation of children within the classroom. Patronizing such children and oversimplifying are two of the dangers in this process. Therefore, constantly presenting students with ever challenging and advancing learning situations is important in classroom achievement.

Immersion classrooms usually have a particular view about **language errors**. Language errors are a typical and important part of the language learning process. Errors are not a symptom of failure. They are a natural part of learning. Errors are not permanent knots that spoil the wood. With time and practice, these knots can be removed. Therefore, immersion teachers are discouraged from over-correcting children's attempts to speak a second language. Just as parents are more likely to correct children's factual errors than their first language errors, the immersion teacher will tend to avoid constant correction of errors. Constant error correction may be self-defeating, negatively reinforcing language acquisition. Language accuracy tends to develop over time and with experience. Constant correction of error disrupts communication and content learning in the classroom. When a child or several children constantly make the same errors, then appropriate and positive intervention may be of value.

In the early stages of immersion, there will be a natural **interlanguage** among children (a simplified 'mixed' language used initially by a second language learner). A child may change round the correct order in a sentence yet produce a perfectly comprehensible message. For example, faulty syntax may occur due to the influence of the first language on the second language. A child may put the pronoun or a preposition in the wrong order: as in 'go you and get it'. Interlanguage is not to be seen as error. Rather it indicates the linguistic creativity of students who are using their latent understanding of the first language to construct meaningful communication in the second language. Interlanguage is thus an intermediate, approximate system. It is a worthwhile attempt to communicate and therefore needs encouragement. Seen as a halfway stage in-between monolingualism and being proficient in a second language, interlanguage becomes part of the journey and not a permanent rest point.

The immersion teacher will assume that proficiency in the first language contributes to proficiency in the second language. Concepts attached to words in the first language will easily be **transferred** into the second language. The acquisition of literacy skills in the first language tends to facilitate the acquisition of literacy skills in the second language. However, not all aspects of a language will transfer. Rules of grammar and spelling may not lend themselves to transfer. The closer a language structure is to the second language structure, the greater the transfer there is likely to be between the two languages. For example, the transfer between English and Spanish is likely to be more than Arabic to English due to differences in syntax, symbols and direction of writing. However, the system of meanings, the conceptual map and skills that a person owns, may be readily transferable between languages.

The focus of immersion classrooms is very much on **tasks and curriculum content**. There is also a place for an analytical approach to the second and the first language in the classroom. An immersion classroom will not just enable children to acquire the second language in an unconscious, almost incidental manner. Towards the end of elementary education, the experiential approach may be joined by a meaning-based focus on the form of language. Children may at this point be encouraged to **analyze their vocabulary and grammar**. At this later stage, some lessons may have progress in the second language as their sole aim. After early sheltering with language, the development of vocabulary and grammar may be dealt with in a direct and systematic manner.

Ten specific techniques that tend to be used by experienced and effective immersion teachers are given below.

(1) Providing plenty of contextual support for the language being used (e.g. by body language — plenty of gestures, facial expressions and acting).
(2) Deliberately giving more classroom directions and organizational advice to immersion students. For example, signaling the start and the end of different routines, more explicit directions with homework and assignments.
(3) Understanding where a child is at, thereby connecting the unfamiliar with the familiar, the known with the unknown. New material is linked directly and explicitly with the child's present knowledge and understanding.
(4) Extensive use of visual material. Using concrete objects to illustrate lessons, using pictures and audio-visual aids, giving the child plenty of hands-on manipulative activities to ensure all senses are used in the educational experience.
(5) Obtaining constant feedback as to the level of a student's understanding. Diagnosing the level of a student's language.
(6) Using plenty of repetition, summaries, restatement to ensure that students understand the directions of the teacher.
(7) The teacher being a role model for language emulation by the student.
(8) Indirect error correction rather than constantly faulting students. Teachers ensure that the corrections are built in to their language to make a quick and immediate impact.
(9) Using plenty of variety in both general learning tasks and in language learning tasks.
(10) Using frequent and varied methods to check the understanding level of the children.

(adapted from M.A. Snow (1990) Instructional methodology in immersion foreign language education. In A.M. Padilla, H.H. Fairchild and C.M. Valadez (eds) *Foreign Language Education: Issues and Strategies*. London: Sage).

E19 My child has been placed in a Withdrawal class for extra language support. How should I react to this?

Induction classes, Withdrawal classes, Transition classes, Reception classes or whatever name is given them have often received a bad press. Such classes provide **language support** for a child. Such extra language help before a child enters a mainstream classroom seems valuable and important. Taking a child out from lessons for a few periods a week, or placed in a special class for a few months, or a special language center for a few months, may provide the language confidence required for the child to swim in the complex language pool of the classroom. However, there are possible negative outcomes, nothing to do with language.

What educationists have spotlighted is the **non-language effects of such classes**. Children placed in these classes may feel stigmatized, separated, ostracized, and feel that they have a deficiency in language. Entry into usual peer group relationships may be made difficult. This leads some educationists to argue for language support **within** the class, avoiding language support in Withdrawal classes or separate language centers. Providing bilingual resources for teachers, use of parents in the classroom and team teaching in the classroom may be ways in which language support is given more subtly to particular children, with less stigmatization and more sensitivity.

Potential problems of a psychological nature that may be caused by extra language help should not detract from language help being given. Particularly where minority language children attend a mainstream majority language school, there is often a need for supplementary language help in the classroom. Such **language support** is not to be questioned. How such support is given to minimize the risk of a loss of face and self-esteem for that child requires discussion. For minority language children, this often means that Withdrawal classes may not always be the best method. A special track or stream in the school for such children, particularly when there are color, racial and ethnic differences between streams, is best avoided. Integration of children in school is a high priority. This means that support, where possible, needs providing in a positive, sensitive and diplomatic way in the mainstream classroom itself. The fewer language minority children in such a school, the more integration in mainstream classrooms is possible and desirable.

Thus many educationists argue for **integration rather than segregation** when there are children with particular language needs. When language minority children are integrated, majority language peers may be used to help such language minority children in the classroom. Majority language children can become language models for the minority language child. Such cooperation may succeed in providing a more integrated and harmonious classroom.

Withdrawal classes or language centers are more defensible for majority language children learning a new, majority language or minority language. Such majority language children may have fewer problems of stigmatization, prejudice or integration because they own a majority language and culture that has high status and prestige.

When a large number of children with a majority language are placed in a minority language school, there is a tendency for minority language children to **switch** to the majority language. The teacher may also switch from previously using the minority language to using the majority language much of the time. When majority in-migrants, for example, change the language balance of the school, there may be an argument for separate provision for those in-migrants. Some induction into the minority language may be considered before attending schools operating in that minority language. This places a responsibility on teachers to ensure there is good integration of children from different language backgrounds when immediate or later mixing occurs.

E20 What kind of education should I give my child if we regularly move to different countries?

This type of question tends to come from those parents who, as part of their employment, have to move regularly across regional and national borders. For example, workers in the Council of Europe, the European Union, diplomats, those working for large international companies, those involved in marketing and commerce in a variety of countries and academics are increasingly moving across borders. Children are resilient and adapt to new circumstances and situations with an ease that many adults do not predict. Nevertheless, for all children, there is a **transition period**, of adapting to new circumstances, new friends, a new school and a new pattern of living. The home and family become an important source of stability, strength and continuity for the child.

Children differ in their accommodation of new circumstances, a new school and new friends. Some meet the challenge with interest and confidence, learning to adapt and enjoy fresh stimulation. Such children adapt to sunshine, snow, wind and rain. They enjoy the seasons, the change of seasons and the benefits of each. At the other end of the dimension, there are those children who are shy, lack confidence in their ability to cope in new circumstances, quickly become apprehensive of a change of circumstances and require much greater support in the home and in the school. Such differences between children not only emanate from child rearing practices, but also from personality, prior experiences in schools and age. Race, color, creed and language also play a part in this.

For parents in this situation, there are sometimes **choices** of sending a child to a boarding school where the home language is used. This may be in the home country. Alternatively, there are sometimes schools in large cities that teach through international languages (i.e. a different language from mainstream schools in the country of current placement).

Another alternative is to leave a child with the extended family or other carers in the home country. This will establish continuity of schooling for the child, allowing the child to return to the family at vacation times and school breaks. Another alternative is for children to accompany their parents as they move. Children attend the local school. This may mean a switch of language. When children are very young, for example under the age of seven, there is usually little problem in switching schools where a different language is used. However, as children become older, adapting to a completely new language environment becomes more difficult in terms of speedy language learning, obtaining sufficient skills in a language to cope in the classroom alongside first language speakers, and understanding a relatively complex curriculum.

Therefore, into the **decision equation** comes: the age of the child (younger children can linguistically and educationally adapt more easily than older children); a decision about children living in the home or being away at Boarding school or remaining at home with friends and carers; the personality and adaptability of the child to a new situation; how effective the new school will be in providing a sensitive transition period for the child and accommodating the language profile of the child; and will the school provide supplementary help and language support. Also, an important part of the equation is the time and effort parents are prepared to play in smoothing the transition to a new language and culture for their child, the language support that they, and those around them, can offer the child, and parents' own goals and wishes for the educational and language development of their child.

E21 How valuable are Saturday Schools and Voluntary Schools outside regular school hours in the development of a minority or second language?

When parents speak a minority language, Voluntary Schools and Saturday Schools may be a path parents choose, where available, to extend that minority or native language. For example, Italian speakers in Britain sometimes have locally supported Saturday Schools where children of Italian origin supplement their education through their heritage language. This is a device used by some mixed language families in certain European countries to maintain and enrich the less practiced language of the home. The reason for such schools is that such children will be taking their education through the medium of the majority language. Parents want the **home language** to be **supported** and extended, for the culture attached to the language to be taught and caught in such schools, and for their children to understand curriculum areas through their native tongue. So long as such schools are a joy rather than a burden, a pleasurable experience for the children rather than making large inroads into their playtime, such schools have great value. A child becomes more bilingual and more bicultural. Many such schools are important in literacy development in the home language.

Such schools work particularly well when they support and extend the language, or one of the languages of the home. When such schools are **effective**, it may increase the motivation of both the children and parents. However, if children see such schools as an imposition, as depriving them of time for sport, playing with friends out of school, and time for personal hobbies and interests, such schools may serve to work against their aims. One **danger** is that the child will see such extra schooling as a negative accompaniment of their minority language and culture. Therefore, such schools need to provide an enjoyable and pleasurable experience for the children.

While some Saturday Schools and Voluntary Schools are enterprising and effective, unfortunately in many such schools, the education is not progressive in style or content. Typical problems include: a lack of trained, qualified teachers; poor working conditions and facilities; outdated, imported materials (e.g. books); large classes; poor attendance and demotivated children; rote-learning rather than activity methods; dogmatic teaching; and few financial resources to pay teachers and buy equipment.

Such Saturday and Voluntary Schools also exist to teach a **new language**, for example a language that the parents have lost. Another example is schools that teach a language for religion and worship (e.g. Arabic, Hebrew, Yiddish, Greek or Russian). When Islam, Judaism or Orthodox Christianity requires an understanding of a different tongue from the home and school, such schools may have the purpose of ensuring children can understand the Koran, the Talmud, the Bible and understand the sacred language of worship in a Temple, Synagogue, Mosque or Church. Given that such schools provide strong links with the child's nuclear and extended family, links with the child's roots and tradition, history and heritage, and teach morals and values, attitudes and beliefs, such schools have great value. The high premium that many Jews place on Hebrew, and Moslems on Arabic, shows the key place that language plays in maintaining religious tradition and ensuring an enculturation that links the past with the present, the precious heritage with a Godly future.

ACHIEVEMENT AND UNDERACHIEVEMENT QUESTIONS

E22 Will my child's performance in school be affected by being bilingual?

This is an important question. Take the child who is bilingual via the home and attends a monolingual school. There is no evidence to suggest that children will be handicapped in their school performance by being bilingual. Bilingual children attending a monolingual school may have some advantages in thinking that have been outlined in the first section. However, this answer needs refining. When children are dominant in a **minority language** and attend a school through the majority language, and where their peers are mostly majority language speakers, there may be potential problems.

Studies in the United States tend to show that children from **language minority homes** whose bilingualism is not valued by the school, who are forced to operate alongside majority language peers in a majority language, can fall behind. Their linguistic skills are being denied. The level of fluency, power of thinking, even literacy skills in the minority language are not recognized by the monolingual school. Instead, such skills are ignored. Children are expected to learn through a weaker language. Such children may feel that their minority language, their parents, their culture, their home and family are being rejected by the school's rejection of their minority language. Their self-esteem, self-confidence and belief in their learning ability may suffer in such a situation.

Such a school is failing to build on the language minority children's current level of understanding or level of **intellectual development** by not using their minority language. Therefore, such children's education may suffer. In comparison with their monolingual, majority language peers, they may fall behind. Initial failure may breed further failure rather than 'success breeding success'. This provides a strong argument for minority language children being educated through their minority language.

When **majority language** children are **educated in a minority language or a second majority language**, international evidence tends to suggest that their achievement does not suffer in school. The first majority language is not under threat, nor is their self-esteem, status nor academic competence. In such an **additive bilingual environment**, majority language children tend to benefit from bilingual schooling, either in a minority language or a second majority language, without negative effects on their achievement. There may be a **temporary lag**. The child is learning a second language, and learning to work in that second language in the curriculum. Hence, there may be a temporary period when a child is behind monolingual peers in mainstream schooling. Canadian research suggests that any such lag between approximately the ages of six and ten years of age is temporary. Children taught through a second language quickly catch up. Indeed the Canadian research tends to suggest that some bilingual children surpass their monolingual peers in performance in the curriculum, perhaps due to the advantages in thinking and self-esteem that two languages give.

If there is an essential **principle** to ensure a child's performance is not being negatively affected by their bilingualism, it is that parents and the school must ensure that a child's language development is sufficiently advanced for that child to be able to **cope with an increasingly complex conceptual level in the curriculum**. In the early years of primary education, the language complexity of the classroom makes relatively few demands on the child's language skills. As a child proceeds through school, there is a removal of actions, physical demonstrations and less body language. Learning is increasingly through abstract words and ideas, and less through object lessons. Therefore, the **bilingual child's language has to be matched to the complexity level of the curriculum in the classroom**. This either means ensuring that the child has sufficiently well developed language to cope in the curriculum. Or, the teacher needs to adapt to the language level of the child, encouraging language development while making sure that over-complex and over-abstract curriculum learning is not introduced too early.

Problems may arise when older children are placed in a classroom and are expected to work in a **language** that is **underdeveloped** or below the level demanded in curriculum activity. This situation will be considered separately in a later question.

If the child is placed in a school which is unable to give language support for the child's home language, the degree of **determination** of the **parents** will be vital in maintaining the language. Such determination and interest in the child's language learning can have a positive knock-on effect. The child's overall motivation to succeed and desire to achieve may be stimulated by parental interest and encouragement. The latent message is that the child is capable: capable with languages, therefore capable in general learning at school.

E23 Are there positive effects of learning through the medium of two languages?

The bilingual has the **advantage** of operating in two languages compared with the monolingual. This usually means later success in two languages when assessed as a curriculum area. For example, the child who is fluent in French and English will usually be highly successful in French in the British, Irish or North American secondary school. It may also mean an increase in employment prospects, cultural biliteracy, and being able to operate in two language groups and two language cultures. In this sense, a child educated bilingually may be more sympathetic and sensitive to language and ethnic diversity in the world, have a wider world view and have more cultural 'costumes' and understandings than the monolingual child.

Canadian research also shows that there may be small performance advantages among 'balanced' or well developed bilinguals in school. Those **children who can work in either language in the curriculum** may show a marginally improved performance in the curriculum. If there are cognitive benefits attached to bilinguals (outlined in Section B), this may bring success in the classroom. If a child has permeated the two cultures attached to the languages, there may be more width of understanding, appreciation and sensibility that can enhance performance in subjects such as History and Geography, Social Studies, the Creative Arts and the Language Arts.

E24 My child is learning through a new language. Will this affect attainment at school?

If the **switch** has been **from a minority language to a majority language,** there is a possibility that attainment will suffer in school. If children feel their minority language, their parents, their home and heritage and culture have all been rejected, such children may feel dislocated, have lower self-esteem and lack academic self-confidence. In cases where the minority language has been rejected and replaced by another, educational performance may suffer.

This pattern of **potential failure** is found in some submersion and transitional bilingual education schools in the United States. When Spanish-speaking children enter such schools, their Spanish is either denied or only allowed for a short period (such as a year). The expectation is that they move as quickly as possible into the majority language (English). Their linguistic resources are denied by the school. The children are expected to begin again in a new language. When they are placed in the mainstream alongside monolingual English speakers, many become low achievers, become segregated and are labeled as deficient or limited in their language proficiency. For example, the official United States term for such bilinguals is Limited English Proficiency children.

Wherever possible, **language minority** children need their language to be represented in the school and to learn through the medium of that language for as long as possible. Research tends to suggest this produces maximal performance for that child.

Where a **language majority child** enters a school and learns through a new language, particularly when this language is learned from an earlier age, attainment is unlikely to suffer. For example, children from English homes learning through the medium of French in Canada have not been found to suffer disadvantages in curriculum performance. Where both their languages are well developed, there are possible curriculum advantages to being bilingual. Another example is when a family moves to a different country. Language majority children, particularly when young, usually adapt to the new language school situation.

Two cases may be less positive in outcome. First, when a **language minority** child moves to a school or different geographical location where their minority language is not valued, even ridiculed, the imposition of a majority language may create lower self-esteem, lower academic motivation and lower school performance. The child's linguistic skills are denied by this subtractive bilingual situation. Second, when an **older child moves school**, the danger is that they will not be able to cope with increasingly complex concepts in the curriculum in a 'new' language.

Part of the equation of success in school is that a child learns a positive academic self-concept. This includes believing that both the owned languages are valued in school, in the home and in society. In this **additive** language environment, the child may become aware that two languages are better than one, that bilingualism means addition rather than subtraction, multiplication rather than division. Hence academic attainment in the primary school and secondary school is unlikely to be different from monolinguals. While there may be a temporary lag in primary school in attainment compared with the monolingual as the child learns a new language, this is temporary and is unlikely to be evident beyond a two- to four-year period.

E25 My child's school teaches through the minority language. Will this affect my child's development in the majority language?

The answer is almost definitely not. Children who learn through the minority language usually pick up the majority language with a degree of ease. There are two main reasons for this. **First**, what a child learns in one language can easily be **transferred** into a second language. The child who learns about evaporation in the environment, about the life cycle of an amoeba, or military strategies in history does not have to relearn those concepts and ideas in the majority language. Such knowledge, skills, ideas and concepts, attitudes and feelings easily transfer into the majority language. So long as the child has the vocabulary in the majority language, what is learned at school is usable in that majority language.

Second, a child's majority language fluency and competence is often well represented through other **experiences in the environment**. On breakfast cereal packets, television, pop music cassettes and compact disks, street signs and posters, newspapers and magazines, comics and catalogs, majority languages are well represented. Also, many children are exposed to the majority language in the playground, in the street and with the growth of the peer group. Often, the majority language is the common denominator language to such an extents that the minority language speakers are expected to switch into that majority language when only one person is present who cannot understand that minority language.

Out-of-school experiences often help children develop in the majority language. Therefore, if the diet of the school is mostly in the minority language, and there is a diet outside school partly in the majority language, children often become bilingual. However, it is also important in school that time is allocated to ensuring fluency and literacy in the majority language. **Over-balancing** towards the minority language and too little development of the majority language is rarely in the best interests of the child. Literacy in the majority language is usually essential for the majority language child.

A child needs a richness of experience in the majority and minority languages. As was expressed in Section A, it is the quality, variety, stimulation of experiences in a language that makes for richness, not just quantity of experience. If the majority language is experienced for large periods of time (e.g. through the television and computer), the majority language may lack vigor, cultural breadth and a wealth of experience. Just as the developing body needs a varied and healthy diet, so does a developing language — majority as well as minority.

E26 Speakers of our home language are often poor and unemployed. Should we ensure our child is educated in the majority language to aid employment prospects?

In some countries of the world, **bilinguals** are over-represented among the poor, underprivileged, unemployed and disadvantaged. The Spanish speakers in the United States, the Welsh in rural areas of Wales, Irish speakers on the west coast of Ireland, Gaelic speakers in north west Scotland, and many lesser-used language groups in Europe, are marked by relatively less affluence, relative disadvantage and poverty. With in-migrants, guest workers, refugees and indigenous languages in remote rural areas, there is a pattern of deprivation, unemployment and poverty. While there are many examples of bilinguals in elite positions, (e.g. in Europe, working for the Council of Europe or European Union and working in transnational companies), most bilinguals don't tend to be in such privileged circumstances.

Speakers of languages that are aligned with poverty, unemployment, less power and political influence, often wonder if **moving to the majority language** will give them more access to advantage, employment and affluence. It is as if changing language might change life fortunes. Bread on the table is more important than bilingualism. It is important for minority language speakers to become fully fluent and functional in the majority language. To compete against majority language monolinguals, it is important to be able to start on relatively equal terms as far as language goes. Access to employment may require a high degree of competence in the majority language. The opportunity to compete for jobs increases when a person has majority language skills.

However, this is an **argument for thorough bilingualism**. It is not an argument for majority language monolingualism. Families and schools can ensure that children are thoroughly competent in the majority language while retaining their minority language. One language need not be removed to improve another. Languages don't exist in a balance: the higher the one, the lower the other. Rather two languages (and more) can be accommodated within the thinking systems of individuals. Retaining the minority language while ensuring that majority language competence is high enables a bilingual child to have more rather than less. If the majority language overtakes the minority language at home, much will be lost. Heritage, family identity, subtle psychological processes that hold families in unity, especially in times of problems and crises, the cultural cement that holds minority families together, will be lost. Loss of the minority language may divide the family. Gaining fluency in the majority language while retaining the minority language will be a multiplication of language skills and culture.

E27 My child seems to be underachieving at school. Is this because of bilingualism?

There are frequent occasions when children are felt to be under-achieving. Most parents believe their children are under-performing, at least sometimes in their educational careers. When language minority or language majority children appear to exhibit under-achievement in the classroom, what may be the explanation? When first, second or third generation in-migrant children appear to fail in the classroom, where is the 'blame' popularly placed? When guest workers' children, indigenous minorities and distinct ethnic groups are shown statistically to leave school earlier, be lower achievers in examinations and tests or receive lower grades and averages, what is the cause?

First, the blame may be attributed to the child's **bilingualism**. Bilingualism itself is often popularly seen as causing cognitive confusion. The explanation given is a picture of the bilingual brain with two engines working at half throttle, while the monolingual has one well tuned engine at full throttle. As Sections A and B revealed, such an explanation is incorrect. Where two languages are well developed, then bilingualism is more likely to lead to cognitive advantages than disadvantages (see the three-tiered house diagram on page 52). Only when a child's two languages are *both* poorly developed can 'blame' be attributed to bilingualism itself. Even then, the blame should not go to the victim, but to the societal circumstances that create underdeveloped languages.

Second, where under-achievement exists, the reason may be given as **lack of exposure to the majority language**. In the United States and England, a typical explanation for the under-achievement of certain language minorities is insufficient exposure to English. Failure or below average performance is attributed to students having insufficiently developed English language skills to cope with the curriculum. Those who use Spanish or French or Bengali at home and in the neighborhood are perceived to struggle at school due to a lack of skills in the dominant, mainstream language. Thus submersion and transitional forms of bilingual education attempt to ensure a fast conversion to the majority language.

A **fast conversion** to the majority language stands the chance of doing **more harm than good**. It denies the child's skills in the home language, even denies the identity and self-respect of the child itself. Instead of using existing language skills, the 'sink or swim' approach attempts to replace those skills. The level of English used in the curriculum may also cause the child to show under-achievement, with consequent demands for more of the same medicine (more English language lessons).

Under-achievement in majority language education (e.g. submersion and transitional bilingual education) may be combated by providing education through the medium of the minority language. When the language minority child is allowed to operate in their heritage language in the curriculum, the evidence suggests that success rather than failure results. Such success includes becoming fluent in the majority language (e.g. English). Thus **lack of exposure** to a majority language (e.g. English) is a popular but **incorrect explanation** of under-achievement. This explanation fails to note the advantages of education in the minority language for achievement. It inappropriately seeks an answer in increased majority language tuition rather than increased minority language education.

Third, when bilingual children exhibit under-achievement, the attributed reason is sometimes a **mismatch between home and school**. Such a mismatch is seen as not just about language differences but also about dissimilarities in culture, values and beliefs. As an extreme, this tends to reflect a majority viewpoint that is assimilationist, imperialist and even oppressive. The child and family is expected to adjust to the system, not the system to be pluralist and incorporate variety. For such an assimilationist viewpoint, the solution is in the home adjusting to mainstream language and culture to prepare the child for school. Past advice by some professionals has been for language minority parents to raise their children in the majority, school language.

The alternative view is that, where practicable, the school system should be flexible enough to incorporate the home language and culture. A mismatch between home and school can be positively addressed by 'strong' forms of bilingual education for language minorities. By bilingual education, through the inclusion of parents in the running of the school, by involving parents as partners and participants in their child's education, the mismatch can become a merger.

Fourth, under-achievement may be attributed to **socioeconomic factors** that surround a language minority group. Typical circumstances are in-migrant and refugee children leading a life of urban poverty or rural isolation, living in deprived dwellings with minimal facilities. In some cases bilingual children live alongside abuse, malnutrition, poor health, ignorance and neglect. Their circumstances reveal a life of ethnic stigma and low status.

Socioeconomic status is a broad umbrella term that points to a **definite cause** of language minority under-achievement. It provides an example of the importance of not blaming the victim, but analyzing societal features that contribute to under-achievement. Such features may be **economic deprivation**, material circumstances and living conditions as well as psychological and social features such as discrimination, racial prejudice, pessimism and immobilizing inferiority.

While socioeconomic factors are a proper partial explanation of language minority under-achievement, two cautions must be sounded. Socioeconomic status doesn't explain why different language minorities of similar socioeconomic status may perform differently at school. **Beliefs, values and attitudes** vary between ethnic groups. Sociocultural factors within and between ethnic groups and not simply socioeconomic status must be assessed to begin to work out the equation of language minority achievement and under-achievement.

This raises another issue. Under-achievement cannot be simply related to one or several causes. The equation of under-achievement is going to be complex, involving a number of factors. Those factors will **interact** together and not be simple 'standalone' effects. For example, umbrella labels such as socioeconomic status need decomposing into more definable predictors of under-achievement (e.g. parents' attitude to education). Home factors will then interact with school factors providing an enormous number of different routes that may lead to varying school success and failure. The recipes of success and failure are many, with varying ingredients that interact together in complex ways. However, socioeconomic and sociocultural features are important ingredients in most equations of under-achievement.

Fifth, part of the language minority achievement and under-achievement equation is the **type of school** a child attends. The same child will tend to attain higher if placed in education that uses the heritage language as a medium of instruction than in programs which seek to replace the home language as quickly as possible. Therefore, when under-achievement occurs in a language minority child or within a language minority group, the system of schooling needs scrutiny. A system that suppresses the home language is likely to be part of the explanation of individual and ethnic group under-achievement where such under-achievement problems exist.

Sixth, types of school is a broad heading under which there can exist superior and inferior submersion schools, outstanding and mediocre Dual Language and Heritage Language schools. Where under-achievement exists, it is sometimes too simple to blame the type of school rather than digging deeper and locating more specific causes. Some of the attributes that affect the **quality of education** for language minority children include: the supply, ethnic origins and bilingualism of teachers, balance of language minority and language majority students in the classroom, use and sequencing of the two languages across the curriculum over different grades, and reward systems for enriching the minority language and culture.

Seventh, under-achievement may be due to **real learning difficulties** and the need for some form of special education. It is important to make a distinction between real and apparent learning difficulties. Too often, bilingual children are labeled as having learning difficulties which are attributed to their bilingualism. As is discussed later in this section, the causes of apparent learning problems may be much less in the child and much more in the school or in the education system. The child is perceived as having learning difficulties when the problem may lie in the subtractive, assimilative system which itself creates negative attitudes and low motivation. In the 'sink or swim' Submersion approach, 'sinking' can be attributed to an unsympathetic system and to insensitive teaching methods rather than individual learning problems.

Apart from system-generated and school-generated learning problems, there will be those who are bilingual and have genuine learning difficulties. The essential beginning is to distinguish between real, genuine individual learning difficulties and problems which are caused by factors outside the individual.

Such a distinction between the real and the apparent, the system-generated and the remediable problems of the individual, highlights the alternatives. When under-achievement exists, do we blame the victim, blame the teacher and the school, or blame the system? When assessment, tests and examinations occur and show relatively low performance of language minority individuals and groups, will prejudices about bilingual children and ethnic groups be confirmed? Or can we use such assessment to reveal deficiencies in the human architecture of the school system and the design of the curriculum rather than blame the child? As this section has revealed, under-achievement often tends to be blamed on the child and the language minority group. Often the explanation lies in factors outside of the individual.

E28 Should my child be placed in a Bilingual Special Education Program?

Categories of special education vary from country to country but are likely to include areas such as: visual impairment, hearing impairment, communication disorders, learning disabilities (e.g. dyslexia and developmental aphasia), severe subnormality in cognitive development, behavioral problems and physical handicaps.

In the United States the Office of Special Education has estimated that nearly one million children from language minority backgrounds are in need of some form of special education. Can we be sure that such a categorization is valid and just, and that such children will benefit from a placement in special education?

The danger is that many children from language minorities may be wrongly regarded as having a 'disability' and, as such, incorrectly placed in special education. The communicative differences of language minority children must be distinguished from communicative disorders. This occurs because **common errors** are made. The child is often assessed in a weaker, second language thereby inaccurately measuring both language development and general cognitive development. For example, in Britain and the United States, in-migrant children are often assessed through the medium of English and on their English proficiency. Their level of language competence in Spanish, Bengali, Turkish or Urdu, for example, is ignored. Thus such children are classed as having a 'language disability' and perhaps a 'learning disability'. Instead of being seen as developing bilinguals (i.e. children with a good command of their first language who are in the process of acquiring a second, majority language), they may be classed as of 'Limited English Proficiency' (LEP in the United States), or even as having general difficulties with learning. Their below average test scores in the second language are wrongly defined as a 'deficit' or 'disability' that can be remedied by some form of special education.

When language minority children are assessed it is important that three different aspects of their development be kept distinct: (1) language proficiency, (2) second language proficiency, and (3) the existence (or not) of a physical, learning or behavioral difficulty. This distinction means that there will be two different groups of bilinguals with regard to special education.

The first comprises those who are bilingual *and* have a physical, neurological, learning, emotional, cognitive or behavioral difficulty. Such children may need some kind of special education or intervention. One estimate in the United States is that 1 in 8 (approximately 12%) of language minority students will fit into this category. Similar figures are quoted in other countries. Most of these children will **benefit considerably from bilingual special education** rather than monolingual special education (e.g. English-medium special education in the United States).

When bilingual or language minority children have been accurately assessed as having special needs, many educators will argue that education solely in the dominant, majority language is needed. In the United States, the advice is often given that Latino children with special needs should be educated in monolingual, English special schools. The argument is that such children are going to live to an English-speaking society. When there is **serious mental retardation**, it seems sensible that a child should be educated monolingually. Such a child develops very slowly in one language.

For other special needs children, the **benefits of bilingual special education** are many. One example is the recently arrived in-migrant, special needs child. Placing such a child in a class where he or she doesn't speak the language of the classroom (e.g. English in the United States) will only increase failure and lower self-esteem. To be educated, the child preferably needs initial instruction mostly in the first language, with the chance to become as bilingual as possible. Most children with special needs are capable of developing in two languages. Many do not reach levels of proficiency in either language compared with peers in mainstream classrooms. Nevertheless, they reach satisfactory levels of proficiency in two languages according to their abilities. Becoming bilingual does not detract from achievement in other areas of the curriculum (e.g. Mathematics and Creative Arts).

Children in bilingual special education share the benefits of those in other forms of bilingual education: dual language, educational, cultural, self-identity and self-esteem benefits. These are discussed more fully in other answers in this section.

The second group comprises those who are bilingual and do **not** have a physical, learning or behavioral difficulty. This is the great majority of language minority children (e.g. seven out of every eight children). Such children will usually prosper in bilingual rather than special education. The optimal education for such children is where their first language is used as a medium of instruction. At the same time, the child learns the second (majority) language, gradually reaching competence in both languages. After a foundation of education in the first language, the second language is developed to the level where the child is able to work in the curriculum through either language.

Separation of these two groups shows that the child's second language proficiency is different from potential problems in an individual's capacities that require specialist treatment (e.g. hearing impairment, severely subnormal in 'IQ'). Neither the language and culture of the home, nor socioeconomic and ethnic differences should be considered as handicapping conditions. The child's level of functioning in a second language must not be seen as representing the child's level of language development. The child's development in the **first language** needs to be assessed (e.g. by observation if psychological and educational tests are not available) so as to paint a picture of proficiency rather than deficiency.

The movement of a bilingual student to special education should only occur after a conclusion is reached that the child's needs cannot be met by a regular (mainstream) school. This holds for those currently in bilingual education who may need special bilingual education. When a bilingual or language minority child requires special education, it is **preferable** for that to be **bilingual special education**.

One example not discussed so far is when a child is **failing** in a mainstream school due to his or her language proficiency not being sufficient to operate in the curriculum. For example, in the United States, some Spanish-speaking children are in mainstream schools (a 'submersion' experience) and, although of normal ability, fail in the system (e.g. drop out of school, repeat grades, leave High School without a diploma) because their English proficiency is insufficiently developed to comprehend the increasingly complex curriculum.

This situation creates an apparent dilemma. By being placed in some form of **special education**, the child is possibly stigmatized as having a 'deficiency' and a 'language deficit'. Such special education may be a separate school (or a special unit within a larger school) that provides special ('remedial') education for bilingual children. Such schools and units may not foster bilingualism. Often, they will emphasize children becoming competent in the majority language (e.g. English in the United States). Such segregation may allow more attention to the second language but result in ghettoization of language minorities. While giving some sanctuary from sinking in second language submersion in a mainstream school, special education can be a retreat, marginalizing the child. Will children in such special education realize their potential across the curriculum? Will they have increased access to employment? Will their apparent failure be accepted and validated because they are associated with a remedial institution? Will there be decreased opportunities for success in school achievement, employment and self-enhancement?

The ideal for children in this dilemma is not mainstreaming or special education. It is education which allows them to start and continue learning in their first language. The second language is nurtured as well — to ensure the development of bilinguals who can operate in mainstream society. In such schools, both languages are developed and used in the curriculum. Such schools avoid the 'remedial' or 'compensatory' associations of special education. Such schools celebrate the cultural and linguistic diversity of their students.

Bilingual education is sometimes in danger of being seen as a form of special education. Even when the 'language delayed' are separated from those who are in the early stages of learning the majority language (e.g. English in the United States), the danger is that the latter will still be assessed as in need of compensatory, remedial special education, including being allocated to bilingual education.

In the United States, Public Law (94-142) gives the **right** to free public education, to tests that are not culturally discriminatory, to tests in the child's native language, to multi-dimensional 'all areas' assessment to all 'handicapped' students. The misdiagnosis of language minority students for special education has led to court cases (e.g. Diana versus California State Board of Education). Such court cases revealed how language minority students were **wrongly assessed** as in need of special education. In some cases, teachers were unsure how to cope with a child whose English was relatively 'weak'. On this basis only, the teacher wanted special education for the 'Limited English Proficient' child.

The litigation showed the importance of separating bilinguals with real learning difficulties from those bilinguals whose second language (e.g. English) proficiency is below 'native' averages. The latter group should not be assessed as having learning difficulties and therefore in need of special education. The litigation also showed the wrongs done to language minority students: misidentification, misplacement, misuse of tests and failure when allocated to special education.

Unfortunately, the fear of litigation by school districts can lead to an **under-identification** of language minority pupils with a real need of special education. In the early 1980s, the trend was (in California, for example), for assuming too many language minority students were in need of special education. Towards the end of the 1980s, this had been reversed. The tendency moved to underestimating the special needs of language minority children. This makes accurate assessment very important. The **assessment** of children from language minority backgrounds in need of special education is considered separately in a later question in this section. However, accurate assessment and placement in different schools is not enough. The development of **effective instruction strategies** and an appropriate curriculum is crucial. So is the need to train teachers for bilingual students in special education.

E29 My child is suffering in school because other children tease him/her about speaking another language. What can I do?

Just as many children are teased about their color, clothes, religious beliefs, creeds and ethnic identity, so there are occasions when children are teased about their language. For bilinguals, the teasing and bullying tends to be from monolinguals. Those without dual language competence tend to tease those who have. It is of little solace to the child, but teasing about language skills often reveals a deficiency in the teaser and not the teased. The problem lies in the perception of the person ridiculing, rather than the one who is ridiculed. Such a situation is experienced by many minority language children. Such ridiculing may be part of a **fear** about difference. When language difference resides alongside color, creed and cultural difference, there is often a fear of the unknown, a fear of the different, and a fear of the 'not understood' in the person making the negative comments.

For parents and children, apart from suffering silently and explaining and discussing where possible, there is often no permanent solution to the immediate cause of the teasing and ridicule. Wherever possible, if bridges of **friendship** can be made with the ones doing the teasing, the abuse may decrease or disappear. Bilinguals often have to be the ones who make the bridges of friendship with those who oppose them. When this is possible, ridiculing and abuse does tend to decrease. The ridiculer is rarely directly concerned about language difference but concerned about the distance it may place between two people. Not understanding a conversation and feeling excluded may be the cause of the ridicule. The bilingual therefore has to be the eternal **diplomat** in breaking down barriers of communication, harmoniously integrating a peer group, and using their two languages to ensure good relationships with both communities of speakers. It is the 'sinned against' and not the 'sinners' who often attempt the roles of mediators and healers. Part of being a diplomat is injecting humor and forgiveness into the situation. Humor and kindness, even when not deserved, is a route to barrier breaking.

Parents can also educate their children as to why teasing and bullying sometimes occurs. While this does not change the situation, it allows understanding. If a child has some understanding of the illogical, irrational motives and reasons behind teasing and bullying, this provides a small shield and a little psychological defense. Such support by parents and a personal understanding may give the child some ability to tolerate some teasing. However, this is no substitute for the real remedy: the education and modification of behavior of the perpetrators.

There is an important role to be played by teachers and education in the furtherance of **multiculturalism**, linguistic diversity and the increase of understanding between different groups of people. For example, getting the monolingual to 'role play' a bilingual in a contrived situation may allow the monolingual to understand the situation of the bilingual. When sensitivity and empathy are taught and caught in the classroom, divisions between languages, between cultures and ethnic groups may be helped. Increasingly, education has become important in **anti-racism** drives, in teaching about language awareness, and encouraging children and teenagers to see the beauty of language diversity in the world.

A poor solution to teasing and abuse is to return the ridicule and abuse. No positive headway is made if a spear is met with a sword. Continuing antagonism, embattled positions and warfare will only be generated. As difficult as it is, hate needs to meet with love, confrontation with information, abusing by the defusing of an emotional situation. There are no quick fixes or certain solutions. There is only a chiseling at the edges of envy and evil. Teasing and taunts are never simply erased or ended. Civilized progress unfairly rests with those who have been wronged — often language minority speakers.

LANGUAGE IN THE CLASSROOM

E30 Will my child be able to learn a new language thoroughly in the school system?

One route to **second language and foreign language learning** used in many countries is approximately one half an hour language lesson per day over five or more years. Even when children have twelve years of such a diet, from primary school through to secondary school, the general finding in Canada, United States and Britain is that few become really fluent in the second/foreign language. While some do become fluent in French, German, Spanish or Italian, and can use the language with ease in a foreign country or study that language at university, the majority fall by the wayside. The seed sown takes root, but does not flower.

Despite many hundreds of hours of second/foreign language learning lessons, it is the few rather than the many who become functionally bilingual. At its best, it produces a small percentage of people who can just about communicate with native speakers in the learned language. Only an elite learn that language thoroughly. Such **drip feed language teaching** tends to produce children who do not use their second/foreign language out of school, and soon lose that language.

In contrast to the United Kingdom and the United States, in some European countries, children seem much better at learning languages through the school system. In countries such as the Netherlands, Belgium, Denmark, Finland, Sweden and Germany, children seem to learn languages via the school with more ease. Sometimes, this is out of the necessity, for employment prospects, for use in a different community, and for frequent travel. Often such students find plenty of second **language support out of school** (e.g. television programs in the second language) to support their incipient bilingualism. Such learners also find opportunities to practice (their English and French for example) in their community with in-migrants, travelers from abroad and guest workers. One special example of successful second and third language learning is the **European Schools Movement** (see a previous question).

A higher probability of learning a new language and becoming bilingual occurs when the new language is also a language of the curriculum in the school. When language learning is joined by that language becoming a **medium of instruction** in a school, a greater depth and width of experience in that second language will be gained. This is the difference between bilingual education (in its strong sense) and second language learning. Second language learning is a thin diet of language lessons in a school. Language is taught as a subject in itself. Bilingual education means language learning plus using that second language as a medium to learn a variety of subjects in the curriculum. In such a way, the second language becomes more embedded, has more use and function, and is more likely to lead to bilingualism.

One important question is **how early or late a child should begin learning a language in a school**. Considerable research suggests that neither young children nor older children have an overall advantage in learning a language. Young children tend to learn a new language more slowly, and older children more quickly and efficiently. However, with young children, the language may become more embedded, with pronunciation more correct and with the potentiality of more years of language learning.

Overall, it is more valuable for a child to begin learning a second language as **early** as possible in the school. Language tends to be acquired more easily and painlessly when young. With young children in the primary school, language is acquired informally, unconsciously, almost accidentally. There is no focus on language as in language learning lessons in the secondary school. Language learning in the primary school can be a by-product of playing, projects and participation in singing, drama and playing games. If such language activity occurs throughout schooling, primary and secondary, and where possible with some medium teaching in that language, the child stands more chance of being bilingual. At the same time, there are fifty, sixty, and seventy-year-olds who have successfully learned a language and become bilingual. No age is too late.

E31 How should two languages be distributed in a bilingual classroom?

Particularly in the early years of primary education, bilingual educators often regard it as important that two languages used in the classroom are compartmentalized. Clear boundaries are needed to keep **languages separated in school**. For example, in **Dual Language schools** in the United States, the policy is often 'one language one day, the other language on the next day'. An **alternating pattern** by day or half day is strictly adhered to by teachers in order for both languages to be given equal practice, equal status and equal instruction time. This means that all curriculum areas will be taught in both languages. For example, Mathematics will be taught in Spanish one day, English the next day. Spanish songs will be sung one day, English songs on the next day. On the door to such dual language classrooms, a notice or a picture indicates the language of that day.

Inside Dual Language classrooms, there is often a **separation of languages** on the wall displays. The idea is not only the equality of status of languages and equality of exposure, but also teaching the child to keep their two languages separate. This is the same principle as the one parent–one language approach to raising children bilingually.

The **reality** of Dual Language schools tends to be slightly different. On English days, children naturally speak Spanish to each other just as on Spanish days, a Spanish child may speak English to a friend who is dominant in English. It feels natural and normal for the child, and to keep that naturalness and avoid imposing punishments, the teacher may allow such variation. Also, the teacher will sometimes switch languages to reinforce an idea, ensure understanding by all children in the classroom, to stress a point and sometimes compare and contrast the languages as interesting information in itself. On wall displays in such dual language schools, there are times when both languages appear side by side. For example, the colors of nature (trees, flowers, the sky and the sea) may be labeled in both languages. In Dual Language schools, there is also a tendency to teach Science and Mathematics increasingly in the English language. This will be discussed in a later question.

In **minority language schools**, the separation that occurs will ensure the minority language dominates, particularly in the early years. The aim is a strong and steady development of a potentially weaker plant. The teacher may accept what the language majority child is saying in their majority language, but always responds in the minority language. In the early years of minority language education, it is usual for all, or almost all, the curriculum to be taught through the minority language. The majority language will be introduced often around seven years of age, sometimes around eight or nine years of age. In such minority language schools, the teacher may teach one topic a day through English, or have English language lessons. Increasingly, the children are allowed to work through the medium of English as they proceed through the primary school.

Often, in such minority language schools, when children reach the ages of eleven and twelve, they are expected to be able to work in **both languages in the curriculum**. At this age, the child may be able to work in Mathematics in either language, and read school textbooks in both the majority and the minority language. Minority language schools often have an 80% to a 100% minority language curriculum at the start of schooling. This will gradually change, increasing the use of the majority language to approximately a 50%–50% distribution. In other minority language schools, the minority language dominates in the curriculum (including literacy development) in all year groups (e.g. two thirds in the minority language, one third in the majority language).

Where **secondary school bilingual education** is available through the medium of the minority language, some 50% to 80% of the curriculum may be taught through the minority language. The aim is still to produce fully bilingual and biliterate children. The policy of developing the minority language in school is partly to balance the dominance of the majority language outside the school gates.

Where a **majority language** is introduced as a new language to a child at the start or middle of primary education, the majority or all the curriculum will initially be through that new language. For example, in the Canadian immersion bilingual education programs, children from English-speaking backgrounds learn through the medium of French for 100% of the curriculum at the start of primary education. They slowly move to around a 50% distribution between French and English by the end of primary education. The aim is to build up the second language strongly at the start of primary education.

By the end of primary education, the child should be approximately equally fluent and biliterate in both languages. Some degree of balanced bilingualism in individual children is encouraged by a thorough immersion in a second language at the start of schooling. This is followed by a slow and gradual movement to using both languages in the curriculum by the end of the primary school years. One special European case is the **European Schools Movement** where children from different European language groups are taught through their home and another language in a European School. This was considered in detail earlier in this section.

E32 Should Science and Mathematics be taught in an international language such as English?

In many minority language, dual language and bilingual schools, there is a trend towards teaching **Sciences, Technology and Mathematics through the medium of English** — or another majority, international language. The rationale is that most Science text books, scientific information, college and university studies of Science and Technology (and lots of other 'ologies', such as Sociology, Psychology, Geology) are in English. For example, in Kuwait University, Art students are taught through Arabic, and Science students through English. In Dual Language schools in New York, Science and Mathematics are often taught in English only. In Welsh-medium secondary schools, where much of the curriculum is taught through the medium of Welsh, it is not unusual to find Science and Mathematics taught in English. This may reflect the textbooks that are available, the preference of English language educated Science teachers, the preference of some to think mathematically in English, or simply the tradition of teaching Science and Mathematics in English.

The **problem** is in the associations that accompany teaching Science and Mathematics through a majority language such as English. Scientific culture is seen as Anglo-American, and increased status is given to the English language. French in France is following a crusade against the scientific dominance of English terminology.

Is the hidden message that the **minority language** is not up to date, isn't capable of scientific and mathematical usage, hasn't the vocabulary to enable scientific and mathematical teaching? Is the minority language therefore connected with history, culture, tradition, folk lore and heritage? Is the majority language connected with modernity, the powerful masculine image of Science, the high status aspects of Science and Technology? Does this make one language more internationally valued and minority languages less valued?

In Spain and Wales, for example, there have been **movements** to try to ensure that science teaching, science textbooks and science thinking can all operate in a minority language (such as Catalan, Basque and Welsh). Considerable attempts have been made to show that a minority language can adapt to being a modern language. New vocabulary needs inventing, sometimes providing extra meaning to a scientific concept, at other times borrowing from the English, Greek or Latin languages.

The language of Science, Technology and Mathematics is a **controversial area** among parents and educators. It tends to split those who fervently seek language minority salvation and those who argue that English is *de facto* the international language of Science and Mathematics, Technology and Computing. It tends to separate those who argue for basic language principles and planning from those who are language pragmatists and 'free market language economists'.

E33 My child's school doesn't support bilingualism. What should I do?

Many bilingual parents find themselves in an environment where a **monolingual school** has little regard for their child's bilingualism. Where monolingualism reigns supreme in the environment, bilingual parents often find themselves at variance with the limited horizons of a monolingual, monocultural school. The child's bilingualism seems neither to be noticed, valued nor celebrated. The love and affection, care and support the child has received at home has been transmitted through the home, minority language. The monolingual school regards that minority language as worthless. This is frustrating for parents who see the educational as well as social and cultural value of their child's bilingualism.

A school's **attitude to bilingual** children should certainly be one factor when there is a choice of schools. This is particularly the case where minority language children enter a majority language school. Often such schools devalue the child's bilingualism. The child's life-style, culture, religion, eating and dietary habits, even the 'foreign' names of in-migrant children are ignored or ridiculed. The child's self-esteem, sense of dignity and self-confidence often suffer.

However, there are also many schools that have a positive attitude to linguistic diversity and cultural diversity. Some schools are particularly good at celebrating the variety of languages and cultures within their school, making them a learning experience for all, and generally reducing prejudice and racism in the locality.

Effective schools value **parent–teacher co-operation**. When a school is sensitive to the wishes and needs of the consumers, is prepared to treat children as important individuals rather than as whole classes, the school often has a vitality. Explain to the teacher that your child can speak two languages or comes from an intercultural marriage. Ask, for example, if the child can sometimes take a book in the non-school language to read in the school. Suggest that occasionally the child be allowed to display something on the classroom wall that is in the non-school language. Sometimes, parents are invited to the school to help the teacher. For example, language minority parents listen to children reading or help the teacher organize classroom activities. This is an important way that bilingual parents help bilingual children in a monolingual school. When the door is open to parents to come and help the teacher in the classroom, this opens up opportunities for other languages than the school language to be supported in the classroom.

Education doesn't just occur at school. There is a difference between schooling and education. Education continues from cradle to grave, from the second of waking in the morning to the second of sleeping in the evening. Therefore, **parents** have time during the latter part of the day and at weekends to add to the educational experience of their children. During these times, a child's second language or non-school language can be fostered, enhanced and celebrated. During **school holidays**, there may be opportunities for bilingual children to join similar others in the locality to play, paint and participate in educational activities through a language not used in school. In Saturday or Sunday schools and Voluntary schools outside formal education, children may participate through their non-school language, enabling that language to develop as a tool of thinking, enculturation and socialization.

E34 Which language should be used to test/assess/counsel a bilingual child? What should be the nature of such assessment?

The answer to a previous question on Bilingual Special Education highlighted how essential it is for the psychological and educational assessment of bilingual children to be fair, accurate, valid, broad and extensive. Too often, tests given to bilingual children only serve to suggest their 'disabilities', supposed 'deficits' or lack of proficiency in a second language. Assessment can too easily legitimize the disabling of language minority students. English language tests and IQ tests administered in the second language are particular examples. Here are some **guidelines** as to how the assessment of bilingual children can be more fairly achieved:

(1) The **temporary difficulties** faced by bilinguals must be distinguished from relatively more permanent difficulties that impede everyday functioning and learning. Brief language delays, temporary adjustment problems of in-migrants and short-term stammering (stuttering) are examples of transient difficulties. Dyslexia, hearing loss and neuroticism are examples where longer-term problems may need treatment. This simple distinction hides different and complex dimensions. The means of distinguishing temporary and longer-term problems follows below.

(2) Diagnosis needs to avoid a few, simple tests and engage a wide diversity of measurement and observation devices. Diagnosis needs to be extended over a time period and avoid an instant conclusion and instantaneous remedy. **Observing** the child in different contexts (and not just in the classroom) will provide a more valid profile (language and behavior) of that child. The family and educational history of the child need assembling. Parents and teachers need consulting, sometimes doctors and social workers as well. Samples of a child's natural communication need gathering, with the child in different roles and different situations.

(3) The choice of **assessors** for the child will affect the assessment. Whether the assessors are perceived to be from the same language group as the child will affect the child's performance (and possibly the diagnosis). The perceived age, social class, powerfulness and gender of the assessor(s) will affect how the child responds and possibly the assessment outcomes. The assessment process is not neutral. Who assesses, using what devices, under what conditions, contributes to the judgment being made.

(4) Children need to be assessed in their **stronger language**. Ideally children need assessing as bilinguals — in both their languages. The tests and assessment devices applied, and the language of communication used in assessment, should ideally be in the child's stronger language. An assessment based on tests of (and in) the child's weaker language may lead to a misdiagnosis, a false impression of the abilities of the child and a very partial and biased picture of the child.

(5) Parents and educators need to make sure the **language used** in the test is **appropriate** to the child. For example, a translation of the test (e.g. from English to Spanish) may produce inappropriate, stilted language. Also, the variety of Spanish, for example, may not that be used by the student. Chicano Spanish-speaking parents will want the tests in Chicano or at least Mexican Spanish rather than Cuban, Puerto Rican or Castilian Spanish. Once Spanish-speaking children have been in the United States for a time, their Spanish changes. English influences their way of speaking Spanish. So a test in 'standard' Spanish is inappropriate. A Spanish test may accept only one right answer, penalizing children for their bilingualism and their United States Spanish. A monolingual standard of Spanish is inappropriate to such bilingual children.

Since there are language problems with tests (as outlined above and continued below), it is important to distinguish between a child's language profile and **performance profile**. The performance profile is more important as it attempts to portray a child's underlying abilities rather than just language abilities. A performance profile seeks to understand the overall potential of the child, not just their language proficiency.

(6) There are times when a test or assessment device cannot be given in the child's stronger language. For example, appropriate language minority professionals may not be available to join the assessment team, tests may not be available in the child's home language, and translations of tests may make those tests invalid and unreliable.

Interpreters are sometimes necessary. Interpreters do have a valuable function. If trained in the linguistic, professional and rapport-making competences needed, they can make assessment more fair and accurate. Interpreters can also bring a possible bias into the assessment (i.e. 'heightening' or 'lowering' the assessment results through the interpretation they provide).

(7) There is a danger of focusing the assessment solely on the child. If the child is tested, the assumption is that the 'problem' lies within the child. At the same time, and sometimes instead, the **focus** needs to

shift to **causes outside of the child**. Is the problem in the school? Is the school failing the child by denying abilities in the first language and focusing on failures in the second (school) language? Is the school system denying a child's culture and ethnic character, thereby affecting the child's academic success and self-esteem? Is the curriculum delivered at a level that is beyond the child's comprehension or is culturally strange to the child? The remedy may be in a change to the school system and not to the child.

(8) The danger of assessment is that it will lead to the disablement rather than the **empowerment** of bilingual children. If the assessment separates children from powerful, dominant, mainstream groups in society, the child may become disabled. The assessment may lead to categorization in an inferior group of society and marginalization. Instead, assessment should work in the best, long-term interests of the child. Best interests doesn't only mean short-term educational remedies, but also long-term employment and wealth-sharing opportunities. The assessment should initiate advocating for the child, and not against the child.

(9) It is important to use the understanding of a child's **teachers** who have observed that child in a variety of learning environments over time. What do the child's teachers think is the root problem? What solutions and interventions do teachers suggest? Have the child's teachers a plan of action? A team of teachers, meeting regularly to discuss children with problems, is a valuable first attempt to assess and treat the child. Such a team can also be the school decision-maker for referral to other professionals (e.g. speech therapist, psychologist, counselor).

(10) Norm referenced **tests** are often used to assess the child. This means that the assessor can compare the child with other 'normal' children. The assessor can indicate how different the child is from the average. Many such tests are built on scores from 'native' language majority children. Thus, comparisons can be unfair for language minority children. For example, tests of English language proficiency may have 'norms' (averages, and scores around the average) based on native speakers of English. This makes them biased against bilinguals and leads to the stereotyping of particular language and ethnic groups.

Such tests are often written by white, middle class Anglo test producers. The test items often reflect their culture. For example, the words used such as 'tennis racquet', 'snowman' and 'credit cards' may be unfamiliar to some in-migrants who have never seen a snowman, played or watched tennis, or know about the culture of plastic money.

Such norm referenced tests are often 'pencil and paper' tests, sometimes involving multiple choice answers (one answer is chosen from a set of given answers). Such tests do not measure all the different aspects of language, of 'intelligence' or any curriculum subject. Spoken, conversational language and financial intelligence, for example, cannot be adequately measured by a simple pencil and paper test.

Some tests report the results in **percentiles** (especially in the United States). Percentiles refer to the percentage of children below (and above) the child being tested. For example, being in the 40th percentile means that 39% of children score lower than the child being tested. Sixty per cent of children of an age group score above the 40th percentile child. The child is in the 40th group from the bottom, all children being assumed to be divided into 100 equal size groups.

Norm referenced tests essentially compare one person against others. Is this important? Isn't the more important measurement about what a bilingual child can and cannot do in each curriculum subject? To say a child is in the 40th percentile in English doesn't tell the parent or the teacher what are a child's strengths and weaknesses, capabilities and needs in English. **Curriculum-based assessment** is called criterion referenced testing, and seeks to establish the relative mastery of a child on a curriculum area. Such criterion referenced assessment of language minority students gives parents and teachers more usable and important information. It details what a child can do in a subject (e.g. Mathematics) and where development should move to next. Such assessment enables an individualized program to be set for the child.

E35 Are teachers trained to help bilingual children?

One problem in bilingual education is that there is little **teacher training** for working in bilingual schools and bilingual classrooms. In the majority of teacher training courses, even in bilingual countries, there are few courses that prepare teachers for educating bilingual children. This is exacerbated by a considerable international lack of bilingual teachers. Very often there is a complete dearth of language minority teachers — Welsh, Asian languages, Spanish speakers in the United States, French bilinguals in English-speaking parts of Canada, and teachers of bilinguals in Asian countries such as Japan, Malaysia and Thailand. With insufficient bilingual teachers, and with insufficient training for bilingual classrooms, much of the current expert knowledge about bilingual children and bilingual education is not filtering through to teachers.

Among those teachers who become Headteachers, Principals, advisers and educational administrators, there is also a surprising **ignorance** about bilingual children and bilingual education. Such administrators, Principals, Headteachers and advisers often have expertise in assessing children, in managing and marketing, but too little information about bilingual children. It is not surprising therefore, that some teachers have a prejudice against bilingual children, find bilingual children awkward and difficult to teach, find bilingualism a strange and worrying phenomena, and do not know how to approach parents who have a keen interest in their children becoming bilingual and biliterate. One surprising aspect about bilingual education is that there are sometimes more parents than teachers who have a good understanding of the state of knowledge about bilingual children and bilingual education. Bilingual **parents** sometimes have more enthusiasm, erudition and educated knowledge of bilingualism. Such parents are often surprised when teachers are lower down the learning curve.

The same situation tends to exist in **language minority schools**. Teachers may be trained to teach through the medium of the minority language — Welsh, Catalan, Basque and Irish. They are trained as monolingual teachers of a minority language. This is much to be applauded. However, such teachers understand little about bilingualism, bilingual classrooms and bilingual education. How to act as a bilingual teacher, encouraging the growth of two languages and cultural diversity is too often a foreign language to them.

Section F

Concluding Questions

F1 Is there a future for bilingualism in the world? The economy and politics of the world is changing. How will this affect bilingualism?

As the global village develops, as the spread of information, telecommunications, mass media breaks down national frontiers, the **danger** is always that major international languages, particularly English, will grow in importance. As travel between continents and countries becomes easier, cheaper and faster, the danger is that minority languages will be less used and majority languages have more utility. As the European Union grows in strength, politically, economically, socially and culturally, as Pacific countries join to form a strong trading area, and as the role of North America continues as important in the world power and politics, the danger is that a few languages will have increasing use and value. At worst, other languages will subsequently be solely connected with sacred history and scattered homes.

Therefore, some commentators believe that there will be a change in the language economy. There may be an increasing movement towards international languages used for trade, information exchange and international relations. If such a **pessimistic view** is believed, minority languages and bilingualism may be in danger. Some pessimists argue that bilingualism is merely a halfway house. Bilingualism is merely a midway point in between a flourishing minority language and a move to monolingualism in a majority language. A history of minority languages in the twentieth century tends partly to support such pessimism. For example, Irish and Welsh were once spoken by over 50% of inhabitants within those countries. The history of the twentieth century is a history of decline in these languages. Around 20% speak Welsh in Wales, 1.4% in Scotland speak Scottish Gaelic, and about one in three people are able to speak some Irish in Ireland, with much less use of that language than such figures suggest. Such a downward movement in minority language usage is evident throughout Europe.

A more positive and **optimistic** view is also possible. For centuries, many people who speak **two** or more **majority languages** have had status and prestige. The ability to speak French and English, German and French, German and Russian, Chinese and English, has always been a valuable asset, much in demand amongst traders, diplomats and travelers. The global village, the breaking down of trade and transport barriers has led to an increase in the value of those who can operate in two or more international languages. In Europe, there seems to be a growing demand and respect for those who can use two or more languages in the European Union.

A different type of **optimism** may be possible with **minority languages**. As there is pressure to belong to the global village, a pressure to be international, to be European and a movement to become part of a bigger whole, so there also may be a reactive need to go back to roots. As the world gets smaller and some differences start to fade, there may be an inner need to find who one is, from where one has come. An anchor is needed in a local identity as well as the larger identity. For example, third and fourth generation in-migrants who have lost their heritage language sometimes become interested in their family and heritage culture.

Some **in-migrants** will assimilate into the majority language and culture. Others are keen to keep links with their past, their ancestors, and buy back some of the cultural wealth of the past. Family history, nostalgia for the heritage of one's ethnic group, an inner need to find rootedness and continuity with the 'glorious past' are powerful conscious and unconscious drives. Such an interest may promote minority languages, reawaken awareness that a minority language provides access to the tradition of that minority culture, enabling a security of self-identity, a sharing of the inheritance of the past and giving some security and status within the 'small and known' rather than the 'large and unknown'.

The plight of '**lesser used languages**' within Europe has become part of European awareness. For example, the European Bureau for Lesser Used Languages has actively supported and greatly promoted the importance of vitality of those minority languages throughout Europe.

If such optimism is possible with minority languages, it is an **argument for bilingualism**. Minority language speakers require competence in the majority language for economic, information and sometimes national integration needs. While many minority languages live under a cloud of pessimism, there are silver linings around those clouds. Languages rarely stay still, they shift as politics, economics, culture, individual needs and personal motivations change. The middle- or long-term future of many minority languages is hard, if not impossible, to predict with assurance. However, there has been growing optimism in the last decade that preserving the variety of languages in the world is environmentally friendly. The diversity of language flowers adds to the wide spectrum of color in the language garden of the world. Bilinguals are environmentally friendly people.

F2 Why is it important for minority languages to survive in the future?

Professor Ofelia García of City College of New York uses a powerful analogy to portray the importance of languages surviving. Her **language garden analogy** commences with the idea that if we traveled through the countries of the world and found field after field, garden after garden of the same, one-color flower, how dull and boring our world would be. If a single color flower was found throughout the world without variety of shape, size or color, how tedious and impoverished the world would be.

Fortunately, there is a wide variety of flowers throughout the world of all shapes and sizes, all tints and textures, all hues and shades. A garden full of different colored flowers enhances the beauty of that garden and enriches our visual and aesthetic experience.

The same argument can be made about the language garden of the world. If there were just one language in the garden, it would be easy to administer, easy to tend. If one of the majority languages of the world (e.g. English) solely existed, how dull and uninteresting our world would be. Rather, we have a language garden full of variety and color. For example, in London alone, there are said to be around 184 different languages being spoken. The initial conclusion is simply that language diversity in the garden of the world makes for a richer, more interesting and more colorful world.

However, language diversity makes the garden more difficult to tend. In a garden, some flowers and shrubs spread alarmingly quickly. Some majority languages, particularly English, have expanded considerably during this century. When the garden is unkept, one species of flower may take over and small minority flowers may be in danger of extinction. Therefore some flowers need extra care and protection. This leads to the second part of Professor García's analogy. A free language economy allowing some flowers to dominate gardens is less preferred than careful **language planning**. When a gardener wishes to create a beautiful garden, there will be both careful planning and continued care and protection. Sometimes radical action may be taken to preserve and protect. The analogy suggests that language diversity requires planning and care. Four examples follow:

(1) **Adding flowers to the garden**. The language garden analogy suggests that, where the majority language is a person's first language, it may be enriching to add a second, even a third and fourth language. For example, in Canada, English speakers learning French may ensure that the colorful diversity of the Canadian multilingual situation is maintained. In mainland Europe, speakers of French, German, Spanish or Italian, for example, often learn a second or third language. In much of the United States, Australasia and Britain, a monochrome language garden seems relatively more common.

(2) **Protecting rare flowers**. In many countries throughout the world, the minority or indigenous language(s) may be under threat from the quickly spreading majority languages. Just as environmentalists in the twentieth century have awoken to the need to preserve the variety of flora and fauna, so in the language garden, it is environmentally friendly to protect rare language flowers. Through education and legislation, through pressure groups and planning, protection of language species in danger of extinction may be attempted.

(3) **Augmenting the numbers of those flowers in danger of extinction**. Where a language species is in danger of extinction, stronger action may be needed than protection. Special efforts to revive a dying language may be needed through intervention. For example, positive economic discrimination towards the Irish language in certain defined heartland areas has attempted to preserve the indigenous language in its traditional strongholds.

(4) **Controlling flowers that spread quickly and naturally**. Flowers which spread rapidly and take the space of other flowers also need supervision and planning. While majority languages for international communication are an irreplaceable part of the Information Society,

language planning may seek to allow spread without replacing and killing endangered species.

It is clear from using Professor Ofelia García's language garden analogy that a *laissez-faire* situation is less desirable than deliberate, rational language planning. Gardeners are needed (e.g. parents and teachers) to plant, water, fertilize and reseed the different minority language flowers in the garden to ensure an enriching world language garden. While there are gardeners (e.g. parents and teachers) tending the language garden, there are landscape engineers who can plan and control the overall shape of the language garden.

The view of language landscape engineers (e.g. politicians, policy makers) is often to regard the language garden as just one part of a wider control of the environment. The dominant power groups who determine the social, economic and cultural environment may see language as just one element in an overall landscape design. For example, the type of bilingual education program that is allowed in a region is part of a design for the total landscape in which the languages are located.

A language landscape engineer who is concerned only for majority language flowers, will regard protecting rare flowers to be expensive and unnecessary, and will wish to standardize on the variety of language in the country. A landscape engineer who wishes to protect rare flowers and increase flowers in danger of extinction may encourage the growth of such flowers alongside majority language flowers within bilingual education. In the United States and England, for example, many politicians prefer monolingualism rather than bilingualism. The preference is for the assimilation of minority language communities into a more standardized, monochrome garden. The dominant ruling group in United States society is monolingual, with little perceived need to know or speak the minority languages of the country. Thus their view of bilingual education is determined by their wider ideology.

One attitude to minority languages is that they must live in a free market language economy. Their survival or death depends on their utility in the language marketplace of the world. This approach is one of **survival of the fittest**. Those language flowers that are strongest will survive. Others will wither and die.

Such an **evolutionist view** follows Darwin's idea of the survival of the fittest. Weaker languages will either have to adapt themselves to their environment or die. However, survival of the fittest is too simplistic a view of evolution. It only accents the killing of languages, language suppression and exploitation. A more positive view of language evolution is that languages are often interdependent rather than in constant competition. Co-operation for mutually beneficial outcomes is just as possible in a language world as exploitation.

The second approach to languages is that of **conservationists**. Conservationists will argue for the maintenance of variety in the language garden. For conservationists, language planning must care for and cherish minority languages. Just as certain animal species are now deliberately preserved within particular territorial areas, so conservationists will argue that threatened languages should receive special status in heartland regions of that language. Catalan in Spain, native North American languages and the Celtic languages in Britain and France have all invoked the conservationist argument. In Ireland, certain areas called Gaeltachta are officially designated for Irish conservation.

The third attitude to languages is that of **preservationists**. Preservationists are different from conservationists by being more conservative and seeking to maintain the status quo rather than develop the language. Preservationists are concerned that any change, not just language change, will damage the chances of survival of their language. Such a group are therefore traditionalists, not modern in outlook. Whereas conservationists may think global and act local, preservationists will tend to think local and act local.

F3 Are monolinguals more common than bilinguals in the world?

One belief of many monolinguals is that they are in the majority in the world. Many monolinguals tend to have the view that the state of monolingualism within an individual and within society is the most logical, acceptable and prevalent in the world. Yet, the reality is that **bilinguals are in the majority in the world**. Various estimates exist of what percentage of the world is bilingual. This is very difficult, because the definition of bilinguals may include or exclude those who have a little fluency in one language. Under the term 'bilinguals' go many different colors with many different shades and hues.

If Pidgins and Creoles are included or excluded from the count, the estimate of the percentage of bilinguals in the world will change. When local dialects are added into the confusion of producing an accurate figure, any percentage will be inaccurate. Published estimates tend to vary **between 60% and 75%** of the world as bilingual. The conclusion is clear. Bilinguals are in the majority in the world, not monolinguals.

One problem for bilinguals is that monolinguals often have greater power and privilege, more status and prestige. For example, in England

and the United States, Australia, New Zealand, France, parts of Germany and Canada, **monolinguals** tend to be over-represented in the ranks of **power elites**, among those with wealth and influence. In England and the United States for example, bilinguals tend to be regarded as an oddity, even a problem, or at best as quaint. English monolingual speakers in England are often amused to find people speaking Welsh or Scottish Gaelic — regarding it as rustic, quaint, but also rude, disruptive and valueless. Therefore, the problem that some bilinguals face is that they are in the majority in the world, but have a minority of power. Their language condition is usual and commonplace, yet it is often regarded by power elites and politicians as pointless and a problem.

F4 Why are many politicians against bilingualism and bilingual education?

In England, France, the United States, sometimes in Canada, Germany and Japan, politicians and newspaper publishers often portray bilinguals, bilingual education and cultural diversity as a problem.

Public and political discussion of bilingual education and languages in society often commences with the idea of language as causing complications and difficulties. This is well illustrated in discussions about the supposed **cognitive problems** of operating in two languages. Perceived problems are not limited to thinking. **Personality and social problems** such as split-identity, cultural dislocation, a poor self-image and rootlessness are also sometimes attributed to bilinguals. At a group rather than an individual level, bilingualism is sometimes connected with national or regional disunity and inter-group conflict. Language is thus also viewed as a **political problem**.

Part of the 'language-as-problem' political orientation is that perpetuating language minorities and language diversity may cause less integration, less cohesiveness, more antagonism and more conflict in society. The perceived complication of minority languages is to be **solved by assimilation** into the majority language. Such an argument holds that the majority language (e.g. English) unifies the diversity. The ability of every citizen to communicate with ease in the nation's majority language is regarded as the common leveler. A strong nation is regarded as a unified nation. Unity within a nation is seen as synonymous with uniformity and similarity. The opposing argument is that it is possible to have national unity without uniformity. Diversity of languages and national unity can co-exist (e.g. as in Singapore, Luxembourg, Switzerland).

The co-existence of two or more languages is rarely a cause of tension, disunity, conflict or strife. The **history of war** suggests that economic, political and religious differences are prominent as causes. Language is seldom the cause of conflict. Religious Crusades and Jihads, rivalries between different religions, rivalries between different political parties and economic aggression tend to be the instigators of strife. Language, in and by itself, is rarely a cause of unrest. In a research study on causes of civil strife, the eminent New York academic, Joshua Fishman found that language was not a cause. Rather, the causes of strife were found to be deprivation, authoritarian regimes and modernization.

A **minority language** is often connected with the **problems** of poverty, under-achievement in school, minimal social and vocational mobility and with a lack of integration with the majority culture. In this perspective, the minority language is perceived as a partial cause of social, economic and educational problems, rather than an effect of such problems. This 'language is an obstacle' attitude is summed up in the phrase, 'If only they would speak English, their problems would be solved'. The minority language is thus seen as a handicap to be overcome by the school system. One resolution of the problem is regarded as the increased teaching of a majority language (e.g. English) at the expense of the home language. Developing bilingualism is an irrelevant or a secondary and less important aim of schooling. Thus submersion and transitional bilingual education aim to develop competent English language skills in minority language children as quickly as possible so they are on par with English first language speakers in the mainstream classroom.

Bilingual education is sometimes perceived by politicians as **causing a language problem**. Such education, it is sometimes argued, will cause social unrest or disintegration in society. Fostering the minority language and ethnic differences might provoke group conflict and disharmony. The response is generally that bilingual education will lead to better integration, harmony and social peace.

Bilingual education should not be connected with causing language problems. Rather, the evidence suggests that developing bilingualism and biliteracy within bilingual education is educationally feasible and can lead to:

- higher achievement across the curriculum for minority language children;
- maintaining the home language and culture;
- fostering self-esteem, self-identity and a more positive attitude to schooling.

Such higher achievement may enable better usage of human resources in a country's economy and less wastage of talent. Higher self-esteem may also relate to increased social harmony and peace.

F5 Is bilingualism a natural right of any individual?

A different orientation to that of 'language as a problem' is thinking of language as a **basic, human right**. Just as there are individual rights in choice of religion, so there should be an individual right to choice of language. Just as there are attempts to eradicate discrimination based on color and creed, so language prejudice and discrimination need to be eradicated in a democratic society.

Language rights may be derived from **personal**, legal and constitutional rights. Personal language rights will draw on the right to freedom of individual expression. It may also be argued that there are certain natural language rights in group rather than individual terms. The rights of language groups may be expressed in terms of the importance of preservation of heritage language and culture communities. A further level of language rights may be **international**, derived from pronouncements from organizations such as the United Nations, UNESCO, the Council of Europe and the European Community. Each of these four organizations has declared that language groups have the right to maintain their language. For example, in the European community, a directive (25th July 1977: 77/486/EEC) stated that Member States should promote the teaching of the mother tongue and the culture of the country of origin in the education of migrant workers' children. However, individual countries have generally ignored such international declarations.

Language rights are not only expressed in legal confrontations (e.g. in the United States) with the chance of being established in law. Language rights are often expressed at the **grass-roots level** by protests and pressure groups, by local action and argument. For example, the *Kohanga Reo* (language nests) movement in New Zealand provides a grass-roots instituted, immersion preschool experience for the Maori people. Beginning in 1982, these language nests offer a preschool all-Maori language and culture environment for children from birth to school age, aimed at fostering development and growth within a context where only the Maori language is spoken and heard.

Another example of a grass-roots expression of 'language as a right' is the recent Celtic (Ireland, Scotland and Wales) experience. In these countries, 'grass-roots' movements created preschool playgroups, 'mother and toddler' groups and adult language learning classes so that the heritage languages can be preserved in both adult social interaction and especially in the young. Strong language activism and insistent demands have led to the establishment of heritage language elementary schools, particularly in urban, mostly English-speaking areas. Not without struggle, opposition and antagonistic bureaucracy, parents have obtained the right for education in the indigenous tongue. Such pressure groups have contained parents who speak the indigenous language, and those who speak only English, yet wish their children to be taught in the heritage language of the area.

In North American and British society, no formal recognition is usually made in politics or the legal system to categories or groups of people based on their culture, language or race. Rather the focus is on **individual rights**. The accent is on individual equality of opportunity, individual rewards based on individual merit. Policies of non-discrimination, for example, tend to be based on individual rather than group rights. Language minority groups will nevertheless argue for rewards and justice based on their existence as a definable group in society. Sometimes based on territorial rights, often based on ethnic identity, such groups may argue for rewards in proportion to their representation in society. **Group-based rights** are often regarded as a way of redressing injustices to language minorities. This may be a temporary step on the way to full individual rights. Alternatively, language minorities may claim the right to some independent power, some measure of decision making and some guarantee of self-determination.

F6 Does my child have a right to bilingual education? (e.g. in law, a natural right)?

Bilingual education has often been promoted by governments for one particular type of bilingual. Where two **majority languages** are used in the classroom (e.g. English, German), there tends to be political and public support for bilingual education. This represents **additive bilingualism** — a second language and culture is added at no expense to the first language. Such bilingual education is seen by those in power as enriching, enhancing employment possibilities and as **civilizing**. 'Finishing Schools' in Europe — attended by princesses and the daughters of the very rich — are one example. The European Schools Movement is another example (see Section E). This support for bilingualism in two majority languages is not claimed as a right. It is granted willingly, and must be viewed as a privilege shared by the already advantaged.

Where **language minorities** exist, bilingual education is not usually granted as a group or individual right. If bilingual education exists, it has usually been fought for by protests, pressure, grass-roots assertiveness and constant campaigning. Parents and language minority activists have often combined to persuade administrators of the value of mother-tongue education. There is often a considerable **struggle** to win small concessions for bilingual education for language minorities. Growth in such bilingual education is usually slow, controversial, disputed by those in power and a source of continuing conflict. Yet paradoxically, in this struggle there is often added enthusiasm and extra commitment. Hearts and minds have to be won. In the fight, there is zeal and passion. A mission is established. The children benefit from the extra commitment and fervor that goes into the establishment of bilingual education. Again, no right to bilingual education is granted. Bilingual education in such circumstances is granted more as a favor, or as a privilege apparently charitably granted by those in power.

In many countries, education **law** is frequently about what is not permissible. 'Thou shall not' is joined by rules about central policy that must be followed by all. Therefore, there are often no expressed 'natural' rights or rights in law for parents to demand bilingual education. Since bilingual education is a minority pursuit, centralized policy sometimes sees bilingual education as an exception to the rule.

Not all countries fit this pattern. For example, in the United States, there are Constitutional **rights** that express personal freedoms, liberties and personal rights. Whereas language minority activists have been taken to court in Spain and Wales, in the United States, language minority activists have taken the government to court. The United States Constitution expresses the rights and freedoms of individuals, rather than the 'Thou shall not' approach.

The rights of an individual and language groups to bilingual education has been tested in the **United States courts**. From the 1920s to the present, United States courts have increasingly established the educational rights of minorities. For example, one famous case was *Brown* v. *Board of Education* (1954). The court ruled that segregation by race in public schools violated the 14th Amendment of the United States Constitution. As an early part of the Civil Rights Movement, this decision helped create rights for minorities. However, the Civil Rights Movement (e.g. the 1964 Civil Rights Act) did not lead to prohibition against discrimination on the basis of language .

A landmark in United States' bilingual education was a **lawsuit**. A court case was brought on behalf of Chinese pupils against the San

Francisco School District in 1970. The case concerned whether or not non-English-speaking students received equal educational opportunity when instructed in a language they could not understand. The failure to provide bilingual education was alleged to violate both the equal protection clause of the 14th Amendment and Title VI of the Civil Rights Act of 1964. The case, known as *Lau* v. *Nichols*, was rejected by a federal district court and a court of appeals, but was accepted by the Supreme Court in 1974.

The verdict outlawed English-only 'submersion' programs for language minority children and resulted in nationwide 'Lau remedies'. The Lau remedies were that something had to be done for students not proficient in English. Such remedies included English as a Second Language classes, English tutoring and some form of bilingual education. The Lau remedies created a small expansion in the use of minority languages in schools. The Lau remedies were withdrawn by the Reagan government and do not have the force of law. The federal government left local politicians to create their own policies. For example, in New York, bilingual education is mandated following an out-of-court consent by the New York City Board of Education in 1974.

The Lau court case is symbolic of the dynamic and continuing contest to establish **language rights** in the United States particularly through testing the law in the courtroom. Further changes in the rights to United States bilingual education are given in the table below. However, often legislation and litigation has led to 'weak' forms of bilingual education (e.g. transitional bilingual education). Also, recent legislation has not tended to increase rights to bilingual education. In the Reagan and Bush years in the United States Presidency, the accent was more on submersion and transitional bilingual education. The right to early education through a minority language failed to blossom in those years.

A summary of major United States events in the rights of language minorities is given in the table below.

There is another side to language rights. Rights may be demanded, fought for, granted or denied. The relationship implied is sometimes that of a subservient minority requesting rights from the powerful majority. The dominant majority language group has the power in law and government to grant such rights through Acts and laws.

While there is a reality about this situation, language minority activists have increasingly suggested that **empowerment** and **enablement** of language minorities is needed. Rather than purely being subservient, dependent, servile, lowly and subordinate, language minorities need

Year	United States Legislation/ Litigation	Implication regarding Bilingual Education
1954	*Brown* v. *Board of Education*	Segregated education based on race made unconstitutional.
1965	Elementary and Secondary Education Act (ESEA)	Funds granted to meet the needs of 'educationally deprived children'.
1968	Elementary and Secondary Education Act (ESEA) Amendment of 1968, The Bilingual Education Act, Title VII	Provided funding to establish bilingual programs for students who did not speak English and who were economically poor.
1974	*Lau* v. *Nichols*	Established that language programs for language minorities not proficient in English were necessary to provide equal educational opportunities.
1974	Reauthorization of Bilingual Education Act Title VII of ESEA	Grants available to include native language instruction in schools to 'effect progress' of students not proficient in English. Bilingual Education was defined as transitional (TBE).
1976	*Keyes* v. *School District No. 1* Denver Colorado	Established bilingual education as compatible with desegregation.
1978	Reauthorization of Bilingual Education Act Title VII of ESEA	Reauthorized funding for bilingual programs (transitional). Poverty criteria for eligibility was removed. The term 'Limited English Proficient' (LEP) introduced, replacing LES (Limited English Speaking).
1984	Reauthorization of Bilingual Education Act Title VII of ESEA	Extended the range of fundable bilingual education programs for students not proficient in English. Transitional (TBE) given 75% of funds. Developmental Bilingual Education (dual language) programs funded as were Special Alternative Instructional programs (SAIP). SAIP provided funding for English-only 'submersion' classes with no instruction in the student's native language.
1988	Reauthorization of Bilingual Education Act Title VII of ESEA	Same as in 1984, but 25% of funding given for English-only SAIP.

education and encouragement to become independent, more self-reliant — particularly economically, more free and autonomous. Through creating employment in language minority areas, through planned growth in the local economy, a language minority may attain more power over their own lives, enabling a rise in self-esteem and self-respect. Through ensuring literacy and biliteracy, children and adults are empowered and enabled. Literacy gives access to information. In information there is power.

'Rights' can give lawful, constitutional power to a language minority (e.g. to promote bilingual education). At the same time, language minorities often need to develop autonomy, freedom to promote their language and culture, to have power over their own lives and the destiny of their language community. Through education, employment and the economy, language minorities can strive to increase their power and their ability to control their own futures.

F7 Language is an important part of our religion. Should my child learn a second language for this purpose?

For Moslems, Jews, Orthodox Christians and some Asian groups, there is a **religious language** that is important for their children to learn. To worship in the Synagogue, Hebrew or Yiddish are often required. For the Greek or Russian Orthodox worshipper, Greek or Russian may be invaluable to penetrate the heart of the Orthodox tradition and its services. For those who worship in a Mosque or Temple, specific languages often need learning to participate, understand and engage in daily religious observances.

For many parents in such religious traditions, there is no debate. It is essential that children learn the appropriate religious language. To partake in **religious custom and worship**, to create a sense of continuity with the religious past, and sometimes to achieve greater holiness and heavenly prospects, religious language becomes crucial. Since religion is part of the home, heritage and happiness of the family, learning a religious language often gives the child pride, a sense of religious, ethnic and family identity, and provides a strong foundation for meeting the uncertain journey through life.

One concern of some parents is the **level of language learning** that is achieved. For example, someone may learn Arabic enough to repeat prayers in the Mosque, yet not understand Arabic in conversations. For the Orthodox Christian or the Jew, the language learned is sometimes specifically and purely for religious purposes. The vocabulary, and the feel for the language, does not exist outside prayers and the place of worship. The language of prayer is not practiced in public places. Outside the Holy Book, the language for religion is not used.

This provides an interesting example of **language boundaries** and language compartmentalization. The child learns a different language, bounded in its function and place of use. This helps ensure languages do not become mixed but evolve in a separate fashion. Such language learning provides a potentiality to extend that language for other purposes. Children have sometimes learned Hebrew for the Synagogue. When visiting other friends or going to Israel they find that they can extend their Hebrew outside the Synagogue. Those who use Arabic in the Mosque and in reading the Koran may later extend that in greeting and meeting Arabic speakers. Providing a religious language provides a potentiality to extend that language.

F8 I use a particular dialect/a Creole/a pidgin language in the home. Is your advice about raising a bilingual child different or similar?

It is often **difficult to define what is a language**. There are often not sharp boundaries between different languages. Where a language stops and a dialect starts can be a debated point. Some dialects have higher status, others lower status. The term 'language' is an arbitrary label attached to a politically recognized and socially accepted dialect. There is often an amusing academic debate about whether English is a language. English is a concoction of Saxon, French, Latin and Greek. It hasn't the 'purity' of continuity that the Basque, Finnish, Welsh or Greek languages appear to have. No language stays the same or is completely standardized for all time. Language change is a sign of an alive, adapting language. A language that doesn't change has little future.

There is **constant change in language**. Reading Old English, Middle English, Chaucer, Shakespeare, Dickens in the English language reveals the speed of change. Read a textbook from the 1950s and see how quickly language (in terms of vocabulary, style and structure) has changed. As Science, Technology and Computers have rapidly changed this century, so has vocabulary in English. Software, programs, fax machines, telex, satellite dishes, hovercraft, are all part of modern vocabulary that our ancestors would not understand.

There are different Englishes in the world as the visitor to New York, Kuala Lumpur, Helsinki, Moscow, Johannesburg, Calcutta, Bombay, London, Trinidad, Kenya or Zaire will soon hear. There is considerable variation among apparent similarity. There are world Englishes rather than one English in the world.

Therefore, with Pidgin languages and with Creoles, it seems possible to argue that the **advice** of this book is no different. A Creole or a Pidgin often has unity within itself, some standardization of language although changing like any other language, and most important, is a living and thinking language for a group of people. Neither a Pidgin nor a Creole has barriers within it or constraints in a child learning to think, communicate or function orally in that language. A Creole or a Pidgin has an embedded experience, a vitality and a continuity of culture within it that is valuably transmitted as language grows. Therefore, the advice of this book covers Creoles and Pidgins.

Dialects can vary in their similarity and difference from each other and the 'standard' language. Dialects of English, for example, often have considerable similarity to each other. People can move inside England and the United States and understand other people speaking their dialect without much real difficulty. Variations in dialect are often a valued and important part of local identity. In this respect, it is often inappropriate to think of someone who has a local dialect and a more 'standard' production of that language owning two different languages. There is so much overlap between the two that use of a dialect is not bilingualism.

However, there are other circumstances where dialects may be very different from each other although part of a wider family. There are local dialects that are considerably different from each other to the point at which two speakers of those dialects have difficulty in communicating with each other. In Africa and India for example this is sometimes the case. At what point two dialects are sufficiently apart to be regarded as two languages is going to require arbitrary and arguable judgement. The more there is mutual intelligibility, the less one can talk about two separate and different languages and hence bilingualism. There are some cases where two 'dialects' are sufficiently apart and mutually different for the advice about bilingualism in this book to hold.

F9 I have a deaf child. Is your advice about raising a bilingual child different or similar?

There is a growing merger between two hitherto distinct groups: those interested in bilingualism and those interested in deaf children. There is a growing recognition that **much of what has been written about bilinguals applies to deaf children**. This has not been so until recently. The 'medical' view — essentially monolingual — has dominated.

The **'medical' view** has historically been that deaf and many hearing-impaired children must be monolingual. To function in mainstream society, sign language must be forgotten, and the vocal and written majority language (e.g. English in the United States) must be learned. This is a deficit view of the deaf and of sign language. Although sign language comes naturally to the deaf, the 'medical' view has been that top priority is integration into mainstream society. Mainstream integration means avoiding Signing which purportedly restricts social and employment opportunities.

The **'bilingual' view** is that deaf and many hearing-impaired children should have sign language as their 'native', first language. For such children, Signing enables immediate, instinctively natural and full communication. Bilingualism is achieved by one (or both) of two routes. The second language can be a written majority (or minority) language, and/or the vocal form of that language. The vocal form of the language may be a deliberate combination of speech and sign, vocalization and gesture (e.g. 'Live English', 'Signed English', 'Sign Supported English').

It is important to understand that there is considerable **controversy** and passion about this area. Some argue for indigenous signs for the deaf, some argue for signs that approximate, for example, English grammar, and those who accent the dominance of vocal speech. Complications arise because most (e.g. nine out of every ten) deaf children have hearing parents, sign language users are not always a geographical community, and some deaf people are against Signing.

As with hearing bilinguals, there is much **transfer** from the first to the second language. The concepts, ideas, knowledge and skills learned through Signing transfer to the second language. They definitely do not have to be relearned through the second language. A second language is learned through building on a child's existing linguistic and intellectual resources gained through Signing.

Sign Language (which is a language in itself) and a second language create **bilingual children**. Deaf children express themselves in a visual mode (Signing) which is a foundation for the development of a spoken and/or written form of language. A vocal/written language is acquired after sign language rather than simultaneously. Each language has different uses and functions with different people. There are language boundaries between each language, as with hearing bilinguals. A combination of Signing and vocal/written language is also a means of identifying with different groups of people.

Having a visual language (Signing) and a vocal/written language (e.g. English, French, German, Spanish) provides a wealth of different means of **expression**. Signing is very expressive, conveying vividly a whole range of feelings, with constant motion and color. Body language (and not just the hands) conveys a frame of mind, and emotions such as joy and jealousy, anxiety and anger. Poetry in motion.

Restricting deaf children to sign language (e.g. American sign language, French sign language, Swedish sign language, British sign language) means they may not acquire their mother's tongue (if living with hearing parents). To expect deaf children to remain monolingual (Signing only) is an unacceptable 'deficit' view of the deaf. **Wider communication**, access to different cultures, further 'worlds of experience' and wider employment opportunities are made possible by deaf children (and adults) becoming bilingual. Similarly, forcing the deaf to avoid Signing restricts their language development and denies them the chance of bilingualism.

With well designed bilingual education and information to parents, deaf children can acquire a second language as well as Signing. **Bilingual education** for the deaf is growing, but very slowly. Each language can be supported in the classroom. Bilingualism can make the deaf more integrated bilinguals into both hearing and deaf societies.

Deaf children are particularly affected by **negative attitudes** to their bilingualism. They often do not have the supporting environment in the family or community that other language minority groups may experience. Deaf people often do not have an ethnic heritage, family traditions or cultural continuity to fall back on or to surround them. Participation, cultural identity and self-respect may be heightened when the deaf are enabled to become bilingual.

Acquiring both a sign language and a second language needs **positive attitudes** among the deaf, their parents, teachers and education administrators. Negative attitudes towards sign language and the subsequent enforced use of a vocal language (e.g. spoken English) in the classroom have led to the same type of under-achievement that has marked language minorities who are forced to learn in their second language. There is a feeling among many deaf people in Britain and the United States that they are held back educationally as a result of school pressure to learn English and through English. **Supporting bilingualism** among the deaf is therefore supporting their first language (Signing) and bilingual education.

This brief consideration of deaf bilingualism suggests that many issues discussed in this book are **relevant to the deaf**. Further information about bilingualism and the deaf is available from Deaf Associations, Special Needs teams in school districts, and in publications from publishers such as Multilingual Matters Ltd (e.g. Danielle Bouvet's book *The Path to*

Language: Bilingual Education for Deaf Children). In the United States, a very useful publication listing many help agencies is *Kendall Demonstration Elementary School: Deaf Studies Curriculum Guide* by M. Miller-Nomeland and S. Gillespie (Washington, DC: Gallaudet University, 1993).

F10 People talk about diglossia. What does it mean?

The term bilingualism is typically used to describe the two languages of an individual. When the focus changes to two languages in society, the term often used is **diglossia**. The term diglossia is originally a Greek word meaning two languages. Often this is two languages for different purposes.

A language community is unlikely to use both languages for the same purpose. A language community is more likely to use one language in certain situations and for certain functions, the other language in different circumstances and for different functions. For example, a language community may use its heritage, minority language in the home, for religious purposes and in social activity. This language community may use the majority language at work, in education and when experiencing the mass media. This is illustrated below. The example below shows that languages may be used in different situations, with one language more likely to be used in informal, personal situations; the other language being used more in formal, official communication contexts.

Context	First Language	Second Language
1. The Home and Family		*
2. Schooling	*	
3. Mass Media	*	
4. Business and Commerce	*	
5. Social & Cultural Activity in the Community		*
6. Correspondence with Relatives and Friends	*	*
7. Correspondence with Government Departments		
8. Religion		*

The table suggests that the different language contexts usually make one language more prestigious than the other. The majority language may sometimes be perceived as more superior, more elegant and educative a language, the door to both educational and economic success.

The concept of diglossia can be usefully examined alongside the concept of individual bilingualism. Four situations will explain the value of the two terms 'bilingualism' and 'diglossia' The **first** situation is a language community containing **both individual bilingualism and diglossia**. In such a community, almost everyone will be able to use both the majority language and a minority language. Each language is used for a different set of functions.

The **second** situation is **diglossia without bilingualism**. In such a context there will be two languages within a particular geographical area. One group of inhabitants will speak one language, another group a different language. One example is Switzerland where, to a large extent, different language groups (German, French, Italian, Romansch) are located in different areas. The official status of the different languages may be equal. Fluent bilingual speakers of both languages may be the exception rather than the rule.

In some cases, the ruling power group will speak the high status language, with the larger, less powerful group speaking another, lower status language. For example, in a colonial situation, English or French may be spoken by the ruling elite, with the indigenous language spoken by the masses.

The **third** situation is **bilingualism without diglossia**. In this situation, most people will be bilingual and will not restrict one language to a specific set of purposes. Either language may be used for almost any different function. Such communities tend to be unstable and in a state of change. Where individual bilingualism exists without diglossia, the expectation is often that one language will, in the future, become more powerful and have more purposes. The other language may decrease in its functions and decay in status and usage. One example quoted is the changed situation of smaller, indigenous languages in the old USSR.

The fourth situation is where there is **neither bilingualism nor diglossia**. One example is Cuba and the Dominican Republic where everyone speaks Spanish and there is little bilingualism. A different example is a small speech community using its minority language for all functions and insisting on having no relationship with the neighboring majority language.

Language shift tends to be more typical than language stability. Changes in the fate and fortune of a language occur because the separate purposes of the two languages tend to change across generations. The boundaries that separate one language from another are never permanent. Neither a minority language community nor the uses that community makes of its minority language can be permanently separated. Even with the **territorial principle** (one language being given official status in one geographical area, the second language being given status within a separate geographical area), the political and power base of the two languages changes over time. However, keeping boundaries between the languages and compartmentalizing their use in society is usually necessary so the weaker language can survive.

Where the **territorial principle** is claimed (e.g. in Wales, Switzerland), geography is used to define language boundaries, with inhabitants of a region classified as a distinct language group. The argument for the survival, maintenance and spread of the language is based on its historic existence within a defined geographical boundary. As the indigenous language of the region, language rights may be enshrined in law.

Welsh speakers have certain language rights in Wales (e.g. using Welsh in courts of law) but not when they cross the border into England. The **territorial principle** benefits the Welsh but has unfortunate implications for other 'in-migrant' language minorities in Britain. The danger and discriminatory nature of the territorial principle is revealed in a set of questions. If Welsh is the language of Wales, is English to be seen as the only rightful language of England? Do languages belong to regions and territories and not to the speakers of those languages or to groups of those languages wherever they may be found? Do Punjabi, Urdu, Bengali, Hindi, Greek and Turkish speakers only belong in the home country? Do such languages have no home in Britain? Under the territorial principle, should language minorities either speak the language of the territory or return to the home country? The territorial principle thus has benefits for some (e.g. the Welsh). For others, it is unacceptable, unfair and untenable.

The term **personality principle** is particularly helpful to minority groups and individuals who cannot claim a language territory principle. The right to use their minority language is claimed due to its character, continuity with the past and links with cultural and ethnic identity. The 'personality' of a language minority group is the sum of its more or less distinctive language attributes (e.g. revealed in customs and rituals, habits and values, culture and beliefs, communication and literature). A language group (e.g. the Pennsylvania Amish community) have ensured the continuity of their language by reserving a special place for their language inside the home and church. English is spoken in school and with 'outsiders'. The personality principle is practiced by **segregating** the two languages through different uses. Each language has specific, separate functions for the language group.

The **personality principle** is an especially supportive concept for in-migrant groups (e.g. community languages in England and the language minorities in Canada and the United States). Such in-migrant groups cannot claim the territorial principal. Instead, they need to 'create space' for their heritage language by applying the personality principle. To destroy the language of an in-migrant group is to attempt to destroy their past, their personality and their cultural character.

The **personality principle** concerns an arrangement of the separate use of two languages by a group of bilinguals. A group needs to claim and recognize the personality principle. If there is no arrangement for the different, independent uses of the two languages, a shift to majority language monolingualism is likely to occur. This is one challenge facing Latinos in the United States. Spanish needs to find a separate, recognized existence among Latinos, acting as a coherent body. Otherwise, a shift to English monolingualism will continue to occur.

F11 Books on child care and child development warn me against bilingualism. How should I react?

Here are two **quotations** from popular best-seller books for parents on child care and child development. The first quotation comes from Drs Andrew and Penny Stanway's book *The Baby and Child Care Book: The Complete Guide to Your Child's First Five Years*:

> '...In general it has been found that one language tends to predominate in the child's mind and that most of these children take longer to become proficient in either language than their single-language contemporaries. Some children may appear to be backward in their language development because of this, whereas in fact they are simply confused.'
>
> '...All children find it easier if they know at least some English words before starting school. In areas with high immigrant populations there are classes for teaching mothers English. They in turn can then teach their preschool children.'

From Hugh Jolly's book entitled *Book of Child Care: The Complete Guide for Today's Parents* comes the following quotation:

> 'Your child will be less confused if you always speak to him in the same language whether this is to be his "first" or "second" language... But having a mother who tries to teach you two names for everything at once leads to confusion and rebellion.'

While in both these books there are some positive comments about bilinguals, such books typically talk about mental and language confusion, of interference between languages and the paramount necessity of developing English language skills in the home. Such books are often written by doctors or child psychologists who know little or nothing about bilingualism, are not conversant with literature on bilingualism nor have read the research on bilingual child development. This is simply not an area where medical writers have the expertise nor often the experience to provide informed or expert comment.

React by thinking about the advice of this book and other similar books mentioned later in this book. Find out **information** from sources where there is informed comment, expert understanding and greater experience and awareness of childhood bilingualism.

F12 How do I contact other parents in a similar situation?

Raising a child bilingually will rarely be a smooth or easy process. Worries and problems are bound to arise along the journey. One valuable way through worries and problems is to talk them out and discuss similar experiences with other parents who are raising bilingual children. Psychologists underline the importance of the 'social comparison process' where we compare ourselves with similar others to ensure that our behavior and attitudes are reasonable and rational. Through social comparison, we obtain catharsis for our anxieties by sharing problems. We gain the experience of others who have been along a similar journey.

How about placing an advert in a local newspaper? It doesn't always matter if bilingual parents who meet in a **local group** have different languages. The problems, anxieties and pleasures are often common. If there are enough local people who can meet as a language group, the exchange of books, cassette tapes, posters as well as experiences will be invaluable.

Another way of finding out about local and other language networks of parents with similar interests and worries is gained through the *Bilingual Family Newsletter*. For over a decade this quarterly newsletter has been found an invaluable asset for like-minded parents of bilingual children. People in the same situation as you will already have joined that network. All languages and situations, all kinds of problems are addressed in the newsletter. For more information and a free sample copy, write to Multilingual Matters (see details at end of the next section).

F13 How do I find out more information about bilingualism?

There are other books that provide extra depth and width to the discussions of this book. These tend to be more academic in nature but are still aimed at thinking parents. Two of the best are:

(1) Lenore Arnberg, *Raising Children Bilingually: The Pre-school Years* (Clevedon: Multilingual Matters, 1987). This book provides a valuable academic introduction to aspects of bilingualism relevant to young children in families, chapters on practical suggestions and some case studies. It is particularly valuable for in-migrant parents and those in language minority situations.

(2) Edith Harding and Philip Riley, *The Bilingual Family: A Handbook for Parents* (Cambridge: Cambridge University Press, 1986). This book is also written from an academic viewpoint. There are case studies of sixteen bilingual families and an alphabetic reference guide. This book is particularly valuable for those families where there are **two majority languages**. The book is written by linguists and has valuable insights from a linguistic point of view.

(3) Another book is a **survey of parents** and their bilingual experience. Representing a variety of parental experience, it lacks in expert advice and a 'state of the art' understanding of bilingualism. The book is by Eveline de Jong, *The Bilingual Experience: A Book for Parents* (Cambridge: Cambridge University Press, 1986).

(4) The next recommended book is by George Saunders, entitled *Bilingual Children: From Birth to Teens* (Clevedon: Multilingual Matters, 1988). Saunders and his wife raised their sons and daughter in English and German in Australia. Even though Saunders was not a native speaker of German, and there was little support for German speakers in the community, they raised their children bilingually. From birth, the mother spoke to the children in English while the father used German. Saunders provides a detailed case study with plenty of illustrations, much analysis and is regarded as a classic case study of the development of bilingualism in a family.

(5) Susanne Döpke's book entitled *One Parent One Language: An Interactional Approach* is published by John Benjamins (Amsterdam/ Philadelphia, 1992) and represents one recent academic research study on bilingualism in the family. Research-based but still readable, there are many insights gained from study of a sample of children brought up in a one language–one parent situation.

(6) For those parents who want to read more about children's language, one best-seller is David Crystal's *Listen to Your Child: A Parent's Guide to Children's Language* (London: Penguin Books, 1986). This follows language development from the beginning through the first, second and third years into preschool and early school years. Delightfully written with transparent sensibility and well informed from linguistic and psychological research, the book is versatile, eminently readable and highly informative.

(7) For those who want a comprehensive introduction to bilingualism and bilingual education, there is Colin Baker's *Foundations of Bilingual Education and Bilingualism* (Clevedon: Multilingual Matters, 1993). This book aims to provide a first introduction to the psychological, sociological, educational, political and cultural aspects that surround bilingualism. Written as a foundation-level textbook for parents, students and teachers, the eighteen chapters cover the crucial issues and controversies about language minorities, language majorities and bilingual education.

(8) An up-to-date and most valuable source of information for parents is the *Bilingual Family Newsletter*. A free sample will be provided on request. Contact: Marjukka Grover, Multilingual Matters Ltd, Frankfurt Lodge, Clevedon Hall, Victoria Road, Clevedon, Avon BS21 7SJ, England.

Glossary

The Glossary gives further information about some terms used in this book. It also includes terms not used in this but regularly found in other books for parents and teachers on bilingualism.

Accommodation: Modifying speech to make oneself understood.

Acculturation: The process by which an individual adapts to a new culture.

Additive Bilingualism: The second language adds to, and does not replace the first language.

Assimilation: A process whereby an individual or group lose their heritage language and culture which are replaced by the language and culture of the dominant group.

Balanced Bilingualism: Approximately equal competence in two languages.

Basal Readers: Reading texts that use simplified vocabulary and grammar.

BICS: Basic Interpersonal Communicative Skills. Everyday, straightforward communication skills that are helped by contextual supports such as gestures.

Big Books: Used frequently in 'whole language classrooms,' they are teachers' books that are physically big so that students can read along with the teacher.

CALP: Cognitive/Academic Language Proficiency. The level of language required to understand academically demanding subject matter in a classroom. Such language is often abstract, without contextual supports such as gestures and viewing objects.

Caretaker Speech: A simplified language used by parents to children to ensure understanding.

Cloze: A procedure whereby every *n*th word is deleted in a text. The child has to guess the missing word. Used to determine the readability of text and the reading ability of a student.

Code Switching: Moving from one language to another, inside a sentence or across sentences.

Cognition: The acquisition, storage, retrieval and use of knowledge.

Common Underlying Proficiency (CUP): Each language serves one underlying, central thinking system. Two languages working in an integrated manner.

Communal Lessons: Lessons in which linguistically diverse students are mixed for common activities, such as working in projects, doing art or physical education. The European Hours in the European Schools are Communal Lessons.

Communicative Competence: Proficiency to use a language in everyday conversations. This term accents being understood rather than being 'correct' in using a language.

Compensatory Education: See Deficit Model.

Comprehensible Input: Language delivered at a level understood by a learner.

Context: The setting, physical or language, where communication occurs. The context places possibilities and constraints on what is said, and how it is said.

Context Embedded Language: Language where there are plenty of clues, shared understandings, and where meaning is relatively obvious due to help from the physical or social nature of the conversation.

Context Reduced Language: Language where there are few clues as to the meaning of the communication apart from the words themselves. The language is likely to be abstract.

Core Language Class: Teaching the language as a subject. Used mostly to describe foreign language instruction.

Core Subject: A subject that is of prime importance in the curriculum. In England, the three core subjects are Mathematics, English and Science.

CUP: See Common Underlying Proficiency.

DBE: Developmental Bilingual Education: Also known as Two-Way Dual Language Programs and Two-way Bilingual/Immersion Programs. Two languages are used for approximately equal time in the curriculum.

Decoding: In learning to read, decoding is the deciphering of the sounds and meanings of letters, combinations of letters, whole words and sentences of text.

Deficit Model: The child has a perceived language 'deficit' that has to be compensated by remedial schooling. The problem is located in the child rather than in the school system or society. The opposite is an enrichment model. (See Enrichment Bilingual Education.)

Dialect: A regionally or socially distinctive variety of a language, often with a distinctive pronunciation or accent.

Diglossia: Two languages existing together in a society in a stable arrangement through different uses attached to each language.

Double Immersion: Schooling where subject content is taught through a second and third language (e.g. Hebrew and French for first language English speakers).

Early Exit/Late Exit Bilingual Education Programs: Early exit programs move children from bilingual classes in the first or second year of schooling. Late exit programs provide bilingual classes for three or more years of elementary schooling. Both programs are found in Transitional Bilingual Education.

EC: European Community.

EEC: European Economic Community.

EFL: English as a Foreign Language.

Empowerment: Those of low status, low influence and power are given the tools to increase their chances of prosperity, power and prestige. Literacy and biliteracy are major means of enabling such individuals and groups.

Enrichment Bilingual Education: Develops additive bilingualism, thus enriching a person's life. Two languages and cultures are developed through education.

Equilingual: Someone who is approximately equally competent in two languages.

ERASMUS: A European program for students to take part of their higher education at one or more European universities as well as their 'home' university.

ESL: English as a Second Language.

Ethnic Mosaic: In-migrants of different geographical origins coexisting in a country (e.g. United States) and retaining the colorful constituents of their ethnicity.

Ethnocentrism: Discriminatory beliefs and behaviors based on ethnic differences.

Ethnolinguistic: A set of cultural, ethnic and linguistic features shared by a social group.

EU: European Union.

First Language: This term is used in different, overlapping ways, and can mean (a) the first language learnt (b) the stronger language (c) the 'mother tongue' (d) the language most used.

Foreigner Talk: The language of native speakers who simplify their communication so that 'foreigners' can understand what is being said.

Gastarbeiter: (German term) An in-migrant or guestworker.

Graphology: The way a language is written.

Guest Workers: People who are recruited to work in another society. Also known as Gastarbeiter.

Hegemony: Domination; the ascendance of one group over another. The dominant group expects compliance and subservience from the subordinate group.

Heritage Language: The language a person regards as their native, home, ancestral language. This covers indigenous languages (e.g. Welsh in Wales) and in-migrant languages (e.g. Spanish in the United States).

Heterogeneous Grouping: The use of mixed ability and/or mixed language groups or classes. The opposite is 'homogeneous grouping' or tracking.

Hispanics: Spanish speakers in the United States. The term is officially used in the United States Census.

Immersion Bilingual Education: Schooling where some or most subject content is taught through a second, majority language.

In-migrants: Encompasses immigrants, migrants, guest workers and refugees.

Instrumental Motivation: Wanting to learn a language for utilitarian reasons (e.g. to get a better job).

Integrative Motivation: Wanting to learn a language to belong to a social group (e.g. to make friends).

Interlanguage: A language, integrating aspects of the first and second language, used by a second language learner while learning the second language.

Involuntary Minorities: Also known as 'caste-like minorities'. They differ from in-migrants and 'voluntary minorities' in that they have not willingly migrated to a country.

L1/L2: First Language/Second Language.

Language Ability: An 'umbrella' term and therefore used ambiguously. Language ability is a general, latent disposition, a determinant of eventual language success. Language ability is also used as an outcome, similar but less specific than language skills, providing an indication of current language level.

Language Achievement: Normally seen as the outcome of formal language instruction.

Language Acquisition: The unconscious development of language that occurs naturally in a young child. Language that is acquired incidentally rather than being learned.

Language Competence: A broad and general term, used particularly to describe an inner, mental representation of language, something latent rather than overt. Such competence refers usually to an underlying system inferred from language performance.

Language Demographics: The distribution of the use of a language in a geographical area.

Language Minority: A group who speaks a language of low prestige or with low numbers in a society.

Language Performance: The outward evidence for language competence. By observing general language comprehension and production, language competence may be presumed.

Language Proficiency: An 'umbrella' term, sometimes used synonymously with language competence; other times as a specific, measurable outcome from language testing. Language proficiency is viewed as the product of a variety of mechanisms: formal learning, informal uncontrived language acquisition (e.g. on the street) and of individual characteristics such as 'intelligence'.

Language Skills: This refers to highly specific, observable, clearly definable components such as writing.

Latinos: Spanish speakers of Latin American extraction. This Spanish term is now used in English, especially by US Spanish speakers themselves. Often preferred to 'Hispanics'.

LEP: Limited English Proficiency (US term). Used to refer to students in the United States who are not native speakers of English and who have yet to reach 'desired' levels of competence in understanding, speaking, reading or writing English.

Lexical Competency: Competence in vocabulary.

Lexis/Lexicon: The vocabulary or word stock of a language, their sounds, spelling and meaning.

LINGUA: A European program to increase majority language learning across Europe. The program funds scholarships, student exchanges and teaching materials to improve language learning and teaching in the 12 European (EC) countries.

Lingua Franca: A common language used between groups of people with different native languages.

Linguicism: The use of languages to legitimate and reproduce unequal divisions of power and resources in society.

LMS: Language Minority Students.

Mainstreaming: Putting a student who has previously been in a special educational program into classrooms for everybody. Language mainstreaming occurs when children are no longer given special support (e.g. English as a Second Language classes) and take their subjects through the majority language.

Majority Language: A language of higher prestige and usually with large numbers in a society.

Marked Language: A minority language distinct from a majority one, and usually lowly valued in society.

Medium of Education: Using a language to teach content. Also medium of instruction.

Melting-pot: The amalgamation of a variety of in-migrant ethnic groups to make, for example, a 'US American citizen'.

Metalinguistic: Language about language. Thinking about one's language.

Minority Language: A language of lower prestige or with low numbers in a society.

Motherese: A simplified language used by parents to children to ensure understanding.

Mother Tongue: The term is used ambiguously. It variously means (a) the language learnt from the mother; (b) the first language learnt, irrespective of 'from whom'; (c) the stronger language at any time of life; (d) the 'mother tongue' of the area or country (e.g. Irish in Ireland); (e) the language most used by a person; (f) the language to which a person has the more positive attitude and affection.

Non-verbal Communication: Communication without words; for example, via gestures, eye contact, position and posture when talking, body movements and contact, tone of voice.

Orthography: Spelling.

Passive Bilingualism: Being able to understand (and sometimes read) in a second language without speaking or writing in that second language.

Parallel Teaching: Where bilingual children experience two teachers working together as a team, each using a different language. For example, a second language teacher and the class teacher planning together but teaching independently.

Personality Principle: The right to use a language based on the history and character of the language. Such use reflects two languages existing together in a society in a stable arrangement through different uses attached to each language.

Phonics: A method of teaching reading based on recognizing the sounds of letters and combinations of letters.

Phonetics: The study of the sound structure of speech.

Phonology: The sound system of a language.

Polyglot: Someone competent in two or more languages.

Process Instruction: An emphasis on the 'doing' in the classroom rather than creating a product. A focus on procedures and techniques rather than on learning outcomes. Learning 'how to' through inquiry rather than learning through the transmission and memorization of knowledge.

Productive Language: Speaking and writing.

Pygmalion effect: The self-fulfilling prophecy. A student is labeled (e.g. by a teacher as having 'limited English'). The label is internalized by the student who behaves in a way that later serves to confirm the label.

Racism: A system of privilege and penalty based on race. It is based on a belief in the inherent superiority of one race over others, and acceptance of economic, social, political and educational differences based on such supposed superiority.

Reception Classes/Centers: For newly arrived students in a country, to teach the language of the new country, and often the culture.

Receptive Language: Listening/understanding and reading.

Register: A variety of a language closely associated with different contexts or scenes in which the language is used (e.g. courtroom, classroom, cinema, church) and hence with different people (e.g. police, professor, parent, priest).

Scaffolding: Building on a child's existing repertoire of knowledge and understanding.

Second Language: This term is used in different, overlapping ways, and can mean (a) the second language learnt (chronologically); (b) the weaker language; (c) a language that is not the 'mother tongue'; (d) the less used language. The term is sometimes used to cover third and further languages.

Self-fulfilling Prophecy: A student is labeled (e.g. by a teacher as having 'limited English'). The label is internalized by the student who behaves in a way that serves to confirm the label.

Semantics: The study of the meaning of language.

Separate Underlying Proficiency: Two languages as existing separately and working independently in the thinking system.

Sheltered English: Content (subject) classes that also include English language development.

Skills-based Literacy: Where the emphasis is on the acquisition of phonics and other language forms, rather than in ways of using those forms.

Standard Language: A prestige variety of a language (e.g. Standard English).

Streaming: The use of homogeneous groups (also called tracking, setting, streaming, banding, ability grouping).

Submersion: Schooling that doesn't allow the child to use their home language for learning. The child works solely through a second, majority language.

Subtractive Bilingualism: The second language replaces the first language.

SUP: See Separate Underlying Proficiency.

Syntax: Word order and grammar. Rules about the ways words are combined and organized.

Target Language: The language being learned or taught.

TBE: Transitional Bilingual Education. Temporary use of the child's home language in the classroom, leading to only the majority language being allowed in classroom instruction. (See Early Exit/Late Exit Bilingual Education Programs.)

TEFL: Teaching English as a Foreign Language.

Territorial Principle: A claim to the right to a language within a territory.

TESOL: (a) Teachers of English to Speakers of Other Languages; (b) Teaching English as a Second or Other Language.

Threshold level: Mostly used to describe a level of language competence a person has to reach to gain benefits from owning two languages.

Tracking: The use of homogeneous groups (also called setting, streaming, banding, ability grouping).

Two-way Programs: Also known as Developmental Bilingual Education, Two-way Dual Language Programs and Two-way Bilingual/Immersion

Programs. Two languages are used for approximately equal time in the curriculum.

UK: United Kingdom (England, Scotland, Northern Ireland and Wales).

UN: United Nations.

UNESCO: United Nations Educational, Scientific and Cultural Organization.

Unmarked Language: A majority language distinct from a minority language, and usually highly valued in society.

US English: An organization committed to making English the only officially functioning language in United States society.

Vernacular: A indigenous or heritage language of an individual or community.

Wanderarbeiter: A nomadic, seasonal worker, usually from a 'foreign' country. An itinerant worker in a 'foreign' country.

Whole Language Approach: An amorphous cluster of ideas about language development in the classroom. The approach is against basal readers (see above) and phonics (see above) in learning to read. Generally the approach supports an holistic and integrated learning of reading, writing, spelling and oracy. The language used must have relevance, purpose and meaning to the child. Language development engages cooperative, collaborative sharing and cultivates empowerment. The use of language for communication is stressed; the function rather than the form of language.

Withdrawal Classes: Also known as 'pull-out' classes. Children are taken out for special instruction.

Acknowledgement

The author wishes to thank Professor Ofelia García, of the City College of New York, for her contribution to this Glossary. Some of this Glossary also appears in *Policy and Practice in Bilingual Education: A Reader Extending the Foundations*, by O. García and C. Baker (Clevedon: Multilingual Matters, 1995).